Reading/Writing Connections
Learning from Research

Judith W. Irwin
University of Connecticut

Mary Anne Doyle
University of Connecticut

Editors

ira
International Reading Association
Newark, Delaware 19714

The International Reading Association attempts, through its publications, to provide a forum for a wide spectrum of opinions on reading. This policy permits divergent viewpoints without assuming the endorsement of the Association.

Director of Publications   Joan M. Irwin
Managing Editor   Romayne McElhaney
Associate Editor   Anne Fullerton
Associate Editor   Karen Goldsmith
Assistant Editor   Kate Shumaker
Production Department Manager   Iona Sauscermen
Graphic Design Coordinator   Boni Nash
Mechanical Preparation   Cheryl Strum
Design Consultant   Larry Husfelt
Typesetting Systems Analyst   Wendy Mazur
Typesetting   Anette Schuetz-Ruff
          Richard James
Proofing   Florence Pratt

Copyright 1992 by the
International Reading Association, Inc.

Library of Congress Cataloging in Publication Data

Reading/writing connections: learning from research / Judith W. Irwin, Mary Anne Doyle, editors.
    p.   cm.
    Includes bibliographical references and index.
    1. Reading (Elementary)—United States—Evaluation.   2. English language—Composition and exercises—Study and teaching—United States—Evaluation.   I. Irwin, Judith Westphal.   II. Doyle, Mary Anne, 1949-
LB1573.R2934   1992   91-41538
372.4—dc20   CIP
ISBN 0-87207-369-6

— CONTENTS —

*T*he authors who contributed to this volume are attempting to redefine literacy, and I applaud their efforts. In their introduction, Irwin and Doyle ask, "Is [literacy] the ability to use reading and writing to understand and transform the world in which one lives?" My answer is yes.

The two chapters reporting research by teachers show students actively using literacy to find their places in the worlds of their classrooms. Throne's student with learning problems became the class's word-processing expert. Timion's first grade students learned to choose the books they read, in part by using their friends as resources for suggestions. As Timion watched them develop into a diverse group of readers, she began to realize the power she had given them and "glimpsed the bigger picture—the way that the commercial, prepackaged reading programs have worked against individuality and promoted conformity."

These students, and also the children in the kindergarten discussed in Sulzby and Barnhart's chapter, learn in classrooms built on social-constructivist theories. This outlook, described by McCarthey and Raphael, encourages classroom cultures in which each child's uniqueness is valued and individuality becomes a hallmark of a reader. Hare's reader-writers showed this in the summaries they wrote, and we take her findings to inform pedagogy.

Several other authors give glimpses of ways to rethink instruction. A common theme among Langer, Spiegel, and Smagorinsky's chapters is the importance to writers of reading well-written prose. Vacca and Linek argue for essay assignments rather than study questions in order that students can use writing as a mode of learning in the content areas.

In all of the chapters, I sensed the desire to create classrooms in which students feel motivated to do their work. Spaulding discusses the notion of motivation in terms of two factors: perception of competence and perception of self-control. Students need to make decisions about the difficulty of the challenges they wish to pursue.

As teachers we hope that our students will develop the competence to tackle real-life issues. Unfortunately, school literacy and real-life literacy are often two different things. Tierney says that he frequently begins a course with this statement: "If thinking critically is our goal, then perhaps we should exclude reading and writing from our classroom." In the discussion that follows, Tierney's students identify the ways school-based literacy subjugates and indoctrinates. Teachers control the floor and define "rightness." Literacy, however, can be used either as a weapon to maintain the status quo or as a tool to challenge it.

When literacy becomes real, students' stories about school will change. They will speak with emotion about issues they care about, write about, work toward, and read about. Their stories will connect them to one another and to distant people. "Stories don't just capture and freeze human intentions, emotions, and actions, they reach out," writes Fitzgerald. However, she goes on to say that "we have no research...that touches the heart or the exquisiteness of stories. Why have we explored certain aspects of stories and not others?... Our methodologies have shaped, and perhaps limited, our understanding.... We have used logico-scientific thinking to investigate its opposite—narrative thought."

Research and instruction are changing, however. As we redefine literacy, our schools and classrooms will show students how to use literacy to reach beyond their classrooms, schools, and communities.

Jane Hansen
University of New Hampshire

Reading/Writing Research: Then and Now

*T*he purpose of this book is to present current reviews of research on reading/writing connections, the instructional implications of this research, and some suggestions for future research. The initial motivation for such a project was a historical study conducted between 1982 and 1985 by the International Reading Association's Reading and Its Relationship to Writing committee. To the committee members' dismay, the study revealed that the research conducted to that date had not come very far in answering important questions about the interaction of reading and writing processes or the best ways to integrate their instruction. Moreover, according to independent raters, much of the research was low in quality and lacking in generalizability and significance. (For a complete description of the nature of the survey and an analysis of its results, see the Appendix, "Reading/Writing Research: 1900 to 1984.")

This situation has clearly begun to change, as evidenced by the research described herein. For instance, questions about instructional procedures now address more explicitly the specific contexts of instruction. Researchers now take into account such influences as classroom environments, teaching methods, social contexts, teacher attitudes and philosophies, and teacher/student interactions.

Excellent examples of this awareness of context are provided throughout this volume. For instance, Timion examines the book-selection strategies of the students in her first grade reading/writing workshop, carefully including details about classroom organization and about her own interactions with the students. Sulzby and Barnhart also look at children's developing notions about reading and writing in natural contexts. In the third part of their chapter, McCarthey and Raphael provide an excellent summary of research based on social-constructivist theories about the role of the cultural context in literacy development.

Second, an examination of recent research also reveals a definite shift toward examining reading and writing as processes. This is leading to a search for connections in terms of specific processes such as using story structure (discussed by Fitzgerald) and other specific organizational patterns (see Langer), making cohesive ties (see Spiegel), and creating summaries (see Hare). In Part Two, the authors review these areas of research and suggest that there is much research left to be done, especially with regard to intervention instruction.

Third, new types of research methodologies are now commonplace. Ethnographic and case study approaches are allowing researchers to develop rich descriptions of the complex contexts in which reading and writing tasks take place. New qualitative measurement techniques (including interviews, probing, and taping recalls, as well as draft, error, and protocol analyses) are being developed and used frequently. Participant-observer studies are also occurring with some regularity.

Again, examples of these trends can be found throughout this book. Smagorinsky describes the results of protocol-analysis research that examined the effects of reading models on writing quality. Spaulding's research also integrates qualitative and quantitative techniques. The teacher research presented in Part Four provides examples of participant-observer research, and Throne's chapter is an excellent example of a qualitative case study.

One of the most fruitful developments in reading/writing research has been the entrance into the field of researchers from a variety of disciplines, all with varying perspectives on literacy. Vacca and Linek summarize the research on integrating reading and writing into other content areas. McCarthey and Raphael describe the cognitive (information processing), Piagetian/naturalist, and the social-constructivist perspectives. We have included in this volume chapters based on various perspectives because we believe that this multiplicity of approaches can only increase what we are able to learn about reading/writing connections. Researchers should consider the merits of each position as they address their research questions.

Unfortunately, current instructional research seems to be divided into two distinct camps: the "traditional" instructional studies that focus on reading and writing as abilities to be acquired with structured intervention, and studies related to what Willinsky (1990) has called the "new literacy":

The New Literacy consists of those strategies in the teaching of reading and writing which attempt to shift the control of literacy from the teacher to the students: literacy is promoted in such programs as a social process with language that can from the very beginning extend the students' range of meaning and connection (p. 8).

The former would probably include studies on instruction based on subskill or cognitive-processing models, including all instruction focused on developing specific reading or writing strategies as ends in themselves. This type of research has tended to be quantitative, and therefore has been largely accepted in the traditional education community and by state governments, school boards, and other political groups that make decisions concerning education.

On the other hand, "new literacy" programs are labeled with terms such as "whole language," "reader response," and "process writing." These programs have been studied using qualitative methods, and, as Willinsky (1990) points out, "the predominant discourse of quantitative studies and standardized measures makes it difficult for New Literacy programs to gain a national hearing" (p. 164). "But," he goes on to note, "to eschew quantitative studies not only denies a fair basis of comparison to the educator trying to assess both sides of the debate, it leaves educators who have embarked on a New Literacy course stranded, adding considerably to their test-anxiety" (p. 165).

We believe that both types of instructional programs should be examined with both quantitative and qualitative research methods so this debate will have some use for decision makers in the field.

A second problem in the literature on reading and writing is that researchers too often fail to address the central issue of how literacy is defined. That literacy is defined differently in different types of communities has been documented (see Heath, 1983, amongst others); that it is defined differently by different educators has only recently received attention (see Giroux, 1987; Lankshear, 1987; and Venezky, Wagner, & Ciliberti, 1990; amongst others). Is literacy the ability to use reading and writing to function adequately in the modern world (to make a living, for example)? Is it the ability to use reading and writing to construct personal meaning? Is it the ability to use reading and writing to understand and transform the world in which one lives? Researchers must become more explicit about the definition of literacy on which their work is based.

Finally, because the work in reading/writing research is not complete, this volume ends with a chapter suggesting future directions. Here, Tierney suggests that current developments are giving rise to new issues for investigation: The meaning of school literacy experiences, the role of intertextuality in school learning, and alternative methods for assessing literacy development are all issues to be studied in the upcoming years.

It is our hope that this collection will contribute to the continuing growth in the quality and significance of the research on reading/writing relationships, and that this research will lead to holistic literacy theories that will enrich the lives of learners. We hope that readers of this book will be inspired to conduct their own research on reading/writing connections—research that is theoretically based, process oriented, contextualized, interdisciplinary, and innovative.

References

Giroux, H.A. (1987). Critical literacy and student empowerment: Donald Graves' approach to literacy. *Language Arts, 6*(2), 175-181.

Heath, S.B. (1983). *Ways with words: Language, life, and work in communities and classrooms.* Cambridge, UK: Cambridge University Press.

Lankshear, C. (1987). *Literacy, schooling, and revolution.* New York: Falmer.

Venezky, R.L., Wagner, D.A., & Ciliberti, B.S. (Eds.). (1990). *Toward defining literacy.* Newark, DE: International Reading Association.

Willinsky, J. (1990). *The new literacy: Redefining reading and writing in the schools.* New York: Routledge.

JWI

MAD

June Barnhart
University of Michigan
Ann Arbor, Michigan

Jill Fitzgerald
University of North Carolina
  at Chapel Hill
Chapel Hill, North Carolina

Victoria Chou Hare
University of Illinois at Chicago
Chicago, Illinois

Judith W. Irwin
University of Connecticut
Storrs, Connecticut

Judith A. Langer
University at Albany, State
  University of New York
Albany, New York

Wayne M. Linek
John Carroll University
University Heights, Ohio

Sarah J. McCarthey
The University of Texas at Austin
Austin, Texas

Taffy E. Raphael
Michigan State University
East Lansing, Michigan

Peter Smagorinsky
University of Oklahoma
Norman, Oklahoma

Cheryl L. Spaulding
University of Connecticut
Storrs, Connecticut

Dixie Lee Spiegel
University of North Carolina
  at Chapel Hill
Chapel Hill, North Carolina

Elizabeth Sulzby
University of Michigan
Ann Arbor, Michigan

Robert J. Tierney
The Ohio State University
Columbus, Ohio

Cheryl Shoesmith Timion
Enfield Public Schools
Enfield, Connecticut

M. Joan Throne
Fairfax County Public Schools
Falls Church, Virginia

Richard T. Vacca
Kent State University
Kent, Ohio

Overview of Reading/Writing Research

Sarah J. McCarthey
Taffy E. Raphael

— O N E —

Alternative Research Perspectives

*I*magine a visit to three fourth grade classrooms where students had just finished reading *Tales of a Fourth Grade Nothing* by Judy Blume. In each classroom, the teacher considered a range of postreading activities but, coincidentally, they all decided to have students write summaries of the tale. As we eavesdrop on the lessons, we notice differences in the way each teacher approaches the writing/reading opportunity.

In one classroom, we see Ms. Anderson at an overhead projector. On the overhead is a blank story map with categories for setting, characters, initiating event, reactions, and so forth. Each student has a copy of the story map form. The discussion focuses students' attention on each element of the story's structure, the recurring nature of these elements, and the relative importance of the different ideas presented. As the discussion closes, Anderson directs the students to use their own maps as a way to organize their ideas and then to use these notes as they write a summary of what they think are the story's most important ideas.

In Mrs. Schwarz's classroom, students are sitting in small groups— some on beanbag chairs in the literacy center, others around tables or on the rug near the classroom library. As students converse about the story and how it relates to some of their own experiences, the teacher moves from group to group, listening, nodding, and asking questions. She occasionally reminds students that when they are finished discussing the book, they are to write a summary that will be shared with others as part of the classroom "Review of Books" in the literacy center.

In Mr. Cosie's classroom, the students are sitting at tables in groups of three or four. This lesson appears to have two parts. Initially, Cosie leads a discussion about a recent episode of a television program that many students have seen. The episode showed the difficulty of walking into a new environment at a new school (in this case, the cafeteria). The students are asked to summarize the main events in the story, working together to relate specific events and asking questions. Cosie prompts students to contribute, pointing out how much they can accomplish by working together. He relates the idea of being in a new situation to the characters in Blume's book and directs students to think about what they remember from that story. He then has students work within their groups to construct a summary of the story.

Each of these scenarios depicts a reasonable and appropriate way to integrate reading and writing. Yet underlying them are different views of knowledge, instruction, the role of the student, and the classroom environment. In essence, each of these scenarios captures a different and prominent theory of learning and development. Anderson's lesson reflects many of the principles consistent with an information processing perspective; Schwarz's lesson is consistent with a naturalist perspective; and Cosie's lesson depends on principles fundamental to a social-constructivist perspective.

In this chapter, we discuss these perspectives and their effect on literacy education. In the first three sections, we describe each of the theories in terms of its underlying assumptions, contributions to research on reading and writing connections, and strengths and limitations. In the fourth section, we focus on implications for the role of instruction and the teacher, the role of the student, and the classroom environment.

Cognitive Information Processing Theories

Information processing has been used to develop several models of both reading and writing processes (de Beaugrande, 1982; Gough, 1972; Hayes & Flower, 1980; Kintsch & van Dijk, 1978; LaBerge & Samuels, 1974; Stanovich, 1980). Based on a positivist philosophical tradition, the models assume the existence of an objective reality that can be measured and modeled.

When applied to literacy, this perspective suggests that the processes of reading and writing are stable across contexts (i.e., they fit an objective and defined reality). It also suggests that we can describe these stable processes in terms of how their underlying knowledge structures are represented. Thus, model building has focused on the processes themselves and on the structure of knowledge.

Basic Assumptions

In building their models, information processing theorists appear to be guided by three basic assumptions: (1) reading and writing consist of a number of subprocesses used to perform specialized tasks, (2) readers and writers have limited capacity for attention so that trade-offs occur across the subprocesses, and (3) competence in reading and writing is determined by the degree of attention needed to operate subprocesses; thus, the less memory needed, the more efficient the operation.

Subprocesses in writing and reading. Like the computer whose components perform specialized functions that interact to complete a task, information processing models of reading and writing divide those processes into subprocesses, each with a different function. For example, Flower and Hayes (1981) describe writing as consisting of three recursive phases: (1) planning, in which writers set goals and make plans; (2) translating, in which writers transcribe ideas into written form; and (3) reviewing, in which writers test the plans and translations. The task environment and the writers' long term memory frame the writing process.

Others have suggested similar information processing models of writing. Collins and Gentner (1980) focus on idea production and text production as the broad categories in which subprocesses may be considered, while Scardamalia, Bereiter, and Goelman (1982) distinguish between metacomponents, used to identify choices and make decisions, and performance components that allow writers to carry out their plans. While these models differ in the division of tasks, activities and specific definitions of the writing process, they share an emphasis on dividing a complex psychological process into smaller components for analysis and description.

Information processing models of reading are similar to those of writing. Scholars such as LaBerge and Samuels (1974) have identified component processes that relate to the functions of different types of memory. Specifically, they describe the roles of visual, phonological, semantic, and episodic memory in reading. At the heart of their model is attention, the process that allocates the reader's efforts to the subprocess or memory type needed for the task at hand. Thus, in this view progress through the subprocesses may not be linear (i.e., from pattern recognition to letter recognition to code),

McCarthey and Raphael

since attention may be allocated to different memories in different patterns. The component processes can be identified, however.

In contrast, Gough (1972) suggests a model that describes the reading process as a letter-by-letter sequence that eventually leads to word recognition. He identifies subprocesses such as developing a visual or iconic image, moving toward letter identification, searching one's lexicon, and accessing memory for meaning.

These models have given way to interactive models (Rumelhart, 1977; Stanovich, 1980) and component models (Carr et al., 1990). Rumelhart has argued that the linear models cannot explain why a string of letters such as "alligator" is easier to recognize than something like "rllaagtio." This phenomenon suggests that reading is not always linear, moving from letter recognition to recognition of letter patterns. Rumelhart's interactive model and Stanovich's interactive-compensatory model explain how higher order knowledge structures can be used in addition to (or to compensate for deficiencies at) the lower order print analysis stage.

Component models (Carr et al., 1990) add context use and strategic control processes to aspects such as short term memory and visual, semantic, and phonological processing. In the component models, these processes are decomposable but interactive; all parts of the system need to be functioning together to be effective.

Limited capacity processors. To continue the computer metaphor, imagine you are using a personal computer, occasionally saving, retrieving, or printing files as you work. You may notice that while the machine is printing one file, it takes longer for the typed letters in your new file to appear on the screen. Or, if you save a document during printing, the printer may pause. This is because computers, though capable of performing multiple activities simultaneously and quickly, must divide their "attention" among different tasks. Information processing theorists use the computer metaphor to describe the limited capacity of readers and writers, who must often juggle several subprocesses at once.

Readers operate at several levels, including word recognition and identification, understanding and using syntactic structures, accessing background knowledge, and operating with fluency as they read (Beck, 1985). Writers must also operate at numerous levels, including planning and organizing their ideas, making decisions about relevant or redundant information, and monitoring their plans as they draft and revise written material (Raphael & Englert, 1989).

Just as the computer cannot attend to everything at once, so are humans limited. In fact, as Beck (1985) suggests, if readers have "to give direct attention to too many things...their reading system [may be] overloaded" (p. 249). How readers and writers come to juggle the subprocesses necessary to read and write successfully is explained in terms of how much attention is actually necessary to perform a given activity and how effectively they switch their attention to the process most useful for a particular task at hand.

Automation of processes.   LaBerge and Samuels (1974) use the term "automaticity" to describe the way skilled readers' subprocesses are instinctive routines. Initially the more specific subprocesses—such as decoding during reading or handwriting during composition—are so demanding that higher level processes, such as metacognitive strategies, cannot be employed. Eventually, however, specific subprocesses are mastered to the point of automaticity and new routines can be learned (Carr et al., 1990). While not all subprocesses become automatic (e.g., comprehension and planning always involve some conscious attention), the more that do become automatic, the better the reader or writer is able to attend to more cognitively demanding activities.

These three assumptions, which form the basis of cognitive information processing models, can be seen in several models of reading and writing. To date, however, there has been little attempt to detail the specific links between reading and writing from within this perspective, although two areas of research have received broad attention. As in the individual models, the research into reading/writing connections within this perspective generally first describes the processes themselves and then studies how readers and writers structure their knowledge about these processes.

Reading/Writing Research

Information processing theory has contributed to our understanding of reading/writing processes and their underlying knowledge structures. In this section, we discuss a few representative studies in this field of research. As noted earlier, a major concern of information processing theorists is describing the reading and writing processes. To do so, they focus on analyzing the components of writing and reading and on the relationships among them in order to understand the effects of one process on the other.

Much of the research described previously illustrates how the information processing perspective has guided questions about the nature of reading and writing. However, only a limited amount of research directly examines the relationship between the underlying knowledge important to each activity. In one series of studies, Shanahan (1984) and Shanahan and Lomax (1986) identified components of the reading and writing processes and examined how the knowledge structures underlying successful literacy learning change as students' abilities develop.

Not surprisingly, these researchers found reading and writing to be interactive processes, particularly in terms of their components. One component of knowledge shared by new readers and writers is sound/symbol relationships. Younger students' ability to use phonics rules in decoding correlates with their ability to spell words when writing. Of particular interest, however, is the way this relationship changes as children mature. In older students such knowledge plays a less important role than does knowledge of vocabulary, story structure, and comprehension strategies.

Shanahan's work illustrates researchers' probing into the way in which writing and reading knowledge influence students' literacy learning and development. Stotsky (1983) wrote a review of the literature examining reading/writing connections and found that in general, better writers tend to be better readers and that better readers tend to produce more syntactically mature writing than poorer readers. Wittrock (1983) similarly concluded that writing experiences influence reading comprehension. He found that students' comprehension of text improved when they wrote paragraph summaries following reading. He also described another study in which students who wrote about their own experiences in relation to texts they had read improved their comprehension of those texts.

Researchers also have looked at the effects of reading on writing. Eckhoff (1983), finding that children's writing reflected the features of the basal texts they had used, concluded that what students had read influenced their writing. In a more recent study, Spivey and King (1989) examined students' ability to synthesize in writing information from different texts they had read. They found that accomplished readers produced elaborate plans and were successful at creating a synthesized work from a variety of sources. Further, their writing reflected the influence of these various texts.

A second type of research common to the information processing perspective is the study of expert versus novice readers and writers. The assumption is that the differences between these two groups will reveal the knowledge structures critical to success in literacy. The importance of underlying knowledge structures has been examined in terms of knowledge of text structure, word meaning, and print conventions.

Recently researchers have examined the importance of text-structure knowledge in terms of its impact on both writing and reading, particularly in reference to expository text. In several studies, results have suggested that both reading and writing abilities benefit from such knowledge (Armbruster, Anderson, & Ostertag, 1987; Raphael & Kirschner, 1985; Taylor & Beach, 1984). Duin and Graves (1987) found that knowledge of word meanings leads to reading comprehension and can improve the quality of writing. Ehri (1989), studying knowledge of print conventions and their relationship to reading and writing, has suggested that reading can direct a writer's attention to these conventions while writing enhances a reader's grasp of alphabetic structure.

However, in spite of the information detailing how reading and writing may be related, information processing theory sheds little light on how to encourage their development, how less successful or novice readers and writers become more skilled, or the kind of environment that fosters literacy development.

Strengths and Limitations

Information processing models and research have explored reading and writing and potential ways in which they relate. As a result of this work, we understand the processes themselves in terms of their complexities, their components, and the knowledge base of skilled readers and writers. However, several limitations affect our understanding of reading/writing connections based on this view; three are particularly relevant if considering implications for instruction.

First, information processing models are often based on differences between expert and novice learners (Hayes & Flower, 1980; Scardamalia & Bereiter, 1986). While these contrasts are useful in identifying critical knowledge that young or naive learners need to acquire, they do not address the important factor of how the novice becomes more expert.

Second, Applebee (1986) suggests that the processes involved in writing may vary depending on the nature of the writing task, goals, and purposes. These processes may also vary depending on the instructional context, the writer's own history, and the writer's knowledge base. Current information processing models tend to overlook or dismiss important features such as the context in which learning literacy skills occurs, social practices, and different cultures' views of the purposes for and ways of carrying out literacy tasks. Denying the importance of such factors may lead to decontextualized learning of subskills or routines, much as we see in some workbook pages from basal reading series.

A third limitation stems from the way in which information processing theories portray reading and writing as a series of subprocesses operating in a rather linear fashion, rather than in a more recursive way (Kucer, 1985). These models may be interpreted as suggesting that instruction also be linear; for instance, some instructors might use the notion of automaticity to defend the practice of teaching routines or subskills before allowing new readers and writers to engage in meaningful literacy acts.

In sum, while research within an information processing theory may provide valuable information about the components of reading and writing processes, its applicability to the teaching of reading and writing is limited. It is important to consider the way individuals interact with the environment in which their abilities develop.

Piagetian/Naturalist Theories

The naturalist perspective of learning focuses on individuals' innate cognitive structures. These structures have been characterized in terms of language ability (Chomsky, 1965) and general cognitive structures (Piaget, 1926). Consistent with an emphasis on innate language abilities and the role of the environment in allowing these abilities to unfold is the whole language approach. Those who have articulated whole language teaching methods suggest that language learning is both personal and social and is driven by the learner's need to make sense of the world (Goodman, 1967, 1986; Goodman & Goodman, 1977; Harste, Woodward, & Burke, 1984; Smith, 1982).

Proponents of this perspective suggest that the development of reading and writing is based on the acquisition of oral language. This view stems from the assumption that written and oral language share the same basic characteristics, one of which being that they develop naturally (Goodman, 1986). Thus, language learning moves from whole to part with no hierarchy of subskills; that is, words are learned before letters, stories are read before sentences, meaning is acquired within the context of reading and writing. Learning to read and write involves actively reading and writing, rather than learning to master specific skills or participating in formal instruction. Literacy learning occurs when "a person invents language all over again in trying to communicate with the world" (Goodman, p. 18). Learners construct knowledge of written language as part of their ongoing attempts at comprehension and composition.

This theory of language learning derives from a phenomenological philosophy (Husserl, 1962) and is related to various aspects of a Piagetian developmental theory of learning (Flavell, 1977; Miller, 1983; Piaget, 1926). According to phenomenological thought, we all are born into the *Lebenswelt* or "life-world." In contrast to the existence of an objective reality, this life-world is the reality that is organized and experienced by the individual (Eagleton, 1983; Husserl).

Phenomenological theory suggests that individuals interpret the natural world and endow objects and people with personal meaning. The self is the source of meaning, and the external world is reflected within and interpreted by the individual's consciousness. Culture is part of the external world that must be interpreted and imbued with subjective meaning; speech and written language are means for humans to participate in interpreting culture. It follows within this view that language is a natural part of the world. The child gradually differentiates and integrates the life-world—including its language—through his own activity (Husserl, 1962; Phelps, 1988).

Basic Assumptions

Three premises, originally articulated in Piaget's theory of development, are critical to this perspective: (1) thinking resembles logico-mathematical structures; (2) the child is inherently active, constructing knowledge and continually trying to maintain equilibrium between him or herself and the environment; and (3) cognitive development depends on the learner acting upon the world.

Thinking resembles logical, universal structures. Humans, like all animals, must be able to adapt to their environment to survive. Unlike more simple creatures, however, humans can do this by using their intelligence. Adaptation for humans occurs through two cognitive processes: assimilation and accommodation. Assimilation involves fitting reality into the learner's current knowledge structures. For example, a child may have an established schema, or concept, of *dogs* that includes two different kinds. When a third breed is encountered, the child assimilates that information into his or her current knowledge structure. In this way, the learner's schemata grow and develop as new information and new ideas are encountered.

The second process, accommodation, involves adjusting the knowledge structure to fit the demands of reality. For example, the child may have a schema for *dog* that includes all four-legged animals. When he or she encounters a horse and learns of specific differences between this creature and others in the dog concept, the child may create a new schema to accommodate the concept of *horse*.

The degree to which assimilation and accommodation are successful relates to the learner's stages of development. These stages are organized patterns of behavior that become increasingly abstract and differentiated over time. They are referred to as the sensorimotor, preoperational, concrete operational, and formal operational periods. Piaget characterized these stages as universal and invariant structural wholes that emerge from and transform previous stages.

With regard to literacy, the Piagetian perspective suggests that children learn oral and written language in order to accommodate and assimilate the print environment. Language use is functional; children are able to make sense of language when it meets real needs. This perspective implies that children have strategies that develop over time as they experience language. These strategies include (1) text intent, in which students expect text to make sense; (2) negotiability, in which children use what they know already to make sense of print; (3) risk-taking, in which students hypothesize about the meaning of print; and (4) fine-tuning, in which students use previously learned language in a new situation (Harste, Woodward, & Burke, 1984).

The child actively constructs knowledge.   The need for activity is essential to the Piagetian perspective, for it is through hands-on activity that the child experiences the world, challenges his or her existing beliefs and schemata, and moves through the stages of development.

Learning to read involves interacting with the print environment. Learning occurs when children actively construct their own meanings and have the opportunity to "become language users by mapping language onto experience" (Newman, 1985, p. 9). The learner gains meaning from imposing his or her own experience on the text and checking possible interpretations against past experience. The learner selects and interprets information from the environment. Thus, a child may see the word "Oreos" on a package of a particular kind of cookie and identify the letter sequence as "cookies." Only after a number of encounters within the print environment, perhaps including attempts to communicate in writing with others, does the child develop the appropriate connections between print and word meaning.

Further, the experiences of the child are continually filtered through the child's current understanding. In reading, this idea implies that when a child encounters a new word in a text, that new word is learned within the context of the rest of the text and is based on the child's existing knowledge of words and meaning. For instance, when a child substitutes a word that shares some graphemes with the word actually in the text and that makes sense in context, the child is building on current understanding. Children are able to correct themselves when what is read does not fit into the meaning they are trying to construct (Newman, 1985). This self-correction can occur because the child is constantly changing and monitoring learning.

Over time and through self-monitoring, the child develops the ability to construct meaning from text. Reading and writing change qualitatively as the child matures and develops. The texts that students read or write become more sophisticated with increased language use; these changes reflect changes in cognitive structures.

Development through stages. In Piagetian theory, internal cognitive structures are formed as the child progresses through universal stages of development. Changes in these structures occur as the result of interaction between the individual and the environment. Physical maturation, experience with physical objects, social experience, and equilibration (a balance between the organism and the environment) promote movement from one stage to another.

Whole language incorporates this view of learning by suggesting that reading and writing are natural processes that occur as the result of maturation and interaction with the language world. Implicit in this idea of language development is the concept of readiness; children will learn to read and write when they are developmentally ready and are engaged in meaningful activities that require them to act upon the world. Since in this view cognitive development depends on the learner *acting*, it is essential that the learner have opportunities to interact with print.

Reading/Writing Research

Since the naturalist perspective suggests that students learn through interacting with the print environment, studies within this perspective have focused on the natural ways in which children acquire language. Reading and writing are connected in that both are grounded in oral language. That is, research has not focused on how reading and writing per se are connected, but rather on how written language develops from students' natural abilities and experiences with oral language.

For example, research in emergent literacy examines the relationship between oral and written language in young children (Clay, 1975; Sulzby, 1986; Teale, 1986). Studies indicate that children make sense of the activities of reading and writing long before formal instruction begins and that they have an awareness of print conventions at a very early age. Naturalist researchers such as Harste, Woodward, and Burke (1984) have studied how young children develop strategies for making sense of text. They suggest that children expect text to make sense, that they use their existing knowledge to understand text, and that they have a risk-taking attitude toward text. Children also use the language they have already encountered as a resource for additional experiences with language. Goodman (1967, 1973) has examined students' miscues as a way of understanding how readers make sense of text. Miscue analysis suggests that during reading, students call into play their knowledge of how meaning is constructed and how language operates.

Instruction from a whole language perspective draws from the research of Graves (1983) and Calkins (1983) on children's development as writers. Graves concluded that writers discover meaning as they write and that there is a strong link between the emerging text and thought. He and Hansen (1984) both found that students' development in writing was related to the drawings they produced, that students "rehearsed" before writing, and that their talk with peers in school facilitated their learning. Calkins found that children could become increasingly sophisticated at revising their texts through continual writing and talking about writing.

Studies of the role of the classroom context highlight the importance of establishing a literate environment for promoting literacy development. In examining the influence of print environment on students' writing, DeFord (1986) found that both the form and the content of writing varied as a function of the classroom context. Revision and rehearsal occurred in literature-based classrooms but not in traditional or mastery learning classrooms, and students' writing mirrored the syntax of their textbooks.

Because of the importance of the classroom environment in the naturalist perspective, future research into reading and writing connections will likely take place within the classroom context and focus on how students make sense of the texts they read and write. Research questions might include these two: How do oral language activities facilitate the connection between reading and writing? How do individuals learn to connect reading and writing through the functional uses of the processes?

Studies might include the tracing of students' oral language in learning to read and write. Case studies could include descriptions of natural settings to find out how children use what they read in their writing and, conversely, how their own writing influences their interpretations and uses of what they read. Further development of miscue analysis could examine the relationships between errors made in reading and children's learning of conventional forms of print in their writing. These research questions highlight some of the strengths of the naturalist views while addressing some of the weaknesses.

Strengths and Limitations

The major strength of the naturalist perspective is its focus on the child as a changing, developing organism rather than as a static processor. Because it follows a developmental model, the theory attempts to account for children's growth from their interactions with the environment. Viewing the child as an active constructor of knowledge focuses our attention on the need to understand individuals and how they acquire language. Because language is functional in this view, children must be involved in meaningful activities to construct knowledge. This belief has encouraged educators to provide literacy experiences that build on children's knowledge and provide many opportunities for students to participate in reading and writing activities.

The naturalist view is not without limitations, however. First, the notion of universal, invariant stages across cultures has not held up empirically because it fails to take into account vast differences in ways of thinking within human society (Laboratory for Comparative Human Cognition, 1983; Scribner & Cole, 1981). Because the theory is biological, it assumes that literacy development occurs in the same sort of stages as physical growth, thereby suggesting that literacy is universal. The lack of social and cultural foci diminishes the role of society and emphasizes the individual child over the larger social organization. The theory does not take into consideration language practices that differ across cultures or historical periods.

Second, the theory assumes that language acquisition occurs through accommodation and assimilation as the learner tests out hypotheses about the meaning of the environment based on previous experience. Yet the theory lacks specificity in describing how assimilation and accommodation actually occur. For instance, how does the process of differentiating the horse from the dog actually take place? Simply stating that reading and writing are natural processes begs the question of how one learns them. Because the theory suggests learning is based on prior knowledge, it fails to account for how a learner generates new knowledge.

The third limitation is that this theory underemphasizes the role of the teacher (Phelps, 1988). If learning occurs naturally through the child acting upon the world, then the teacher's role becomes secondary to that of the environment itself. While this perspective may recognize that the teacher is critical in enriching or structuring the environment, it is difficult to infer exactly what should be done instructionally.

In sum, while this perspective suggests the kind of environment in which students may acquire the knowledge bases identified by information processing theorists, it fails to provide pedagogical information about how learners actually acquire new knowledge, relying heavily on the belief that such knowledge is simply acquired "naturally."

Florio-Ruane and Lensmire (1989) suggest that "Learning to write involves not only achieving propositional and procedural knowledge of language structure and norms, but also acquiring beliefs, values, and attitudes about self, others, and text. A mature writer can perceive and use writing as a tool for communicating and also as a means of furthering his or her own thinking and learning of new subject matter." How the mature writer develops, and what constitutes the environment in which such development occurs, is addressed more thoroughly by social-constructivist theorists.

Social-Constructivist Theories

A social-constructivist view of learning has its philosophical roots in the work of Wittgenstein (1953) and Mead (1934), and has been further articulated in the work of Harré (1984) and others. These philosophers share with Kuhn (1962) the conceptualization of knowledge as a social artifact that is maintained through a community of peers. Knowledge, then, is not based on an objective reality that can be measured and quantified, but rather is consensually formed through social interaction (Bruffee, 1984, 1986).

The psychological roots of social constructivism are based on the theories of Vygotsky (1978, 1986; cited in Wertsch, 1985) and others who have developed and modified his views (Bruner, 1985; Cole, 1985; Rogoff, 1986). In this view, knowledge is constructed by the interactions of individuals within society; all thought is social in nature. Learning is an internalization of social interaction that occurs first between individuals and then within an individual. Internalization occurs in the "zone of proximal development" through "adult guidance or in collaboration with more capable peers" (Vygotsky, 1978, p. 86).

Basic Assumptions

A social-constructivist theory of human learning is predicated on three assumptions: (1) knowledge is constructed through the individual's interaction with the sociocultural environment; (2) higher mental functions, including reading and writing, are social and cultural in nature; and (3) knowledgeable members of a culture can help others learn.

Interactive nature of knowledge. Social constructivism assumes that knowledge is constructed through consensus by communities of knowledgeable peers (Kuhn, 1962). In contrast to information processing theories, social constructivism suggests that there is no objective reality that can be measured or mirrored; nor is reality structured by the individual, as suggested in the naturalist perspective.

The changing definition of literacy provides an example of how knowledge is formed through consensus and can evolve and change over time. In the 17th and 18th centuries, literacy was understood to be the ability to decode words aloud to the satisfaction of an examiner, with no requirement for comprehending or applying the information. In the 1920s, students were expected to read silently and answer comprehension questions in order to be considered literate (Resnick & Resnick, 1977). Today some definitions of literacy require students to draw inferences about the material they have read. These changing definitions reflect the consensual nature of knowledge that is inherent in a social-constructivist view.

Individuals use socially constructed sign systems to act on the environment, including interactions between the culture and the individual (Langer, 1987; Vygotsky, 1986). Topics and conventions change over time as the individual interacts with the culture (Scribner & Cole, 1981). Within the culture of American classrooms students learn the skills of decoding words, forming letters, reading for comprehension, and drawing inferences—all conventions of this society. As they achieve these skills, they are able to influence the context of the classroom while they interact with others. The interactions of the individual with others in the society is bound to the second assumption of social-constructivist theory—that all thought is essentially social in nature.

The social nature of higher mental functions. Vygotsky (1986) characterizes higher mental functions (such as reading and writing) as those that require voluntary self-regulation, conscious realization, and the use of signs for mediation. Such functions are social in nature and depend on communication across generations and between individuals. The acquisition of such functions begins with the interaction of individuals such as a parent and child, siblings, or teacher and students. Vygotsky describes such learning as occurring first on an interpsychological plane—or between people—and then on an intrapsychological plane—within the individual. The role of language and dialogue is critical since it is through speech and social interaction that the learner acquires new abilities.

For example, children may scribble in their early attempts to write. Simply leaving them alone to explore print and "naturally" develop their writing ability may not be effective for all learners. Vygotskian perspectives suggest that students learn about the functions of print, and about the conventional forms that allow print to communicate, through interaction with a more knowledgeable adult or peer. Through the modeling and thinking aloud of the more expert person, students learn the role of writing within our culture, the relationships between writing and reading, different ways of thinking when planning to read or write, and so forth.

The term "zone of proximal development" (ZPD) has been used to describe how learners develop higher mental functions. The ZPD is defined as the "distance between a child's actual developmental level as determined through independent problem solving and potential development as determined through problem solving under adult guidance or a collaboration with more capable peers" (Vygotsky, 1978, p. 86). Three interrelated assumptions underlie the ZPD: (1) there is a difference between what the child can accomplish now and his or her potential for further learning; (2) what can be achieved alone is different from what can be achieved with the help of a knowledgeable adult or peer; and (3) a deliberate transfer of control from the more knowledgeable to the less knowledgeable person takes place. How the adult—or more knowledgeable person—assists the student in taking control of the process is integral to social-constructivist theory.

Assisted learning. Assisted instruction has been compared to a scaffold in that it is temporary and adjustable, and provides support (Applebee &

Langer, 1983; Wood, Bruner, & Ross, 1976). This educational scaffolding involves structuring tasks through instruction, modeling, questioning, and feedback until the learner can operate independently. Cazden (1983) describes how mothers provide assisted instruction for their children in games such as peek-a-boo. Mothers model the game for their children and say the words aloud, providing feedback until the child can initiate the process with others. Pearson (1985) describes this process as one that begins with a period of modeling and thinking aloud, moves toward a period of joint responsibility, and ends with students assuming control of the strategy.

For example, to teach awareness of the availability of different sources of information for answering questions (Raphael, 1986), the teacher could model reading a paragraph, asking a question, thinking aloud about what kinds of information are relevant to the question, exploring the text and her knowledge base as she searches for this information, and, finally, constructing an appropriate answer to the question. Over time, teachers and students assume joint responsibility for the activities within the strategy until eventually students can create their own texts or mental representations from reading, generate questions related to their texts, consider sources of information for answering their questions, and evaluate the most appropriate information for their response. Similar approaches have been used by Palincsar and her colleagues (Palincsar, 1984; Palincsar & Brown, 1984) in teaching comprehension strategies and by Englert and Raphael (1989) in developing expository literacy skills. As these examples demonstrate, dialogue is essential to improved performance in the social-constructivist point of view.

Reading/Writing Research

The basic assumptions of a social-constructivist position argue for the social nature of relationships between reading and writing; that is, social constructivism would emphasize that reading and writing are connected through their uses within the culture and through the role dialogue plays in the development of literacy. To date, little research on reading/writing connections from this perspective exists. Rather, social constructivists have focused on issues related to the role of culture in literacy practices and in cognition (Bruner, 1985; Greenfield, 1966; Heath, 1982; Scribner & Cole, 1981).

Scribner and Cole's (1981) study of the Vai people of Liberia has provided much insight about the role of cultural practices and contexts in relation to literacy. They found that different forms of literate activity required different cognitive operations and that these abilities depend on the functions

McCarthey and Raphael

they serve in the society. These findings alert us to the importance of the role of the culture in reading and writing.

Class structure, the relationship between literacy practices in schools, and the value of literacy within communities are important aspects of the role of culture in cognition. For example, Heath's (1982) studies of the preschool environment of students from three distinct socioeconomic communities provide insight into the advantages mainstream students bring with them when they begin school. These children had already been initiated into patterns of literacy behavior that included responding to questions for which the asker already had the answer, labeling and grouping items, linking text characters to events in real life, and listening quietly to stories read by others.

In contrast, students from the two working-class communities either had some experiences but did not make links between book experiences and real-world literacy, or they had not participated in school-type literacy experiences at all. Students from these backgrounds were not as successful in school as the middle-class students whose experiences matched those of the school environment. As Heath (1982) suggests, "knowing more about how these alternatives are learned at early ages in different sociocultural conditions can help the school to provide opportunities for *all* students to avail themselves of these alternatives early in their school careers" (p. 73).

These findings suggest important questions to explore about the relationship between reading and writing, recommendations for establishing appropriate environments for literacy development, and instructional practices to promote reading/writing connections.

Social-constructivist researchers interested in examining reading and writing connections might be interested in these questions: Does the interpsychological become intrapsychological in the same way for reading and writing? Because of the centrality of the role of discourse in the theory, researchers might explore in depth the role of dialogue in promoting reading and writing connections. How does dialogue facilitate students' ability to make connections between reading and writing? Since the teacher is the society member responsible for assisting students, social-constructivist researchers might be interested in exploring the role of the teacher in making reading/writing connections.

Strengths and Limitations

Social constructivism has several strengths for examining literacy. First, it avoids the extremes of suggesting either that there is an objective world that we try to recreate in our minds (as in information processing theory) or that reality consists of our interpretations of subjective experiences (as in the naturalist perspective). Rather, a social-constructivist perspective makes a compelling case for a view of knowledge based on consensus.

Second, a social-constructivist theory accounts for variations among cultures in language practices and in the ways children learn to read and write in different settings. The theory highlights the role of social context and brings our attention to the need to be sensitive to the values and practices of different cultural groups in schools.

Third, because social constructivism is a developmental theory, it avoids expert-novice contrasts and explains how children acquire new learning. The focus on language as a cultural tool is both explanatory in terms of how new learning is acquired and helpful in formulating pedagogical goals and strategies.

The limitations of social constructivism stem largely from the difficulty of testing the theory. Because the theory neither lends itself to being reduced to components as information processing does nor is totally holistic in the way naturalist theories tend to be, testing is difficult. Research questions and methodological issues become more complex when a social-constructivist approach is used. Neither traditional quantitative studies that seek to specify and find regularities nor naturalist case studies that focus on individuals can satisfactorily capture the complexity of the interaction between the individual and the sociocultural environment.

Social constructivism is further limited by the relationship between enculturation and transformation of the mind. The social-constructivist theory explains how a child is led to adapt to a prevailing culture, but it fails to account for the individual's ability to be inventive. The tension between enculturation and transformation is unresolved and merits further theoretical and empirical work.

Like information processing and naturalist theories, social constructivism suggests implications for instruction in classrooms. In the next section we contrast information processing, naturalist, and social-constructivist perspectives in terms of their instructional implications in reading and writing.

Instructional Implications

Views of learning influence how we structure classroom environments, select instructional methods, and define teachers' roles. Information process-

McCarthey and Raphael

ing, naturalist, and social-constructivist theories result in different visions of appropriate literacy instruction. In his meta-analysis of writing instruction, Hillocks (1984) identified three modes of instruction: presentational, natural, and environmental. These three modes relate closely to the theoretical perspectives described here; they are relevant to reading as well as writing. In this section, we use Hillocks' categories to discuss the roles of instruction and the teacher, students, and the classroom environment.

Instruction and the Teacher

Hillocks (1984) describes the presentational mode of instruction as having these characteristics:

> (a) relatively clear and specific objectives...; (b) lecture and teacher-led discussion dealing with concepts to be learned and applied; (c) the study of models...[to] illustrate the concept; (d) specific assignments...[that] involve imitating a pattern or following rules that have been previously discussed; and (e) feedback coming primarily from teachers (p. 147).

Such features are consistent with the perspective that there is an objective reality that can be transmitted to the naive learner through direct instruction by a teacher.

Because reading and writing consist of component processes with related strategies learned to the point of automaticity, instruction from an information processing perspective would focus on the teaching and learning of strategies related to the subprocesses. For example, prediction skills have been shown to be important in planning one's reading (Hansen & Pearson, 1983) in much the same way that writers predict information as they plan their writing (Englert et al., 1988).

From an information processing perspective, teachers should help students become as skilled in predicting as possible. Instruction might begin with a lecture or teacher-led discussion about what a prediction is, followed by several simple prediction activities. As students become proficient, materials of increasing difficulty would be introduced until the students are ready to practice prediction in the context of reading or writing a text. Successful predictions would be judged by the teacher, who would provide practice materials that fit students' ability levels. Texts that students read as well as what they write would be well structured and hierarchical since skills build on one another.

Unfortunately, such an approach can be interpreted as support for the teaching of isolated skills using highly structured materials—workbook pages and the infamous "ditto sheet"—rather than teaching skills in more meaningful contexts. Materials may be artificially created so students can learn (eventually to the level of automaticity) specific letter sounds, words (e.g., Dolch word lists), or skills (e.g., finding the main idea). Actual links between reading and writing may be neglected until students have "mastered" related strategies within each area. While information processing theorists do not necessarily promote such an interpretation, the potential for this approach is worth noting.

In contrast, the whole language approach deriving from a naturalist perspective emphasizes the wholeness of language. Hillocks (1984) characterizes such an approach as the natural mode of instruction. Specific features include broad objectives (e.g., to increase fluency), use of journals so student writers can explore topics of interest, writing for a real audience (such as peers), opportunities for revision, and high levels of peer interaction.

Because language learning is natural, teachers should "lead from behind," letting students explore areas of interest to them. The curriculum in the whole language approach derives from naturally occurring print (e.g., signs, labels), predictable books, trade books, and children's experiences in the world. Since students can learn without deliberate assistance (Smith, 1982), the teacher's role is that of facilitator, establishing an environment in which students can explore literacy. As Newman (1985) states, "Our role is to create situations in which children can discover the predictability of print for themselves" (p. 21).

In this approach, teachers do not lecture but rather provide opportunities for students to learn by encouraging them to explore language, asking open-ended questions and promoting opportunities for writing and shared and sustained silent reading. Students have many choices about activities in which to participate, books to read, and writing topics. From such a perspective, children would learn specific skills such as prediction through natural interactions with printed text, just as they learn to generate hypotheses in oral language activities.

Instruction from a social-constructivist view is more directed than in whole language classrooms but less directed than in information processing classrooms. Hillocks (1984) identifies this perspective as the environmental mode of instruction, characterized by (1) clear and specific objectives (e.g., make predictions or brainstorm to prepare for writing), (2) selection of materials and problems that encourage students to work together on specified processes important to some aspect of literacy learning, and (3) activities conducive to peer interaction.

Teachers give few lectures, instead making introductory comments before having students undertake independent work. As in the presentational mode, instructors teach principles, but within meaningful contexts that inherently promote those principles.

Teaching about predictions from this perspective might take the form of instruction, as in Palincsar's (1984) reciprocal teaching procedure. In this approach, the teacher first models a strategy (e.g., prediction) while reading an expository selection with students. Initial discussions focus on how predicting relates to text comprehension. Students then take turns being the teacher, leading discussions that focus on making predictions. The teacher supports the students in their initial attempts, sometimes helping them get started or making suggestions about the content of their predictions. This support gradually diminishes as students become better able to assume the responsibilities themselves.

Two key features characterize instruction in a social-constructivist classroom: the conscious use of dialogue and the development of particular ways for students to internalize dialogue. Instruction is structured in that teachers model by thinking aloud, but students gradually assume control of the processes. The teacher's role is to provide assistance through dialogue so that students gradually take control.

The Role of the Student

In each of the three perspectives, the role of the student is inversely related to the role of the teacher; that is, the more active the teacher is in directing learning, the more passive the student is in making decisions about what to read and write, how to initiate projects, and so forth. Thus, whereas the teacher is very active in the information processing model, providing information and structuring tasks, the student is relatively passive, following the teacher's lead in learning specific skills.

In contrast, students are very active in a whole language classroom; they discover the meaning of language when *they* are ready. It is the students' responsibility to interact with the environment; the teacher provides the opportunities. "Children...become writers (and readers) by learning to make these decisions for themselves.... Children must feel comfortable exploring written language in whatever way interests them" (Newman, 1985, p. 31).

With social constructivism, teachers and students construct knowledge together; both are active. Teachers have a responsibility to base their instruction on the background their students bring to the strategy or activity to be learned. However, students are expected to participate actively as they develop these strategies in meaningful contexts and work toward specific literacy goals.

The Role of the Classroom Environment

Information processing theories have little to say about the context in which literacy skills are developed because of their basic assumption that these processes are stable across contexts. However, in both the naturalist and social-constructivist perspectives the role of the classroom environment is critical because of the primacy of social interaction.

Differences between the naturalist and social-constructivist perspectives can be predicted from the discussion of the roles of teachers and students. In a naturalist, or whole language, setting, the important features include a print-rich environment with a range of books, many opportunities for writing on topics selected by students, chances to share with peers, and the freedom to experiment without risk. A social-constructivist classroom environment is likely to have many of these features, with the critical difference being an emphasis on dialogue between teacher and students and among peers. In a whole language classroom, writing and reading are considered social because they involve an audience and because students can assist one another. In a social-constructivist classroom, however, dialogue plays a more prominent role. The dialogue itself is not merely facilitative but actually formative in the development of the students' thinking about literacy.

Many current practices in creating a literate environment and providing social interaction in literacy learning are advocated by both naturalists and social constructivists. In fact, observations across classrooms suggest that instructional practices may borrow from different theories. It is unlikely that a classroom would reflect totally the principles of a single theory. Although both types of classroom appear similar, they may vary because of the teacher's individual style and grounding in different psychological perspectives.

An example can be seen in the widespread use of Graves and Hansen's (1983) "Author's Chair," where students sit to share their own writing, the writing of their peers, or that of a professional author. From a whole language view, the Author's Chair provides an opportunity for students to develop their oral language abilities and to share their writing. From the social-constructivist perspective, it provides students with an opportunity to use language about writing and reading and engage in dialogue that will lead to their assuming control of their own cognitive processes.

Dialogue journals (Atwell, 1984) may also have different underlying purposes when considered from these two perspectives. Teachers' and students' ongoing written responses to reading provide a window into the students' thinking for the social constructivists while serving as an example of purposeful writing for those who adhere to the naturalist perspective.

Concluding Comments

It is tempting to assume that the existence of different theoretical perspectives suggests that we must search for the accurate theory, testing one against the other until we have discovered the "truth" about reading/writing connections. However, it may be more realistic to recognize that each perspective contributes to an understanding of different aspects of literacy processes and how they relate.

As we have described, the three perspectives suggest different ways in which reading and writing are related. Further, these relationships have differing implications for instruction. For instance, the focus on component parts in information processing theory implies that reading and writing are connected by matching individual components. In contrast, the naturalist theory suggests that reading and writing are naturally connected through oral language. Social constructivism implies that a teacher, as a knowledgeable member of a culture, needs to make the links between reading and writing through dialogue and directed activities.

The three theories can work together to build a picture of the converging processes of reading and writing. The information processing lens focuses on questions related to the components of writing and reading, relationships among the components, effects of one process on the other, expert/novice and good/poor reader differences, and the structure of knowledge. The lens of the naturalist theory focuses on questions related to the type of environment that facilitates and supports reading and writing, issues in creating child-centered curricula, and children's underlying cognitive structures. Finally, social-constructivist theories focus our attention on the issues of the social origins of reading and writing, emergent literacy (including connections between oral and written language), the developmental priorities of reading, writing, and oral language, how language and literacy tools have been used historically and across cultures, and how children learn to use literacy in unique and personal ways.

References

Applebee, A.N. (1986). Problems in process approaches: Toward a reconceptualization of instruction. In A.R. Petrosky & D. Bartholomae (Eds.), *Teaching of writing* (pp. 95-113). Chicago, IL: University of Chicago Press.

Applebee, A.N., & Langer, J. (1983). Instructional scaffolds: Reading and writing as natural language activities. *Language Arts, 60,* 168-175.

Armbruster, B.B., Anderson, T.H., & Ostertag, J. (1987). Does text structure/summarization instruction facilitate learning from expository text? *Reading Research Quarterly, 22,* 331-346.

Atwell, N. (1984). Writing and reading literature from the inside out. *Language Arts, 61,* 240-253.

Beck, I.L. (1985). Five problems with children's comprehension in the primary grades. In J. Osborn, P.T. Wilson, & R.C. Anderson (Eds.), *Reading education: Foundations for a literate America* (pp. 239-253). Lexington, MA: Lexington Books.

Bruffee, K.A. (1984). Collaborative learning and the "Conversation of mankind." *College English, 46,* 635-652.

Bruffee, K.A. (1986). Social construction, language, and the authority of knowledge: A bibliographic essay. *College English, 48,* 773-790.

Bruner, J.S. (1985). Vygotsky: A historical and conceptual perspective. In J.V. Wertsch (Ed.), *Culture, communication, and cognition: Vygotskian perspectives* (pp. 21-34). Cambridge, UK: Cambridge University Press.

Calkins, L. (1983). *Lessons from a child.* Portsmouth, NH: Heinemann.

Carr, T.H., Brown, T.L., Vavrus, L.G., & Evans, M. (1990). Cognitive skills maps and cognitive skill profiles: Componential analysis of individual differences in children's reading ability. In T.H. Carr & B.A. Levy (Eds.), *Reading and its development: Component skills approaches.* San Diego, CA: Academic.

Cazden, C.B. (1983). Adult assistance to language development: Scaffolds, models, and direct instruction. In R. Parker & F. Davis (Eds.), *Developing literacy: Young children's use of language* (pp. 3-18). Newark, DE: International Reading Association.

Chomsky, N.A. (1965). *Aspects of a theory of syntax.* Cambridge, MA: MIT Press.

Clay, M. (1975). *What did I write?* Portsmouth, NH: Heinemann.

Cole, M. (1985). The zone of proximal development: Where culture and cognition create each other. In J.V. Wertsch (Ed.), *Culture, communication and cognition: Vygotskian perspectives* (pp. 146-161). Cambridge, UK: Cambridge University Press.

Collins, A., & Gentner, D. (1980). A framework for a cognitive theory of writing. In L.W. Gregg & E.R. Steinberg (Eds.), *Cognitive processes in writing* (pp. 51-72). Hillsdale, NJ: Erlbaum.

de Beaugrande, R. (1982). Psychology and composition: Past, present, and future. In M. Nystrand (Ed.), *What writers know: The language, process, and structure of written discourse* (pp. 211-267). San Diego, CA: Academic.

DeFord, D.E. (1986). Classroom contexts for literacy learning. In T.E. Raphael (Ed.), *Contexts of school-based literacy* (pp. 163-180). New York: Random House.

Duin, A.H., & Graves, M.F. (1987). Intensive vocabulary instruction as a prewriting technique. *Reading Research Quarterly, 22,* 311-330

Eagleton, T. (1983). *Literary theory.* Minneapolis, MN: University of Minnesota Press.

Eckhoff, B. (1983). How reading affects children's writing. *Language Arts, 60,* 607-616.

Ehri, L.C. (1989). Movement into word reading and spelling: How spelling contributes to reading. In J.M. Mason (Ed.), *Reading and writing connections* (pp. 65-81). Needham Heights, MA: Allyn & Bacon.

Englert, C.S., & Raphael, T.E. (1989). Developing successful writers through cognitive strategy instruction. In J. Brophy (Ed.), *Advances in research on teaching. Vol. 1, Teaching for meaningful understanding and self-regulated learning.* Greenwich, CT: JAI Press.

Englert, C.S., Raphael, T.E., Anderson, L.M., & Fear, K.L. (1988). Students' metacognitive knowledge about how to write informational texts. *Learning Disability Quarterly, 11,* 18-46.

Flavell, J.H. (1977). *Cognitive development.* Englewood Cliffs, NJ: Prentice Hall.

Florio-Ruane, S., & Lensmire, T. (1989). The role of instruction in learning to write. In J. Brophy (Ed.), *Advances in research on teaching. Vol. 1, Teaching for meaningful understanding and self-regulated learning.* Greenwich, CT: JAI Press.

Flower, L., & Hayes, J. (1981). Plans that guide the composing process. In C.H. Frederiksen & J. Dominic (Eds.), *Writing: The nature, development, and teaching of written communication* (pp. 39-58). Hillsdale, NJ: Erlbaum.

Goodman, K. (1967). Reading: A psycholinguistic guessing game. *Journal of the Reading Specialist, 6,* 126-135.

Goodman, K. (1973). *Miscue analysis: Application to reading instruction.* Urbana, IL: National Council of Teachers of English.

Goodman, K. (1986). *What's whole in whole language?* Portsmouth, NH: Heinemann.

Goodman, K., & Goodman, Y. (1977). Learning about psycholinguistic processes by analyzing oral reading. *Harvard Educational Review, 47,* 317-333.

Gough, P.B. (1972). One second of reading. In J.F. Kavanagh & I.G. Mattingly (Eds.), *Language by ear and by eye* (pp. 331-358). Cambridge, MA: MIT Press.

Graves, D. (1983). *Writing: Teachers and children at work..* Portsmouth, NH: Heinemann.

Graves, D., & Hansen, J. (1983). The Author's Chair. *Language Arts, 60,* 176-183.

Greenfield, P. (1966). On culture and conservation. In J.S. Bruner et al. (Eds.), *Studies in cognitive growth* (pp. 225-256). New York: Wiley.

Hansen, J. (1984, November). *Elementary teachers provide rehearsal time.* Paper presented at National College of Teachers of Education, Detroit, MI.

Hansen, J., & Pearson, P.D. (1983). An instructional study: Improving the inferential comprehension of fourth grade good and poor readers. *Journal of Educational Psychology, 75,* 821-829.

Harré, R. (1984). Social sources of mental content and order. In J. Margolis, P.T. Manicas, R. Harré, & P.F. Secord (Eds.), *Psychology: Designing the discipline* (pp. 91-127). Oxford, UK: Basil Blackwell.

Harste, J.C., Woodward, V.A., & Burke, C.L. (1984). *Language stories and literacy lessons.* Portsmouth, NH: Heinemann.

Hayes, J.R., & Flower, L.S. (1980). Identifying the organization of writing processes. In L.W. Gregg & E.R. Steinberg (Eds.), *Cognitive processes in writing* (pp. 3-30). Hillsdale, NJ: Erlbaum.

Heath, S.B. (1982). What no bedtime story means: Narrative skills at home and at school. *Language in Society, 11,* 49-75.

Hillocks, G., Jr. (1984). What works in teaching composition: A meta-analysis of experimental treatment studies. *American Journal of Education, 93,* 133-170.

Husserl, E. (1962). *Ideas: General introduction to pure phenomenology* (W.R.B. Gibson, Trans.). New York: Collier.

Kintsch, W., & van Dijk, T. (1978). Toward a model of text comprehension and production. *Psychological Review, 85,* 363-394.

Kucer, S. (1985). The making of meaning: Reading and writing as parallel processes. *Written Communication, 2,* 317-336.

Kuhn, T.S. (1962). *The structure of scientific revolutions.* Chicago, IL: University of Chicago Press.

LaBerge, D., & Samuels, S.J. (1974). Toward a theory of automatic information processing in reading. *Cognitive Psychology, 6,* 293-323.

Laboratory for Comparative Human Cognition (1983). Culture and cognitive development. In W. Kessen (Ed.), *The handbook of child psychology: History, theory, and methods* (pp. 295-356). New York: Wiley.

Langer, J. (1987). A sociological perspective on literacy. In J. Langer (Ed.), *Language, literacy, and culture: Issues of society and schooling* (pp. 1-29). Norwood, NJ: Ablex.

Mead, G.H. (1934). *Mind, self, and society from the standpoint of a social behaviorist.* Chicago, IL: University of Chicago Press.

Miller, P.H. (1983). *Theories of developmental psychology.* New York: Freeman.

Newman, J. (1985). Insights from recent reading and writing research and their implications for developing a whole language curriculum. In J. Newman (Ed.), *Whole language: Theory in use* (pp. 7-36). Portsmouth, NH: Heinemann.

Palincsar, A. (1984). The quest for the meaning from expository text: A teacher-guided journey. In G. Duffy, L. Roehler, & J. Mason (Eds.), *Comprehension instruction: Perspectives and suggestions* (pp. 251-264). White Plains, NY: Longman.

Palincsar, A., & Brown, A. (1984). Reciprocal teaching of comprehension-fostering and comprehension-monitoring activities. *Cognition and Instruction, 1,* 117-175.

Pearson, P.D. (1985). Changing the face of reading comprehension instruction. *The Reading Teacher, 38,* 724-738.

Phelps, L.W. (1988). Literacy and the limits of the natural attitude. In L.W. Phelps (Ed.), *Composition as a human science* (pp. 108-130). New York: Oxford University Press.

Piaget, J. (1926). *The language and thought of the child.* Orlando, FL: Harcourt Brace Jovanovich.

Raphael, T.E. (1986). Teaching Question Answer Relationships, revisited. *The Reading*

Teacher, 39, 516-522.

Raphael, T.E., & Englert, C.S. (1989). Integrating reading and writing instruction. In P. Winograd, K.K. Wixson, & M.Y. Lipson (Eds.), *Improving basal reader instruction* (pp. 231-255). New York: Teachers College Press.

Raphael, T.E., & Kirschner, B.M. (1985). *The effects of instruction in compare/contrast text structure on sixth-grade students' reading comprehension writing products* (Research Series No. 161). East Lansing, MI: Michigan State University, Institute for Research on Teaching.

Resnick, D.P., & Resnick, L.B. (1977). The nature of literacy: A historical exploration. *Harvard Educational Review, 47,* 370-385.

Rogoff, B. (1986). Adult assistance of children's learning. In T.E. Raphael (Ed.), *Contexts of school-based literacy* (pp. 27-40). New York: Random House.

Rumelhart, D. (1977). Toward an interactive model of reading. In S. Dornic (Ed.), *Attention and performance VI.* Hillsdale, NJ: Erlbaum.

Samuels, S.J., & Kamil, M. (1984). Models of the reading process. In P.D. Pearson (Ed.), *Handbook of reading research* (pp. 185-224). White Plains, NY: Longman.

Scardamalia, M. & Bereiter, C. (1986). Research on written composition. In M. Wittrock (Ed.), *Handbook of research on teaching* (3rd ed., pp. 778-803). New York: Macmillan.

Scardamalia, M., Bereiter, C., & Goelman, H. (1982). The role of production factors in writing ability. In M. Nystrand (Ed.), *What writers know: The language, process, and structure of written discourse* (pp. 173-210). San Diego, CA: Academic.

Scribner, S., & Cole, M. (1981). *The psychology of literacy.* Cambridge, MA: Harvard University Press.

Shanahan, T. (1984). The nature of the reading-writing relation: An exploratory multivariate analysis. *Journal of Educational Psychology, 76,* 466-477.

Shanahan, T., & Lomax, R. (1986). An analysis and comparison of theoretical models of the reading-writing relationship. *Journal of Educational Psychology, 78,* 116-123.

Smith, F. (1982). *Understanding reading* (3rd ed.). Orlando, FL: Holt, Rinehart & Winston.

Spivey, N.N., & King, J.R. (1989). Readers as writers. *Reading Research Quarterly, 24,* 9-26.

Stanovich, K.E. (1980). Toward an interactive-compensatory model of individual differences in the development of reading fluency. *Reading Research Quarterly, 16,* 32-71.

Stotsky, S. (1983). Research on reading/writing relationships: A synthesis and suggested directions. *Language Arts, 60,* 627-643.

Sulzby, E. (1986). Writing and reading: Signs of oral and written language organization in the young child. In W.H. Teale & E. Sulzby (Eds.), *Emergent literacy* (pp. 50-89). Norwood, NJ: Ablex.

Taylor, B.M., & Beach, R.W. (1984). The effects of text structure on middle-grade students' comprehension and production of expository text. *Reading Research Quarterly, 19,* 134-146.

Teale, W.H. (1986). Home background and young children's emergent literacy development. In W.H. Teale & E. Sulzby (Eds.), *Emergent literacy* (pp. 173-206). Norwood, NJ: Ablex.

Vygotsky, L. (1978). *Mind in society.* Cambridge, MA: Harvard University Press.

Vygotsky L. (1986). *Thought and language.* Cambridge, MA: MIT Press.

Wertsch, J.V. (1985). *Vygotsky and the social formation of mind.* Cambridge, MA: Harvard University Press.

Wittgenstein, L. (1953). *Philosophical investigations* (G.E.M. Anscomb, Trans.). Oxford, UK: Basil Blackwell.

Wittrock, M. (1983). Writing and the teaching of reading. *Language Arts, 60,* 600-606.

Wood, B., Bruner, J.S., & Ross, G. (1976). The role of tutoring in problem-solving. *Journal of Child Psychology and Psychiatry, 17,* 89-100.

Specific Reading/Writing Processes

— T W O —

Reading, Writing, and Genre Development

Although students' literacy knowledge and ability are at the core of education, too often the way knowledge and ability develop and change is overlooked. It is, of course, important to understand the knowledge, structures, and strategies that are called on during literacy activities; however, it is at least as important to know how knowledge shifts and grows over time.

My own work in children's literacy development has been motivated by my optimism about what learners can do rather than what they cannot, and by my conviction that reading and writing are inextricably bound to language and thought—that research and practice in one domain should inform research and practice in the other. In particular, I am concerned that the research of the 1960s (Brown & Bellugi, 1964; Bruner, Goodnow, & Austin, 1956; Weir, 1962), which helped us understand a great deal about the development of children's spoken language, has been neglected in our present-day attempts to understand reading and writing acquisition.

Studies suggest that children develop their own rules in acquiring oral language. These rules for language use are natural and consistent, but different from adults'. Further, teaching children to use adult rules has proved to be unproductive. For those of us interested in literacy, this work may suggest that as with oral language, children will develop their own rules for structuring written language, and that these rules will guide the ways in which they make sense of what they read and write. Further, with time and experience, these rules will change for both oral and written language until children come to use the rules of expression commonly accepted by adults in their community.

Much current research and practice in reading and writing (whether process or product oriented) runs counter to these notions and attempts to identify adult strategies and teach them to young children. In contrast, Vygotsky (1978) suggests that we support children in developing "those functions that have not yet matured, but are in a state of maturation, functions that will mature tomorrow but are currently in an embryonic state. These functions could be termed the 'buds' or 'flowers' rather than the 'fruits' of development" (p. 86). I have tried, in my work, to bridge the theoretical gap between child language research and literacy instruction and to learn from children what new knowledge and behaviors they embrace, so that we might better match classroom instruction to children's developmental journey.

Reading and writing are deeply related activities of language and cognition that are shaped through use (Langer, 1986). The structures and strategies that readers and writers use to organize, remember, and present messages are generally the same in reading and writing. These structures and strategies change in similar ways as the language user matures. However, all reading and writing activities are not the same, and the way in which children approach a reading or writing task is based on their reasons for doing the task in the first place. In literacy activities, form follows function; the structure of the message and the strategies used to formulate and organize it are driven by purpose. Thus, cultural experiences are an intrinsic aspect of the literacy skills that children learn. For example, in the United States, shopping lists often follow a particular brief and disconnected organizational form because of the purpose they serve—the purpose drives the form that both the writing and the reading will take. Similarly, stories often are shaped by organizational features that guide writers and readers through an imaginary journey, and the organizational forms of writing or reading for information are generally shaped by the need to present or obtain and use information. Because reading and writing activities have purpose, those of us who wish to study literacy development in ways that will inform instruction need to look beyond reading and writing activities in general and toward children's knowledge of particular forms for particular purposes—and the ways in which this knowledge changes over time—within a particular culture.

This chapter focuses on exposition, the type of prose that accounts for approximately 80 percent of the reading and writing experiences students in the United States encounter during their school careers. It will describe a range of ways in which third, sixth, and ninth grade mainstream students structure exposition. I believe that instruction can be more productive if we understand where students are coming from and going to within their own rule systems for particular literacy activities.

In an earlier study (Langer, 1985, 1986), I was able to show that beginning at about third grade, students have a systematic and well-developed knowledge of exposition (in the case of this study, exposition consisted of reports) and this knowledge organizes what they read and write. The structures they use to present and remember exposition are logical. Although third and sixth graders demonstrate less control of the adult forms of report organization than ninth graders, they tend nonetheless to be consistent in the forms they do use. Further, although younger students have less control of adult forms of report organization than they do of stories, this gap narrows considerably between grades 6 and 9. The findings also suggest that it is simplistic to assume that young students do not have control of any report form. I conjectured that although the forms these students know and use are rule-governed and predictable, they differ sufficiently from the adult expository forms that they are not generally recognized as valuable antecedents that teachers need to nurture rather than ignore.

Exposition is information-sharing prose. Those of us who take the time to listen to young children know that they share information all the time. Vygotsky (1986), in fact, suggests that children begin using oral and written language as tools to get things done. Bissex (1980) describes how her five-year-old son put written language to a variety of informational uses. "Show and tell" in kindergarten is a form of information-telling, and the different types of oral reports kindergartners make (e.g., about a trip to the zoo or how to play a computer game) follow consistent structures. Although these expository forms may follow different patterns or contain fewer linguistic devices than appear in adult forms, the structure and sense of purpose are clear.

In the remainder of this chapter I take a closer look at the range of structures mainstream American children use and how they change. The evidence I refer to is drawn from student writing, although my earlier studies show that the structures students use to frame their writing are the same ones they use to make sense of and remember reading.

The reports written by a sample of 16 third graders, 36 sixth graders, and 15 ninth graders were analyzed using an adaptation of Meyer's prose-analysis system (Langer, 1985, 1986). This system generates tree diagrams to depict interrelationships between central content and the ways in which children subordinate, link, and elaborate their ideas (see the Figure). Every oral or written text has an overall organizing idea, which is represented as the top level of the tree. This can be any of the four rhetorical predicates defined in the Figure or the main idea or thesis of the piece (its lexical predicate). All other content in the text elaborates on this idea. The placement of each content unit within the tree indicates its relationship to the whole as well as to other units.

Figure
Analysis of Structure with Tree Diagrams

Level 1

Rhetorical predicates function as the overall organizing frames under which all other levels of content follow. Lexical predicates, which act as rhetorical predicates representing the gist (of a story) or the thesis (of a report), are used only when none of the other top-level rhetorical predicates listed below dominate the text's structure.

Rhetorical predicates:

- Causal—antecedent and consequent specified at equal levels in the content hierarchy; these are not attributed to the text without explicit causal markers (e.g., so, because).
- Response—problem/solution, remark/reply, question/answer specified at equal levels in the hierarchy.
- Alternative—two or more equally weighted views or options compared or contrasted.
- Sequence—steps, episodes, or events ordered by time at equal levels in the hierarchy; other rhetorical predicates could serve as events.

Level 2

Embedded under the top-level predicates are any number of further structural levels. Nodes in these levels can be composed of any rhetorical predicates listed above, as well as five further types that occur only at lower levels:

- Description—a variety of types of subordinate elaborations, including manner, attribution, specific, equivalent, setting, identification, epilogue.
- Evaluation—opinion or commentary about ideas or events found elsewhere in the text.
- Evidence—supporting argument.
- Explanation—causal antecedents subordinate in staging to the main idea or event being explained (require explicit causal marker).
- Adversative—comparison between alternatives, where one is less favored and subordinate; the dominant alternative is related to a higher node.

The tree diagrams that follow permit us to inspect two aspects of students' writing: (1) the ways in which the pieces are organized, and (2) the ways in which the students connect one idea with another.

The Range of Structures

· If children are asked to write a report on something they know a lot about (one of the simplest forms of expository writing), their writing will take one of five forms, each representing a different approach to the problem of how to structure the whole expository message and elaborate on its parts: (1) simple description, (2) topic with description, (3) topic with description and commentary, (4) topic with elaboration, or (5) point of view with defense. In simple descriptions, children present ideas in a series (often listing descriptions, events, or directions about some general issue or activity), with no overall structure holding them together—much like the "and then...and then" connections young children use to move their stories along. In topic with description, topic with description and commentary, and topic with elaboration, children focus on a particular topic that serves as their overall organizing frame. But their topical information is supported in different ways depending on the approach—with descriptions alone, with comments about the descriptions, or with a focused discussion about some aspect of the topic along with subordinate information. In point of view with defense, instead of a general topic, students present a point of view and discuss, explain, or defend it. Thus, the structures students use differ not only in the ways they organize information, but also in the kinds of messages they convey.

These five types of organizing structures seem to follow a developmental trajectory; minor subordinating devices used by young children become more important organizers later on. Simple descriptions, for example, very rarely appear in ninth graders' writing, and point of view with defense are virtually unknown in third and sixth graders' writing (see the Table). However, all the other structures appear at each grade level, with different structures being more popular at different ages, along a developmental continuum. Let us examine each type of expository structure separately.

Simple Description

Children use simple descriptions to present strings of information in a sequence of related ideas about an issue, but with no overarching topic, thesis, or controlling idea. These ideas are generally not elaborated beyond one

Langer

Table
Percent Use of Expository Structures in Each Grade Surveyed

Grade	Simple Description	Topic with Description	Topic with Description and Commentary	Topic with Elaboration	Point of View with Defense
3	29	43	14	14	0
6	8	31	39	22	0
9	0	1	30	39	30

subordinate level of information. Students who write simple descriptions either begin their pieces with a topic sentence ("Horses are animals") or a general introduction ("I know a lot about horses") or simply with the first fact ("Horses have four legs"). These pieces are quite brief, often no more than a few sentences.

Marvin's writing about soccer is a good example of the way a third grader uses a list of simple descriptions to structure a report:

How to Be A Good Goalie
[1] How to be a good goalie is to move quickly and [2] keep an eye on the ball [3] and you have to be a good kicker. [4] Also you have to be smart because to tell the kids to guard who [5] and hold on to the ball tight because kids can kick it out of your hands [6] and that's how to be a good goalie.

A tree diagram representing Marvin's report would look like this:

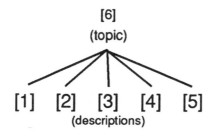

Marvin clearly understands what his report is supposed to do—to tell what he knows about goal-tending in soccer. Although he provides almost no elaboration, he does add two explanations in his "because" clauses. But Marvin has left out a lot of information: he hasn't thought to mention that the sport is soccer and he provides no explanation of what a goalie is or does.

Mike, also in third grade, bases his report about puppets on the other simple descriptive approach to structure—using an unelaborated sequence of steps:

how to make a puppet

[1] first you have to have an idea what puppet you want to make [2] then you take clay and make the head [3] then you cover it with paper strips Dipped in bleach and Let them dry [4] then you cut the puppet open and take the clay out [5] then over the cut line you put more paper strips in bleach so it's whole again and let them dry [6] then you paint it [7] and its Done!

The corresponding tree diagram looks like this:

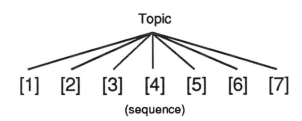

Mike knows a lot about the uses of exposition. He knows that informational writing not only tells "what" but can also tell "how." He clearly knows a lot about making puppets, and his readers can follow the report—provided they already know how to make puppets. But as a set of instructions for readers who *don't* know, Mike's piece is rather bare because it lacks the elaborative information necessary to explain the procedure.

Steve is in grade 6, but his piece is structured in a similar way to Mike's:

[1] Castro took over the government of Cuba and turned it communist which the US didn't like. [2] The US was having fights with Cuba which caused Russia to install missiles pointed for the US. [3] They found out from a US spy plane looking at Cuba. [4] Some people on the US. staff wanted to attack Cuba. [5] But President Kennedy said no.

[6] So finally Kennedy put a sea blockade in between Russian ships and Cuba. [7] The Russians turned back before they crossed the blockade. [8] They agreed to Kennedy's offer that if they took missiles out of Cuba then the US wouldn't bother or attack Cuba again.

The tree diagram looks like this:

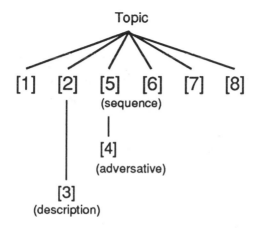

Although the content of Steve's paper is more "academic" than Mike's, the organizing structure he uses to present his ideas is nearly identical; it differs only in having an adversative and a descriptive clause, which are not elaborated.

Although Marvin, Mike, and Steve know what expository language is for and have stable structures for presenting their information, the structure they use lacks the complexity needed to get their ideas across to others. And it is clear from these reports that although sixth graders write longer, more school-related papers and use more developed vocabulary, syntax, and mechanics than do third graders, they do not necessarily present their ideas in a coherent or well-elaborated manner.

It is possible that the simple description structure is similar to the structures these children have used successfully in oral communication, where they share a context with their audience and the audience can ask questions when elaboration is needed. It is also possible that they use this form because, as children, they are often surrounded by people who know more about the topic than they do; thus elaboration is rarely necessary. Whatever the source, it is clear that for school-type exposition, this structure is only a beginning.

If we refer back to the Table, we see that, indeed, simple description is a form that is used primarily (although not exclusively) in younger children's writing. It was used by almost a third of third graders in the study and fewer than 10 percent of the sixth graders; however, it never appeared in this particular group of ninth graders' writing.

Topic with Description

In writing that involves topic with description, children generally go beyond a bare bones set of related descriptors to focus more clearly on a point they wish to make. In doing so, they present and discuss a main topic, but the elaboration is done primarily through description. There is often no discussion at all, and if it does appear, it remains as an aside with no elaboration. Descriptions and sequences ordered by time are generally elaborated on by other descriptions or other sequences, but these are not woven into the central fabric of the text; they extend to a maximum of two levels below the initial content node. Occasionally, more complex language (such as causals, explanations, evaluations, or adversatives) begins to appear in subordinate comments at the lower levels of the content hierarchy, but these are tagged on to a description.

Third grader Nancy's report on chipmunks provides a good example of a topic with description structure. Nancy knows a lot about chipmunks; she introduces her topic, keeps to it, and elaborates on her descriptions. She even uses the beginning of an adversative structure, although it isn't connected to any other information.

Chipmunks   by Nancy
[1] A chipmunk lives in farms and meadows, gardens. [2] They eat all kinds of nuts. [3] you can feed them from your hand [4] they have pouches in there mouths that they carry food in. [5] Chipmunks make

there homes in burrows. [6] In the winter they sleep [7] and sometimes they wake up to eat something. [8] In the spring they look for a mate. [9] A chipmunks baby has no fur when it is born. [10] But you can see five black stripes and for white ones [11] a chipmunk is considered full grown when it is two months old.

The tree diagram looks like this:

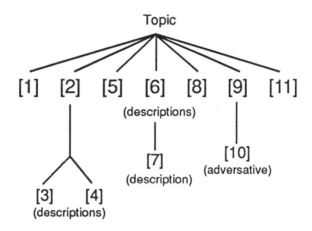

Dana's report for sixth grade is similar. She has a lot to say about Leggo plastic building blocks, but her paper, like Nancy's, consists of a series of descriptive statements that are not very well elaborated:

[1] Leggo's are little bricks that are used to keep little kids amused. [2] Leggo's are to build with. [3] They come in different sizes. [4] Leggo's come in different colors, like black, red, blue, yellow, and white. [3] Some Leggo's are different sizes. [5] Some of them are flat and [6] some of them are tall. [7] Some of them are in the shape of a door to make houses with doors. [8] Some of them have plastic inside a skinny border to form windows. [9] Some of them are rounded at the corners with lines across them to make shutters.
[10] Leggo's are shaped like little boxes with dots on top so they stick together.

Her tree diagram looks like this:

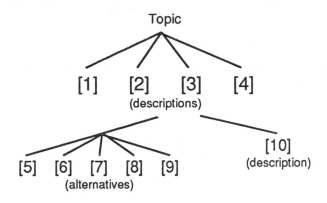

Nancy's and Dana's papers are the first we have encountered that "look" like school reports. They have an academic sound to them: they are factual, terse, and organized around the type of information generally taught in school (e.g., where animals live, what a particular kind of material is used for).

Jake's paper exemplifies a ninth grader's use of the topic with description structure:

Diamond Vision

[1] On April 22, the Oakland A's are going to use the newly installed "Mitsubishi Diamond Vision." [2] This Diamond Vision is something that is new to the sports world. [3] The first Diamond Vision was built around 1979 and installed in Dodger stadium. [4] Since then, many stadiums have put one in.

[5] What the Diamond Vision is is just one big TV screen. [6] It is composed of 3600 light bulbs which each give off different colors and brightness. [7] You can play instant replays, video tapes, and other TV programs on the screen. [8] Since its opening, the company has made a tremendous success with it. [9] Around 50% of all major league parks have this added feature.

[10] Panasonic, another company, is also building a type of Diamond Vision which will surpass the Mitsubishi in quality and price.

[11] The A's have a smaller, temporary one up right now. [12] The public's reaction will determine the fate of this expensive TV in the Oakland Coliseum.

His tree diagram looks like this:

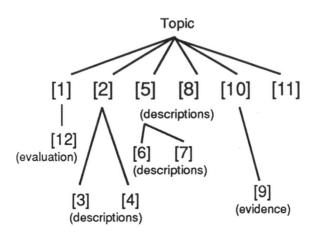

As with Nancy and Dana, Jake introduces his topic, keeps to it, and uses an appropriate closing. Also like them, he fails to develop his ideas—he has not elaborated beyond description, except in providing one small example of evidence. Because these children know what to include in reports about a particular topic, their papers contain the beginning of elaboration of information and some structural embedding. However, elaborations with discussion, opinions, analyses, or comparisons are missing.

Topic with Description and Commentary

Descriptive language continues to dominate in topic-centered pieces of this type, but the beginnings of elaborating comments (such as causals, explanations, alternatives, and evaluations) also appear—and these more complex relationships are themselves elaborated on. Children writing at this structural level begin to cluster selected information into related subtopics, which appear at the lower levels.

For example, third grader Molly wrote a report that presents a topic with descriptions and the beginnings of vague commentary:

Swimming
[1] Swimming is a fun sport. [2] I like it a lot. [3] I am on a swim Team. [4] I go to workout every day for hour in a half. [5] I have lots of ribbons and medals. And 1 trophy. [6] Are Coaches names are Dick and Tim Oliver.

[7] Lots of my friends are in it also. [8] This weekend we had a swim meet at our pool. [9] It was very fun.

The tree diagram looks like this:

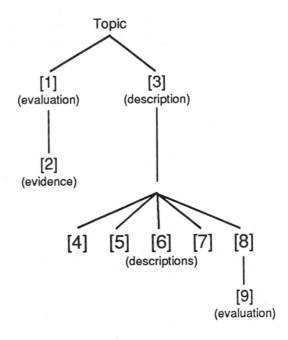

Molly's piece has an identifiable beginning and ending, showing one kind of organizational control. She uses her evaluative opening to move her piece beyond a simple description. Her lower level descriptions also serve to add subordinating complexity to her piece, with particular information clusters being formed. She begins to add commentary by going beyond her stated rhetorical predicates and adding evidence to her evaluation. Characteristic of writing at this level, the elaborating structures she uses go beyond description and sequence to include use of evidence and evaluation and thereby create a more complex written structure.

Sarah, a sixth grader, wrote another example of topic with description and (vague) commentary:

Braces
[1] Braces are silver bands than an orthodontist cements on to your teeth.

[2] They straighten your teeth. [3] They come in all different types and sizes. [4] They have bands which I will describe and braces. [5] People with the brace sort of shaped like small square 5 millimeters call them door knobs.

[6] When you go to the orthodontist to get bands the orthodontist will sit you in a chair and fit bands on your teeth. [7] He will make them fit the exact size and shape of your tooth. [8] They will be on your teeth unglued for about 15 minutes.

[9] Then he/she will take them off one by one and glue/cement them on. [10] After that he will fit a wire the shape of your mouth. [11] This wire is called an arch wire. [12] Then with the holes through the brace he will weave in a way the arch wire. [13] Depending on how crooked your teeth are you can either get some small rubber bands on your teeth to hold the arch wire. [14] If your teeth are very crooked he/she will put a small crooked wire weaving in and out the arch wire. [15] This hurts but you get your teeth straightened.

[16] If you have so/so bottom teeth he will put two bands on your end teeth, [17] and then put a wire about 2-3 millimeters wide on the back of your teeth. [18] That really hurts. [19] If you have really crooked teeth he will put on bands.

[20] WARNING! [21] If you have a loose brace or band, call the ortho. right away. [22] Do the same if you loose one. [23] If you dont, you'll be in big trouble.

Her tree diagram looks like this:

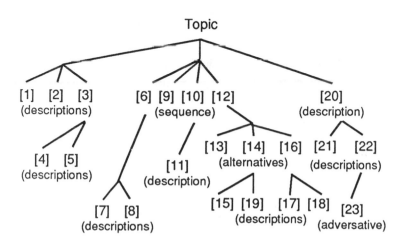

Although Sarah's paper is dominated by descriptions of the kinds of braces that are available and how they are fitted, her use of alternatives and their elaborations as well as her use of an adversative provide fairly complex commentary.

Both Molly and Sarah elaborate on their ideas by going beyond the token use of such rhetorical predicates as evaluation, evidence, alternatives, and adversatives; they not only use them but weave them into the message itself by elaborating on the ideas. This is in contrast to Nancy's and Dana's topic with description papers, where alternatives were used, but not elaborated on. Thus, in topic with description and commentary, Molly and Sarah use descriptions but also some more complex language patterns to build more defined messages about their topics through clusters of related information.

Children at all three ages use this structure to organize their writing, but this pattern seems to be a primary organizational structure for the sixth graders. It is likely that earlier use of simple descriptive forms and unelaborated rhetorical predicates provides the practice older children need to use the same structures in more complex ways. Although the commentary in these two examples is still weak, it does develop the message.

Topic with Elaboration

Students using a topic with elaboration structure present tighter and better developed messages. The topics are defined and organized by pertinent elaborations using a variety of linguistic devices. Papers of this type contain more complex rhetorical relationships (such as causals, alternatives, evaluations, evidence, explanations, and adversatives) than do papers of the topic with description and commentary form, and these occur at a higher level of the content hierarchy to shape the information clusters that become the report's focal issues. Third grader Leslie's piece is typical:

My Report on Math   by Leslie

[1] Addition and subtraction is easy for me now. [2] so is multiplication. [3] But long division I kind of forget. [4] I guess its because I haven't done any dividing this year. [5] I think I better start doing some dividing at home. [6] I can almost solve every problem from 1x1 to 10x10. [7] But from 11x2 it's kind of hard. [8] all I did to do is practis. [9] But I have lots of things to do. [10] To name one it's that I have to swim every day. [11] I have to do my violin homework, school homework and extra homework I

do at home. [12] and I have to do somethings from the cubscout book to earn wolf badge. [13] and right now I have to finish my pinewood derby car and [14] people said that soon Im going to have GATE homework. [15] So, I'm not sure I'll have time.

The tree diagram looks like this:

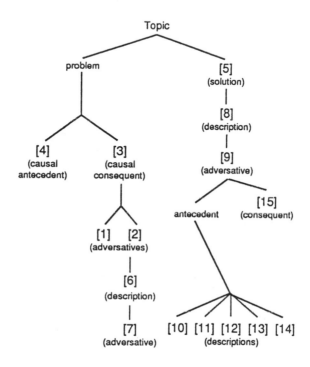

This report is better developed than the other third grade papers we have seen because it clusters information in ways that advance the clarity and complexity of the message. Leslie has organized his piece around a problem rather than using a topic/description structure. He elaborates his ideas with lower level causals, adversatives, and also some descriptions.

Nicole, who is in grade 6, uses a slightly different topic with elaboration structure. She organizes her topic around a series of descriptions, one of which is highly elaborated. Although this is a descriptive piece, the ideas are presented using a variety of rhetorical predicates to elaborate on the descriptions and develop greater complexity:

> [1] Dogs are very loveable animals [2] Some dogs are big [3] and some are small. [4] If you are interested in getting a dog there are many places to find them. [5] One place you can get a dog is the dog pound. [6] There dogs are usually strays that have been taken off the streets [7] but they make good pets. [8] You may also get a dog from a pet shop but [9] they may not live long because some are not very healthy. [10] And a third plce would be straight from the breeder. [11] There you can get top quality dogs and a background on the dog. [12] Once you have the dog you must take good care of it. [13] You must feed the dog at least once a day depending on how hungry the dog is. [14] You must also brush it a lot if it has long hair. [15] It is important to do this so the dog will not get fleas, and so it will look nice. [16] Some people treat them badly [17] and many dogs get hurt. [18] That is why if you are selling a dog make sure the owners are fairly nice.

The tree diagram looks like this:

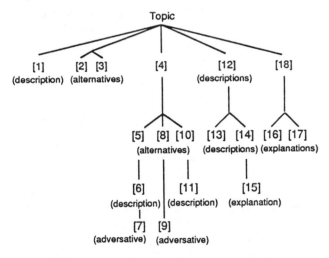

Michelle, a ninth grader, organized her report around a description structure, but she uses a series of looser descriptions in a sequence rather than in a collection to present her key ideas. Like Nicole, she elaborates on one description, which serves as a focal point for her piece. Like Leslie and Nicole, Michelle uses a variety of rhetorical predicates to move her piece along.

[1] Fame, so many people want it, [2] so many people dream of it. [3] Fame has a huge price, bigger than most think. [4] Breaking in is just the beginning. [5] Every morning I look through the performing arts section in the paper. [6] Then, if I am lucky enough, I just might find somewhere to audition. [7] As I gather up my resume that took me a month to make and the portfolio that cost my parents two hundred dollars. [8] Once I reach the address specified in the ad I realize that it is a sleezy ally apartment. [9] Knowing that I've been fooled, I return home to the next paper.

[10] Connections! [11] No one can make it with out them. [12] There is no possible way that one can make it in the business without knowing someone. [13] I often get information about auditions from friends of my parents and so on.

[14] Now that you understand how hard it is just to get an audition, I must tell you that that is the easy part. [15] Once at the studio you are often not even let through the door. [16] It is either because you are too small or too big or your not a blonde and on and on the list goes. [17] If I am lucky enough to get inside and to even audition for some one the chances of getting a call back are so slim you can forget it. [18] Hey just what if I did get called back and maybe even got the part! [19] It would just be another small part in a play or an extra in a commercial. [20] One more item to add to the resume. [21] Most struggling actors never make it past these fetes, [22] but you never know [23] that small commercial might just be a lead in the next Broadway production.

Her tree diagram looks like this:

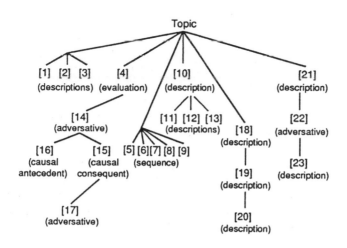

All papers of the topic with elaboration structure are qualitatively more complex than those examined previously. The writers use more discrete clusters of information to give form to the piece, and they elaborate on these clusters with a variety of subordinate information. All the papers have strong, structurally relevant introductions and closings; they also provide explanations and elaborations through use of causal and response structures, as well as adversatives, evaluations, and descriptions. These pieces are also usually more interesting to read. In addition to providing information, students who write this way often attempt to inject some humor or commentary into their writing and can usually manage to control the added structural complexity of the task; they let the reader know why they've commented as they have.

Students in all three grades used the topic with elaboration type of structure in their writing; it is the organizing structure most frequently used by the ninth graders in the study.

Point of View with Defense

Papers organized around this type of structure are different from those that focus on a topic. Here, the writer sets out to present and elaborate on a thesis. Reasons, explanations, and defenses are given for points of view. Papers of this sort are similar (and sometimes identical) to the thesis-support structure students are asked to use in high school.

Only the ninth grade participants in this study used this structure. Wayne's paper about driving is an example:

[1] Driving is harder than people think. [2] People think of driving as steering a wheel in the direction they want the car to go and pushing a pedal to go faster or slower. [3] Well, this is the least of it. [4] Driving is not going from one place to another in a car, [5] it's how the driver gets there. [6] the driver has to be aware of all the things that *could* happen while he is driving. [7] For instance, if someone is driving along a busy street, he has to watch the parked cars to see if one will pull out in front of him, or if a person opens the door toward the street. [8] While doing this, he also has to be aware of cars being operated, and pedestrians. [9] A driver has to think the worst possible situation will come up. [10] One problem that makes driving hard is that most people don't take it as seriously as they should. [11] This makes it harder for all the other drivers. [12] One has to have his full attention on the road in order to be a safe

driver. [13] If everyone who drives a car would take it more seriously and concentrate on the road, maybe driving could become a little easier for everyone.

His tree diagram looks like this:

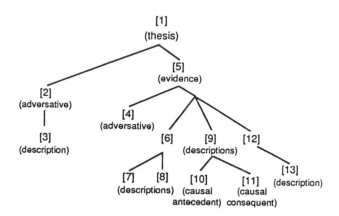

Wayne has focused on a particular point he wished to make about safe driving, rather than merely describing the act itself. He uses a variety of elaborating and linking devices to develop his thesis. This is evident in the tree diagram, which is divided into information clusters beginning at the second level, thus providing successive elaborations of the point he wishes to make.

Other ninth graders whose papers fall into this category compare or contrast actions. In these cases, two parallel clusters are formed, with two alternatives being discussed and elaborated.

In this particular study, 30 percent of the ninth graders used the point of view with defense structure. This appears to be a structure that is late forming, perhaps growing out of the topic structures that seem to predominate in the earlier grades.

Implications for Reading/Writing Connections

What do these analyses add to our knowledge of making connections between reading and writing? First, if we understand the development of sophistication in writing, we will begin to value and guide it. This development helps us understand what a particular student knows and is reaching toward, and moves us away from the tendency to treat less-than-adult structures as wrong.

Because knowledge of the organizational patterns that underlie reading and writing varies with a student's literacy experiences, some reading and writing difficulties are probably a function of a particular student's lack of organizational patterns to call upon and use. Knowledge of only the most basic structures may, for example, limit a student's comprehension or recall of a text written with a more complex pattern. In such a case, providing that student with opportunities to engage in literacy activities requiring use of the more complex patterns may be useful—more so than the more commonly prescribed practice exercises in comprehension and recall. Examination of students' recall, both in writing and discussion, will give teachers clues as to which patterns their students know and which ones they are reaching toward.

Second, because reading and writing activities make use of similar organizing structures, new and known patterns in one can be used to support growth and development in the other. Children's literacy knowledge grows in more than one direction—in the sophistication of topic, language, and syntax, and also in the organizing frames they have available to structure their messages. However, more "academic" language and more complex organizational presentation do not necessarily go hand in hand. While some students' reports are simply longer and sound more academic (particularly some of the older students' papers), we have seen that they sometimes are organized around relatively simple structures. On the other hand, papers that address simple topics with simple language sometimes orchestrate ideas within more sophisticated structures. Knowing which structures students use may help teachers provide support in developing children's reading comprehension and sophistication in writing.

Furthermore, a number of major developmental shifts seem to occur in children's writing, and each shift seems to lead naturally to the next. The unelaborated descriptions and sequences that dominate the simplest structures become better controlled and are used in increasingly varied ways to organize as well as elaborate on information. Further, certain linguistic devices—like evaluation, adversatives, explanation, evidence, and causality—which appear as subordinate devices in one phase later become more central and elaborated, either serving as a central organization or as ways to cluster relevant ideas in better ways.

The five types of expository structures may be thought of as alternative ways to organize information, rather than as more or less preferable ways. It is likely that as children develop, they search for flexibility and greater control over the language they use for the purposes they set. Thus, what they knew before becomes available for use in new forms, for other purposes. Complexity is not always better—a match between form, function, and intended audience is the goal, and students need to learn these distinctions just as they need to expand their repertoire of linguistic devices. For example, descriptive papers with commentary might at times be more appropriate than a point of view with defense, simply because of the purpose the writing will serve. And some exposition is intended to describe, or tell how, not to take a point of view and argue its value. Simple descriptive listings may be the most appropriate form for certain sets of directions. Thus, the developmental course of expository writing permits children to add needed elaborative information within known structures and to use features of text organization in new ways as they learn other ways to organize their messages.

This study involved only children who attended school in a middle-class neighborhood in the United States. It is possible that these writing structures will be present in different proportions, or that different structures will be present, among other groups of children. This, of course, needs to be studied. However, there is plentiful evidence that these five types of text structure serve as organizing literacy patterns for these mainstream students.

Although it is interesting to identify the pattern used by most children at a particular grade level, for instructional purposes it is even more informative to learn that within each grade level a wide range of types is used. And it is useful for teachers to become familiar with these types. Such knowledge, combined with sensitive eyes and ears that look for and hear what the students are trying to say and how they are trying to say it, will provide the reflective teacher with a wealth of information about students' understandings of reading and writing connections—about what connections to make, and when to move on, and where.

References

Bissex, G.L. (1980) *Gnys at work*. Cambridge, MA: Harvard University Press.

Brown, R., & Bellugi, U. (1964). Three processes in the acquisition of syntax. *Harvard Educational Review, 34*, 133-151.

Bruner, J.S., Goodnow, J.J., & Austin, B.A. (1956). *A study in thinking*. New York: Wiley.

Langer, J.A. (1985). Children's sense of genre. *Written Communication, 2*(2), 157-187.

Langer, J.A. (1986). *Children reading and writing: Structures and strategies*. Norwood, NJ: Ablex.

Vygotsky, L.S. (1978). *Mind in society*. Cambridge, MA: Harvard University Press.

Vygotsky, L.S. (1986). *Thought and language*. Cambridge, MA: Harvard University Press.

Weir, R. (1962). *Language in the crib*. The Hague: Mouton.

— T H R E E —

Linguistic Cohesion

$\mathcal{T}$ he following paragraph is an example of writing that does not make effective use of cohesive devices. As a result, readers are likely to have trouble comprehending the passage.

> Bob and Fred went shopping. He wanted to buy a belt and a shirt. The store didn't have the right kind. He bought a blue one.

Who wanted to buy a belt and shirt? Was the store lacking the right kind of shirt or the right kind of belt? Why did "he" buy a blue one? And one what?

The source of the comprehension problems in the paragraph is unclear writing. Had the writer used more effective cohesive devices, most readers would have little trouble comprehending the message:

> Bob and Fred went shopping. *Fred* wanted to buy a belt and a shirt. The store didn't have the right kind *of belt. Therefore, Fred* bought a blue *belt* instead.

Comprehension problems can also arise because the reader is unable to use the cohesive devices the writer provides:

> After three weeks of trying to match their schedules, Amaryllis and Placido at last were able to go shopping together. She wanted to buy a découpaged armoire. By juxtaposition, he was searching for jicama. Patently, the two friends wanted to go to different stores.

Some readers may have difficulty fully or easily understanding that paragraph. They may not be able to make use of the cohesive device "she" because they are unsure of the sexes denoted by Amaryllis and Placido. They may not know what a découpaged armoire and jicama are, and they may not understand the signals of "by juxtaposition" and "patently." As a result, these readers may have to work hard to construct the ironic situation the author has intended: The two friends have such different shopping lists that they may have been better off shopping separately.

Cohesion has been associated with success in reading comprehension (Barnitz, 1980; Cirilo, 1981; Freebody & Anderson, 1983; McClure & Steffensen, 1985; Moe & Irwin, 1986); with the ability to summarize text (Irwin, 1980a); with memory for text (Irwin, 1986; Marshall & Glock, 1978; Moe & Irwin, 1986; Smith & Elkins, 1985; Trabasso, Secco, & Van Den Brock, 1984); and with affecting information processing (Clark, 1986; Kintsch & van Dijk, 1978; Moe, 1979). It has been suggested that analyses of cohesion can provide insights into readability (Geva & Ryan, 1985; Gottsdanker-Willekens, 1986; Irwin, 1979, 1980b; Moe & Irwin, 1986) and help determine the focus of discourse (Holloway, 1981).

Cohesion is an important and reciprocal factor in reading and writing, with the skill of both the reader and the writer playing an important role in the communication's success. In this chapter I explore definitions and descriptions of cohesion, theories about the source of cohesion and how it works, and ways of measuring it. Then I review the research on the relationships between cohesion and reading and writing. My goal is to help readers understand this most basic reading/writing connection and gain an enhanced sense of the degree to which reading and writing are intertwined.

What Is Cohesion?

Any discussion of linguistic cohesion and its relationships with reading and writing must surely begin by defining "cohesion." That is not as simple as it might seem, however. Cohesion has often been ill defined and used without precision in even the most scholarly writing. As a result, one often does not know if an author is referring to cohesion, coherence, or something altogether different.

The confusion about the definition of cohesion stems primarily from a tradition, only recently broken, of treating cohesion and coherence as virtually synonymous (Bain, 1890; Bamberg, 1984; Haslett, 1983). When writers do intend the terms to have different meanings, often they cannot agree on what label to use. Van Dijk and Kintsch (1983), for example, use "local coherence" in place of "cohesion"; Irwin (1986) and McCutchen and Perfetti (1982) use "local connectedness." Another source of uncertainty is that theorists cannot agree on the nature of the relationship between cohesion and coherence. Many writers view cohesion as one aspect of coherence (Bamberg, 1983; Cooper, 1983; Halliday & Hasan, 1976; Irwin, 1982; McCutchen & Perfetti; van Dijk & Kintsch). They tend to agree that cohesion and coherence interact (Fitzgerald & Spiegel, 1986; Goodin & Perkins, 1982; McCulley, 1985; Witte & Faigley, 1981), but the exact nature of that interaction remains obscure (Fitzgerald & Spiegel; Gutwinski, 1976; Spiegel & Fitzgerald, 1990; van Dijk & Kintsch).

Cohesion is often defined as the set of surface-structure markers or text indicators of the coherence of a piece of discourse. For example, van Dijk and Kintsch (1983) describe cohesion as the "specific grammatical manifestations underlying semantic coherence" (p. 149). Gutwinski (1976) suggests that relationships among sentences and clauses of a text are signaled at the grammatical and lexical levels, but that these signals are themselves reflections of a coherent structure at a higher, semologic level (p. 26). Scardamalia, Bereiter, and Goelman (1982) also speak of surface versus deep structure to differentiate cohesion and coherence: cohesion "refers to the linguistic means by which coherence is displayed in surface structure," whereas coherence is "the tying together of meanings in text" (p. 197).

Cohesion is often considered necessary for, but not sufficient to produce, coherence (Bamberg, 1983; Carrell, 1982; Markels, 1984; Moe, 1979; Morgan & Sellner, 1980; Witte & Faigley, 1981). That is, a piece of discourse must be cohesive to be coherent, but cohesiveness will not in itself guarantee coherence. However, the belief that cohesion is absolutely necessary for coherence is not held universally (Keenan, Baillet, & Brown, 1984; Scardamalia, Bereiter, & Goelman, 1982; Winterowd, 1985).

For the purposes of this chapter, cohesion is defined as the surface-structure linguistic features of text that signal connections between sentences and therefore help a sequence of sentences hang together (Halliday & Hasan, 1976, p. 18). Cohesion is thus distinguished from coherence, which is understood to mean "the larger, global quality of text structure" (Smith, 1984, p. 9), the overall discourse level of unity, or how well a text holds together (Bamberg, 1984; Hasan, 1984; van Dijk, 1980).

Cohesive Ties

Although there is considerable dispute about the nature of cohesion, there is general agreement that Halliday and Hasan's (1976) description of cohesive ties or devices provides a useful system for recognizing the linguistic features that signal cohesion. Cohesive devices have been likened to a map, without which "a reader is lost in a labyrinth of ideas" (Chapman, 1984, p. vii), "a semantic back-up system to ensure that the reader follows the direction of movement [in text]" (Sloan, 1984, p. 175), and "a specification of the way in which what is to follow is systematically connected to what has gone before" (Halliday & Hasan, p. 277).

Cohesive ties are linguistic elements that presuppose the existence of other elements (called referents or antecedents) that appear either earlier in the text (anaphora), later in the text (cataphora), or outside of the text (exophora). Thus, the interpretation of the tie depends on some other element of discourse (Morgan & Sellner, 1980) or some outside referent (e.g., referring to "the fork" when no fork has specifically been mentioned but the text does describe someone eating a meal). Halliday and Hasan's system identifies five kinds of cohesive ties in text: reference, substitution, ellipsis, conjunction, and lexical (see Figure 1).

Figure 1
Examples of Cohesive Devices

Reference:	Bob is at the beach. *He* is happy.
Substitution:	Bob wanted a new bathing suit. He got a plaid *one*.
Ellipsis:	Bob went swimming yesterday. He also went [swimming] today.
Conjunction:	Bob used to be a good diver. *But* now he is out of shape.
Lexical—	
same item:	sing/sing
synonym:	boy/lad
superordinate:	instrument/cello
general item:	play/playing
collocation:	school/teacher, big/little, collies/beagles/retrievers

Based on Halliday and Hasan's (1976) list of cohesive devices.

Theoretical Issues

Several theoretical issues must be explored if we are to gain a full understanding of cohesion and its relationship to reading and writing. Opinions differ on the source of cohesion, how it works, the role of prior knowledge in the effective use of cohesive devices, the influence of competence versus performance, and how cohesion should be measured.

The Source of Cohesion

Not surprisingly, the source of cohesion in text is disputed. One point of view, that cohesive devices produce or help to produce a coherent text, is often ascribed to Halliday and Hasan (1976)—although some assign blame rather than credit (Mosenthal & Tierney, 1984). Chapman (1983) supports this view, suggesting that anaphora functions to maintain meaning across boundaries (p. 52). A second point of view is enunciated by Carrell (1982): "Cohesion is not the cause of coherence; if anything, it's the effect of coherence" (p. 486). Morgan and Sellner (1980) are even more forceful: "The source of coherence would lie in the content, and the repeated occurrence of certain words would be the *consequence* of content coherence, not something that was a *source* of coherence" (p. 179).

A more moderate view is that cohesion is a reflection of already existing coherence (de Beaugrande, 1980; Gutwinski, 1976; McCutchen & Perfetti, 1982; Moe & Irwin, 1986; Morgan & Sellner, 1980; Mosenthal & Tierney, 1984; Winterowd, 1970; Witte & Faigley, 1981). Cohesive devices serve as pointers that help the reader discover and understand the coherence that resides in a text's underlying semantic structure (Witte & Faigley). Thus, cohesion is viewed as a text-related, surface-level phenomenon (Moe, 1979; Smith, 1984; Winterowd, 1985; Witte & Faigley), whereas coherence is perceived as arising from the interaction of the deep structure of the text and the reader (Bamberg, 1984; Bellert, 1970; Crothers, 1979; Witte & Faigley).

How Cohesion Works

Linguists, psychologists, and other theorists and researchers have investigated how cohesion functions in reading and writing from a variety of perspectives. Overall, they have found that cohesive devices serve as signals that help the reader integrate text or build an organized structure of a piece of discourse. These devices let the reader know how new information relates to information already provided; they influence comprehension by affecting processing efficiency, storage or memory efficiency, and rehearsal.

Cohesive devices as signals. Cohesive devices provide a road map for the reader to follow in reconstructing the author's meaning (Bartlett & Scribner, 1981; Bracewell, Hidi, & Hildyard, 1981; Brostoff, 1981; Lesgold, 1972; Meyer, Brandt, & Bluth, 1980; Pulver, 1986; Sloan, 1984). Successful use of cohesive devices appears to be enhanced by the skill of both the writer and the reader: less skilled writers are not as adept as more skilled writers in determining readers' need for signals (Rentel & King, 1983), and less skilled readers are less adept at using signals that do exist (Golden, 1987).

These devices help the reader keep track of incoming information (Bartlett & Scribner, 1981) and relate that information to previously encountered information (Mosenthal & Tierney, 1984). Cohesive devices also guide the reader's search for an intended referent: the writer (or speaker) must signal unambiguously which of all potential referents in the discourse is the intended one (Bartlett & Scribner). Clark and Haviland (1977) have labeled this the maxim of antecedence: "Try to construct your utterance such that the listener has one and only one direct antecedent for any given information and that is the intended antecedent" (p. 4). Failure to follow this advice may result in unacceptable, or at best awkward, discourse.

Cohesion as an aid to integrating text. When a piece of discourse is cohesive, it helps the reader reconstruct and organize the writer's underlying meaning structures into an integrated whole. Cohesive devices such as anaphora and lexical repetition help readers infer these structures by reminding them to integrate new information with old (Baumann & Stevenson, 1986; Clark, 1986; Fishman, 1978; Hottel-Burkhart, 1980; Meyer, Brandt, & Bluth, 1980). Devices such as conjunctions make explicit the connections between units of text (Irwin & Pulver, 1984), thereby helping the reader integrate these units into a coherent structure (Keenan, Baillet, & Brown, 1984; Kintsch & van Dijk, 1978; Meyer, Brandt, & Bluth; Moe, 1979; Mosenthal & Tierney, 1984; Smith & Elkins, 1985; Trabasso, Secco, & Van Den Brock, 1984; Webber, 1980). Cohesive devices also signal the reader as to what is important and needs to be emphasized in any reconstruction of text (Fahnestock, 1983; Meyer, Brandt, & Bluth; Smith & Elkins).

The given-new contract. As stated earlier, cohesion ties discourse together by focusing the reader or listener on the relationship of new to old information. The speaker or writer assumes that the audience already knows old, or "given," information, either from previous parts of the discourse or from an outside source. The speaker or writer presents new information on the assumption that it is unknown to the receiver (Clark & Haviland, 1977).

According to Clark (1977), the given-new strategy works in the following manner: First, the listener (or reader) identifies a piece of information in discourse as either given or new. If the information is identified as new, the listener searches his or her memory for a previously existing proposition—the antecedent—that approximates or is related to it. The incoming information is then added to memory by integrating it with its antecedent (p. 246). Thus, cohesion—the linking of new information to given information—serves to integrate the text and strengthen coherence.

Cohesion and psychological processes. According to de Beaugrande (1980), cohesive devices contribute to processing efficiency through "(1) the *compacting* of surface expressions; (2) the *omission* of surface elements; (3) the *carrying forward* of materials to be *expanded, developed, modified,* or *repudiated*; (4) the signaling of *knownness, uniqueness,* or *identity*; and (5) a workable balance between *repetition* and *variation* in surface structure as required by the considerations of *informativity*" (p. 134). As part of this theory, de Beaugrande interprets the economy principle as dictating that, whenever possible, accessing already activated content is preferable to activating new content.

Other researchers emphasize that cohesion improves processing efficiency by avoiding gaps in the structure of the discourse (Clark, 1986; Golden, 1987; Meyer, Brandt, & Bluth, 1980; Moe, 1979). Whenever such gaps exist, the reader must use up limited processing ability to infer the relationships between discourse parts, thereby restructuring the amount available for other comprehension processes. A similar view holds that lack of cohesion may result in "nonspecific degradation of [comprehension] performance because of increased cognitive load" (Freebody & Anderson, 1983, p. 286).

It has been suggested further that cohesion improves memory for discourse by indicating linguistic information that can be stored in the reader/listener's memory as a single integrated unit (Lesgold, 1972; McKoon & Ratcliff, 1980), thus lightening memory load (Webber, 1980). Another view is that cohesion enhances memory for discourse by increasing the rehearsal of information connected by cohesive devices (Smith & Elkins, 1985).

The Role of Prior Knowledge

Many theorists emphasize the role of the reader's prior knowledge in making use of cohesive devices (e.g., Barnitz, 1986; Bracewell, Hidi, & Hildyard, 1981; de Beaugrande, 1980; Fishman, 1978; Kameenui & Carnine, 1982; Markels, 1984; Morgan & Sellner, 1980; Stotsky, 1983; Trabasso, Secco, & Van Den Brock, 1984; van Dijk & Kintsch, 1982). In this view, readers reconstruct the author's meaning by following the guideposts of cohesive devices while drawing "on their own knowledge and expectations to bridge gaps and fill in assumed information" (Bamberg, 1984, p. 6). In other words, cohesive devices are not sufficient to produce a coherent text if the propositions they connect do not match the reader's understanding of the real world. Chapman (1984) refers to a "path of connection between unique and discrete individuals" (p. viii) that is made up of the writer's textual cues but also by the experiential cues shared by the reader and the writer.

Those who emphasize the role of prior knowledge in the functioning of cohesion criticize Halliday and Hasan's (1976) work for being too limited. Because Halliday and Hasan deal only with the surface-level expressions of cohesion, their system is cited for ignoring the "underlying connectivity of text-knowledge and world-knowledge that makes these devices possible and useful" (de Beaugrande, 1980, p. 132). As a result, the Halliday and Hasan description provides little insight into the means by which writers construct meaning and readers reconstruct that meaning; instead, it maintains an artificial division between the text and the real world that does not advance understanding of the processes of reading and writing (de Beaugrande, 1980; Doyle, 1982).

On the other hand, some theorists and researchers de-emphasize the role of prior knowledge in cohesion. The research on the effect of topic (or prior knowledge) on cohesion is contradictory, with some studies showing a strong effect (Fitzgerald & Spiegel, 1986; Tierney & Mosenthal, 1983) but others finding no effect of note (McCutchen & Perfetti, 1984; Spiegel & Fitzgerald, 1990).

Competence versus Performance

Do writers' or readers' failures to use cohesive devices indicate that they are unaware of (or do not understand) the devices' function, or do such failures mean simply that they have not used the devices successfully? Several researchers have suggested that the ability to use cohesion does not develop in an all-or-nothing way but is subject to the effects of medium (oral or written; writing or reading) (Bracewell, Hidi, & Hildyard, 1981; Cox & Sulzby, 1984), discourse type (exposition or narration) (Kameenui & Carnine, 1982), and other communication contexts and linguistic factors (Bartlett & Scribner, 1981; Bridge & Winograd, 1982; Golden, 1987; Witte & Faigley, 1981). The inconsistencies found in both understanding and using cohesive devices—even by the same person—may result "not so much from lack of basic awareness of the referential requirements inherent in these contexts or from any basic inability to choose appropriate linguistic devices, but rather from more momentary and transient performance factors specific to the context in which referencing occurs" (Bartlett & Scribner, 1981, pp. 165-166).

Measuring Cohesion

Although most theorists acknowledge the value of Halliday and Hasan's (1976) description of cohesion in English, opinions vary about how one should *measure* it. Researchers often measure cohesion simply by counting occurrences of Halliday and Hasan's different cohesive ties (Fitzgerald & Spiegel, 1986; Marshall & Glock, 1978; Norris & Bruning, 1988; Witte & Faigley, 1981). However, many researchers are dissatisfied with frequency counts, noting that this procedure may provide a distorted picture of the cohesiveness of a piece of discourse. For example, Crowhurst (1987) argues that use of lexical repetition—which would result in a high cohesion score—might actually indicate immature writing skills in younger writers, who often simply repeat the same word in the same way. Among older writers, though, lexical repetition might reflect a mature tendency to elaborate and summarize arguments. McCutchen and Perfetti (1982) argue that simply counting word repetitions may cause researchers to overestimate the coherence of texts produced by young writers.

Numerous writers object to frequency counts because of more theoretical grounds. Such a system is essentially bottom-up and ignores the structural properties of text (Mosenthal & Tierney, 1984). Furthermore, frequency counts are based solely on surface structure but are used to interpret deep structure. This use is contradictory because a deep structure can have many different surface structures, some of which might use lexical repetition and some of which might not (Markels, 1984). Doyle (1982) argues that Halliday and Hasan's use of the sentence as the unit of interest in cohesion analysis forces an artificial focus on surface structure.

Another criticism of Halliday and Hasan's measure of cohesion is that their system does not take into account the effectiveness of the cohesive ties used (Hartnett, 1984; Moe & Irwin, 1986; Pritchard, 1986). Cohesive errors—when an author uses an inappropriate tie or fails to supply a needed tie—are not part of Halliday and Hasan's system, yet they could be considered as indicators of *lack* of cohesion (Fitzgerald & Spiegel, 1986; Monson & Gonzales, 1984).

Halliday and Hasan's system is also criticized for its lack of clarity in defining terms, particularly repetition (Stotsky, 1983) and collocation (McCutchen & Perfetti, 1982; Stotsky, 1983). Stotsky points out that derivatives and even repeated words may or may not have the same meanings or functions; yet Halliday and Hasan's system would always count them as repetitions. (For example, *table* would be counted as a repetition in "I put the book on the table. The book was about the low water table in our state.")

Hasan (1984) recognized that in the original description, lexical categories of cohesive ties were especially troublesome. She suggested that the following categories be used: repetition (sing/sing, sing/singing), synonym (shout/yell), antonym (hot/cold), hyponym (animal/dog, dog/fish/gerbil), meronym (foot/toe, Europe/Italy), and equivalence (Mr. Bush/president of the United States). However, this refined system also has its detractors. Friedman and Sulzby (1987) suggest that the relatedness of certain items depends on pragmatics (readers' and authors' purposes), yet Hasan's system assumes that many of these categories of lexical ties are text-independent. Thus, a mention of *canary* in one part of a discourse could be considered hyponymous with a mention of *wolf* in another part, even though the mention of two animals might be coincidental and bear no relationship to either the author's or the reader's purposes.

Implications for Reading

Various aspects of cohesion have been found to be related to reading comprehension. Some studies have focused on the relative difficulty of various anaphoric structures. These studies show generally that readers of various ages have trouble comprehending anaphora, but there is no consensus on which forms present the most difficulty. Fishman (1978) found no effect for reference ties on comprehension, while Kameenui and Carnine (1982) found that references had an effect on expository passages but not on narrative. Other studies have found that ambiguous references impede comprehension (Beck et al., 1984; Cirilo, 1981; Golden, 1987). The distance between a referent and its tie has also been studied, with some results suggesting that longer distances are related to poorer comprehension (Cirilo; Clark & Sengul, 1979; Moberly, 1978) and some studies suggesting the opposite (Barnitz, 1980; Richek, 1976). Research into the effects of the direction of anaphoric relationships has found that forward relationships are easier to comprehend than backward (Barnitz).

Conjunctions have often been associated with decreased comprehension. When conjunctions are misused—such as when they join two widely separated propositions (Clark, 1986)—they can interfere with comprehension. Implicit conjunctions are more difficult to comprehend than explicit ones (Irwin, 1980b; Irwin & Pulver, 1984; Marshall & Glock, 1978). Even if conjunctions are explicit and appropriately used, they are more difficult to comprehend than referential or lexical items (Bridge & Winograd, 1982; Geva & Ryan, 1985; Irwin, 1979; McClure & Geva, 1983).

Good versus Poor Readers

Several studies have investigated how different aspects of cohesion affect comprehension among good and poor readers. One set of studies concluded that poor readers have less knowledge of cohesive devices than do good readers (Geva & Ryan, 1985) and less control over the use of cohesive devices to enhance comprehension of text (Bridge & Winograd, 1982; Chapman, 1983; Cox & Sulzby, 1984; Richek, 1976; Smith & Elkins, 1985). In reporting the results of their study on conjunctions, McClure and Steffensen (1985) suggested that readers who fail to understand these cohesive devices "may comprehend each sentence or clause but fail to understand the passage as a whole" (p. 218). Thus, inability to use cohesion may result in a reader's inability to construct a coherent text.

Researchers have also examined the effects of the explicitness of cohesive devices on good and poor readers' comprehension. Although Beck et al. (1984) found that comprehension improved among both groups when references were clearly related to their antecedents, the more general finding is that cohesion explicitness enhances the comprehension of poor (and sometimes average) readers, but not of good readers (Irwin, 1982; Meyer, Brandt, & Bluth, 1980; Roen, 1981). Marshall and Glock (1978) explained this finding by suggesting that the not-so-fluent reader "does not communicate efficiently with the author. He comprehends what the author says rather than what the author means" (pp. 51-52). Therefore, if a connection with what the author says explicitly is not made, poor readers are unable to infer what the author is trying to communicate implicitly.

Several studies have dealt with the reading/writing connection by investigating cohesive devices in the writing of good and poor readers. The consistent finding, regardless of age, is that better readers have better control over using cohesive devices in their writing (Marshall & Glock, 1978; McClure & Geva, 1983; McClure & Steffensen, 1985). For example, Henderson (1980) found that poor college readers actually overcompensated in their use of conjunctive adverbs, using them unnecessarily even if this resulted in a breach of appropriate register. Cox and Sulzby (1984) suggest that young children with more advanced reading skills know more about the rules of written language than do less advanced readers, and that this reading-related knowledge enables the better readers to monitor their own writing more successfully.

Developing Understanding of Cohesive Devices

General agreement exists that development of the ability to comprehend different cohesive devices is relatively slow, especially for more complex structures (Bormuth et al., 1970; Chapman, 1983; Geva & Ryan, 1985; McClure & Geva, 1983; Richek, 1976) and is still incomplete in the middle grades. Not surprisingly, the details of this development vary from study to study. For example Barnitz (1980) found that by grade 6 children could understand most pronoun-referent structures. On the other hand, Gottsdanker-Willekens (1986) found eighth graders still having trouble with anaphora, and McClure, Mason, and Barnitz (1979) found ninth graders ignoring conjunction cues to sentence order. Implicit connectives may remain a problem even for college students (Irwin, 1980b; Irwin & Pulver, 1984). The order of development is also unclear (Barnitz, 1986; Moberly, 1978; Monson, 1982).

Implications for Writing

The relationship between cohesion and writing has been studied from several perspectives. Some researchers have investigated cohesive errors, particularly exophora (inappropriately referring to someone or something outside of the text) and ambiguous references (Golden, 1987; Pritchard, 1986). Bartlett and Scribner (1981) found that writers still make such errors even as late as grade 6; they note, however, that when students in grades 3 to 6 make these errors it is not so much because they don't understand how to use

referencing but rather because of "more momentary and transient performance factors specific to the context in which referencing occurs" (p. 166).

In their study of the use of conjunctions, McClure and Steffensen (1985)
found that positive conjunctions are easier to use than negative. McCutchen
and Perfetti (1982), in their study of violation of the given-new contract,
suggest that failure to provide new information in a sentence results in tedious, repetitive text. Stotsky (1983), Witte and Faigley (1981), and Brostoff
(1981) emphasize the role of vocabulary knowledge in successful writing.
They suggest that better writers have a larger repertoire of words with which
to express relationships and to elaborate and extend concepts by making use
of cohesive devices.

From a more theoretical point of view, McCutchen, Perfetti, and Basick
(1983) and Rentel and King (1983) conclude that one of the most important
aspects of learning to write is perceiving text itself as distinct from the text's
content and being able to realign the text-forming strategies used in speech to
meet the needs of writing. On the other hand, McCutchen and Perfetti (1982)
stress that a "developing sensitivity to the demands of local connectedness in
discourse seems to be related to the development of the children's sensitivity
to topic constraints" (p. 11).

Good versus Poor Writers

Several investigators have successfully studied the differences in the use
of cohesion by good and poor writers. One finding is that better writers
provide many textual cues to "guide the reader in constructing a coherent
text-world" (Golden, 1987, p. 3). Brostoff (1981) suggests that poorer writers may fail to supply these cues because they do not know where or when
to do so, they do not know what words to use, or they are not aware of the
reader's need for such cues. Cox and Sulzby (1984) suggest that better readers may be better writers because they have more knowledge of the rules of
written language.

Several studies have examined how the number of cohesive ties used
affects writing quality. The findings are contradictory. Atwell (1981) and
Witte and Faigley (1981) found that the total number of cohesive ties used
correlates positively with writing quality, but Hagen (1971) and Pritchard
(1986) found that the number of ties has no effect on writing quality. Monson
and Gonzales (1984) found that the number of ties does have a significant
effect on quality, but their finding is unusual in that most of the ties they

found were cohesive errors, which suggests that a lack of cohesion may result in higher quality compositions! Few studies have found any evidence of a significant relationship between the number of specific kinds of cohesive ties and quality (Pritchard, 1986; Witte & Faigley, 1981), although McCulley (1985) found that synonyms, hyponyms, and collocation together had a .39 correlation with quality.

Developing Use of Cohesive Devices

A host of developmental trends have been found in the use of cohesive devices in writing. As writers mature, increases have generally been found in the number of connections they make between ideas (Chall & Jacobs, 1983; McCutchen & Perfetti, 1982), as well as in the variety (Haslett, 1983; King & Rentel, 1981) and complexity of cohesive devices they use (Haslett, 1983; McCutchen & Perfetti, 1982). However, Bracewell, Hidi, and Hildyard (1981) found no differences between grades 3 and 5 in either the number or the variety of cohesive ties used; similarly, Crowhurst (1987) found no differences across grades 6, 10, and 12 in overall use of cohesive devices.

Crowhurst (1987), Fitzgerald and Spiegel (1986), King (1989), King and Rentel (1981), and Monson and Gonzales (1984) have all found that as writers develop they tend to use more lexical ties; the ability to use remote ties effectively and to employ more diverse vocabulary has been noted by Crowhurst. The use of pronominal references and anaphora in general has been found to increase with age in some studies (Haslett, 1983), but to decrease in others (Cox & Sulzby, 1984; Fitzgerald & Spiegel; King). The use of conjunctions has been found to increase as writers develop (King & Rentel; Klecan-Acker & Lopez, 1985; McClure & Steffensen, 1985), although contradictory evidence exists (Crowhurst; Fitzgerald & Spiegel; Monson & Gonzales). Cohesive errors seem to decrease with grade level (Crowhurst; Fitzgerald & Spiegel; King & Rentel; Klecan-Acker & Lopez; McClure, Mason, & Barnitz, 1979; McCutchen & Perfetti, 1982; Monson & Gonzales; Rentel & King, 1983). The number of remote connections and the distance between ties have also been found to decrease (Fitzgerald & Spiegel; McCutchen & Perfetti).

Estimates of when children master the use of particular cohesive devices vary. Evidence has emerged that as early as grade 2 children exhibit "strong control" over several different cohesive devices in narratives (King & Rentel, 1981; Rentel & King, 1983). Other studies are less enthusiastic in their assessment, finding that young writers do master certain basic uses of specific devices quite early (Hagen, 1971), but that as late as grade 8 (McClure & Geva, 1983) or grade 9 (Hottel-Burkhart, 1980; McClure, Mason, & Barnitz, 1979) they still lack the ability to make consistently effective use of other devices. In their study of children in grades 1 and 3, Klecan-Acker and Lopez (1985) concluded that the use of pronouns "continues to improve throughout the early grades and possibly is still being refined in the middle grades" (p. 314).

Discourse Type

Several studies have compared quantities and patterns of cohesion across two discourse types, usually the more familiar narrative form and a less familiar expository form, such as argument. Most have found some differences. For example, Bracewell, Hidi, and Hildyard (1981) found that third and fifth grade writers used more cohesive devices, left greater distances between ties and their referents, and included more reference ties in narratives than in arguments. McCutchen and Perfetti (1982) examined the writing of students at grades 2, 4, 6, and 8 and found more connections and fewer cohesive errors in narratives than in essays. Text-type effects for lexical cohesion emerged with adults in Odell and Goswami's study (1980). Matsuhashi and Quinn (1984) found no significant differences in number of connectives in the two discourse types, but differing patterns in reporting and generalizing essays emerged. On the other hand, Monson and Gonzales (1984) compared cohesive devices in narratives and dialogue and found differences only for conjunctions (which may have been due to overuse of "and" as a filler in the dialogues).

Interpretation of these results is fairly uniform across studies. Different discourse types appear to be constructed with different informing principles. As a result, no universal formula for prescribing optimum use of cohesive devices is viable (Markels, 1983; Odell, 1981). Different patterns will prevail for different text types. Furthermore, these differences do not appear to reflect a need for writers to learn new skills for new discourse types; rather, the task is to transfer skills and strategies already used with familiar genres to less familiar genres (Bracewell, Hidi, & Hildyard, 1981; McCutchen & Perfetti, 1982). McCutchen and Perfetti's findings suggest that the same *sequence* of development in the use of cohesive devices is found in narrative and expository writing; the sequence simply has an earlier beginning with narratives.

Implications for Further Research

We know much about cohesion and good and poor readers and writers, although there is still a great deal to be learned. Good writing makes comprehension easier for readers; poor writers (and many young writers) impede the comprehension of average and less able readers when they fail to provide a road map of cohesive devices. Reciprocally, effective reconstruction of a writer's message depends on the reader's skill in using the provided signals or inferring meaning when signals are not explicit. Better readers make more effective use of cohesive devices to retrieve and remember the author's intended message.

The research that led to these conclusions is, however, based on widely used but still suspect measures of cohesion. Both Halliday and Hasan's (1976) initial approach to describing cohesion and Hasan's (1984) modification are less than satisfying. Both systems explore only the surface structure of text, measuring cohesion with frequency counts of surface elements. This approach is likely to overestimate cohesion by failing to distinguish between lexical and semantic repetition.

Furthermore, both measures focus on the sentence, a relatively superficial element of discourse. For example, in most current systems of analysis, *he* and *his* in "Paul went to the store, but he forgot his shopping list" are not counted as cohesive devices because they are in the same sentence. The artificiality of that distinction is obvious when the same deep structure is conveyed by a surface structure that varies only slightly: "Paul went to the store. However, he forgot his shopping list." Because *however* begins a new sentence, the two pronouns are now considered cohesive devices. Research is needed to find measures of cohesion that take into account the complex relationships between surface and deep structure and examine larger units of discourse.

Another related area needing investigation concerns the role of prior knowledge in cohesion. Readers need to fill in gaps left by writers by inferring from their own prior knowledge, but we do not really know how they do this; nor have we found an acceptable way to measure this blending of real world and text world. The effects of prior knowledge on writers are even less clear.

Third, although the reciprocal nature of reading/writing connections is evident when one examines the research on cohesion, what is still unknown is whether and how these connections can be strengthened through intervention. One promising strand for research might take advantage of reading/ writing connections by investigating the effects on reading of teaching students to use cohesive devices more effectively in their writing, and to investigate the effects on writing of instruction in using cohesive devices while reading.

Implications for Instruction

Given that we are uncomfortable with the ways in which we measure cohesion, unsure of the psychological processes through which cohesion is used by readers and writers, and unclear about the effects of intervention efforts, implications for instruction should be interpreted cautiously. However, several guidelines for instruction flow logically from what we do know about cohesion in reading and writing. In most cases these guidelines are not unique to the development of competence with cohesion.

Guideline 1. Be sure students understand the importance of cohesion in both reading and writing.

Duffy et al.'s (1987) work shows us the importance of students' knowing the answers to these general questions at the end of each lesson: What was it that I was supposed to learn? When would I use that strategy, or why is learning that important? How do I do that? Cohesion is a powerful tool for both readers and writers, but some students may need to be convinced of that power. After all, the words involved are often unsophisticated—words like *he, these, but,* and *one.*

The importance of using cohesive devices can be highlighted through a variety of activities. Learners can examine paragraphs and longer pieces of discourse that have no explicit cohesive markers. The confusion that will result in reading such text can be explored through questions, generated by teachers or students. Since so many children are test conscious, the teacher might even set a pretend "test." The test would involve reading a portion of text and answering questions, but the questions would point out ambiguities in the paragraphs. Students are likely to become indignant when they are unable to answer the questions. The class could then repair the ineffective text by inserting appropriate cohesive markers.

Many students will enjoy writing *ineffective* paragraphs once they understand the role of cohesive devices. A contest format might even be used: authors write two versions of their paragraphs, with the "correct" version serving as an answer key (so teachers can be sure that the "errors" in cohesion were purposeful and not just poor writing). Points for authors would be scored by counting cohesion-related differences between the two versions. Readers would then score points by correcting the poor versions.

Sometimes when we teach children something new, they come to the conclusion that more is always better. To help readers and writers keep a balanced perspective on the use of cohesive devices, pairs of paragraphs might be compared. One paragraph would use too few pronouns, resulting in repetitive, tedious text along these lines: "Sally went to the store. Sally picked up bread. Sally looked longingly at a big chocolate doughnut. But Sally did not buy the doughnut. Sally paid for the bread. Sally left the store." The second paragraph would use too many: "Sally went to the store. She picked up bread. She looked longingly at a big chocolate doughnut. But she did not buy it. She paid for it. She left there."

Children may profit from manipulating cohesive devices to impart differing messages. This manipulation may take many forms. For example, students could be given the base sentence "Maria, _____ Diane, was elected class president" and be asked to complete it in two different ways. One sentence should indicate that Maria and Diane both were elected (perhaps at different schools or in different years). For that sentence *like* might be inserted. A second sentence should convey that Diane lost the election; in this case *not* or *instead of* would be inserted.

Another way for young children to manipulate cohesive devices is through art. Three or four children could be given short scenes to illustrate. The scenes would differ only in their use of pronouns. For example, Picture A could illustrate "Bob and Sally have hats. His hat is blue. Her hat is green"; Picture B would represent "Bob and Sally have hats. Her hat is blue. His hat is green"; and Picture C, "Bob and Sally have hats. His hat is blue. Her hat is blue, too." When the pictures are completed, another group of children could match each story with its picture.

Young children might also enjoy acting out simple scenes. Sentence sets A, B, and C above could be written on the chalk board. A pair of actors could secretly select one set of sentences to act out and the audience could identify the sentences chosen.

Very young learners might gain a sense of the importance of pronouns by using self-sticking removable notes to change a story about a girl to one about a boy. Thus, *she* and *her* would be altered to *he* and *him*.

Guideline 2.   Help writers to think like readers and readers to think like writers.

The reciprocal nature of cohesion can be emphasized by encouraging students to examine their own writing from the perspective of a reader and to become metacognitively involved in their own reading by trying to think along with the author and follow the text's road map. We want both readers and writers to be aware that they are actively constructing or composing knowledge (Squire, 1984; Tierney & Pearson, 1983).

Many of the activities described under Guideline 1 are also appropriate here. Writers might also be encouraged to make graphic representations of their text's road maps (see Figure 2 for an example), using arrows and other signals to indicate how they have consciously used cohesive devices to connect ideas. Readers might make similar road maps of text they are reading. Students might learn much from each other if student writers could see how their peers mapped their work and if readers could examine how writers intended the road map to look.

Figure 2
A Cohesive Road Map

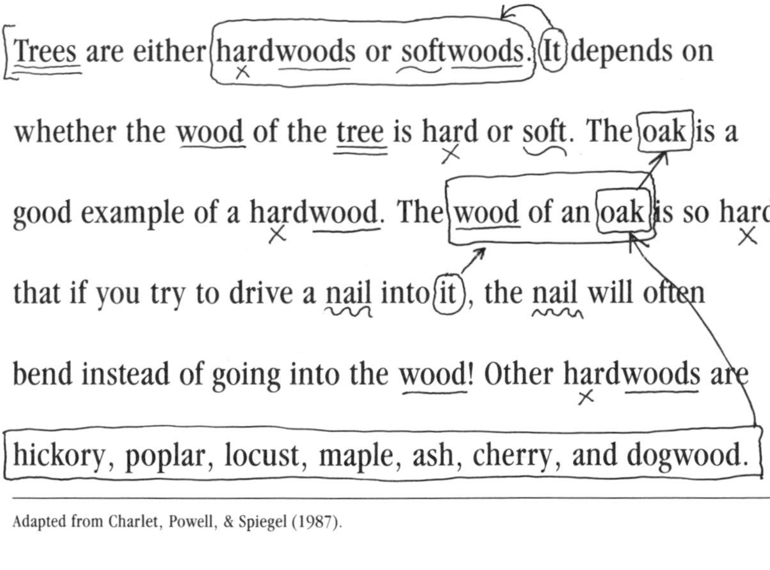

Trees are either hardwoods or softwoods. It depends on whether the wood of the tree is hard or soft. The oak is a good example of a hardwood. The wood of an oak is so hard that if you try to drive a nail into it, the nail will often bend instead of going into the wood! Other hardwoods are hickory, poplar, locust, maple, ash, cherry, and dogwood.

Adapted from Charlet, Powell, & Spiegel (1987).

Guideline 3.   Be sure that learners have the experiential background to profit from cohesive devices.

Bamberg (1984) suggests that understanding the functions of cohesive devices will not be sufficient to reconstruct an author's message if the reader lacks the experiential background to understand that message. Thus, a reader might understand fully the function of the conjunctive phrase *even though* in "Jordan took the point position, even though Ewing was better trained for that job and had more experience" but still not be able to make sense of the sentence.

The point is that students may lose faith in their own ability to make use of cohesive devices or in their teacher's ability to instruct them if they are asked to construct messages for which they have incomplete backgrounds or false information. A logical solution presents itself here. First, use only schemata familiar to learners when teaching lessons about cohesion (or anything else, for that matter). Thus, students have to focus on only one unfamiliar aspect during the lesson. Then extend cohesion lessons to embrace less familiar schemata, but explicitly teach children how to recognize when they are in the wrong ball park. That is, students may need to be shown how to identify the source of their incomplete understanding and to differentiate between a schema problem and a lack of knowledge about a particular cohesive device.

Guideline 4.   Ensure that what children read is written in fully formed language.

Critics of traditional reading programs have often argued—justifiably— that what children read in those programs is frequently unnatural and stilted (Beck et al., 1984). Such ambiguous use is made of cohesive devices ("Look here, Bob. See this. It is big.") that children may learn to distrust or dismiss cohesive markers. If teachers must use a traditional program that provides relatively unnatural text lacking good use of cohesive devices, they may need to use the time they read aloud to the class to provide literature models that are more cohesively rich. Teachers might also design lessons to show their young students how to interpret the pictures and words in their readers together in order to form a cohesive and coherent whole.

If a literature-based or whole language program is being used, teachers might be wise to do a quick check of the literature to get a sense of the completeness of the language modeled. "Real" literature may not use cohesive markers appropriately either!

The guidelines offered above are speculative. They make sense in light of what we know about reading and writing in general and about good and poor readers and writers specifically. The next step is to investigate instructional interventions systematically and find out what actually does work.

References

Atwell, M.A. (1981). *The evolution of text: The interrelationship of reading and writing in the composing process.* Paper presented at the annual meeting of the National Council of Teachers of English, Boston, MA.

Bain, A. (1890). *English composition and rhetoric* (English ed.). London: Longmans, Green.

Bamberg, B. (1983). What makes a text coherent? *College Composition and Communication, 34,* 417-429.

Bamberg, B. (1984). Assessing coherence: A reanalysis of essays written for the National Assessment of Educational Progress, 1969-1979. *Research in the Teaching of English, 18,* 305-319.

Barnitz, J.G. (1980). Syntactic effects on the reading comprehension of pronoun-referent structures by children in grades two, four, and six. *Reading Research Quarterly, 15,* 268-289.

Barnitz, J.G. (1986). The anaphoric jigsaw puzzle in psycholinguistic and reading research. In J.W. Irwin (Ed.), *Understanding and teaching cohesion comprehension.* Newark, DE: International Reading Association.

Bartlett, E.J., & Scribner, S. (1981). Text and content: An investigation of referential organization in children's written narratives. In C.H. Frederiksen & J.F. Dominic (Eds.), *Writing: The nature, development, and teaching of written communication. Volume 2, Writing: Process, development, and communication.* Hillsdale, NJ: Erlbaum.

Baumann, J.A., & Stevenson, J.A. (1986). Identifying types of anaphoric relationships. In J.W. Irwin (Ed.), *Understanding and teaching cohesion comprehension.* Newark, DE: International Reading Association.

Beck, I.L., McKeown, M.G., Omanson, R.C., & Pople, M.T. (1984). Improving the comprehensibility of stories: The effects of revisions that improve coherence. *Reading Research Quarterly, 19,* 263-277.

Bellert, I. (1970). On a condition of the coherence of texts. *Semiotica, 2,* 335-363.

Bormuth, J.R., Carr, J., Manning, J., & Pearson, P.D. (1970). Children's comprehension of between- and within-sentence syntactic structures. *Journal of Educational Psychology, 61,* 349-357.

Bracewell, R., Hidi, S., & Hildyard, A. (1981). *Cohesion in children's stories and arguments: An instrument for examining writing skills.* Paper presented at the annual meeting of the American Educational Research Association, Los Angeles, CA.

Bridge, C.A., & Winograd, P.N. (1982). Readers' awareness of cohesive relationships during cloze comprehension. *Journal of Reading Behavior, 14,* 299-312.

Brostoff, A. (1981). Coherence: "Next to" is not "connected to." *College Composition and Communication, 32,* 278-294.

Carrell, P.L. (1982). Cohesion is not coherence. *TESOL Quarterly, 16,* 479-488.

Chall, J.S., & Jacobs, V.A. (1983). Writing and reading in the elementary grades: Developmental trends among low SES children. *Language Arts, 60,* 617-626.

Chapman, L.J. (1983). *Reading development and cohesion.* Portsmouth, NH: Heinemann.

Chapman, M.T. (1984). Foreword. In R.B. Markels, *A new perspective on cohesion in expository paragraphs.* Carbondale, IL: Southern Illinois University Press.

Charlet, J.D., Powell, W.S., & Spiegel, D.L. (1987). *North Carolina: Our people, places, and past.* Durham, NC: Carolina Academic Press.

Cirilo, R.K. (1981). Referential coherence and text structure in story comprehension. *Journal of Verbal Learning and Verbal Behavior, 20,* 358-367.

Clark, C.H. (1986). Assessing comprehensibility: The PHAN system. In J.W. Irwin (Ed.), *Understanding and teaching cohesion comprehension.* Newark, DE: International Reading Association.

Clark, H.H. (1977). Inference in comprehension. In D. LaBerge & S.J. Samuels (Eds.), *Basic processes in reading: Perception and comprehension.* Hillsdale, NJ: Erlbaum.

Clark, H.H., & Haviland, S.E. (1977). Comprehension and the given-new contract. In R.O. Freedle (Ed.), *Discourse production and comprehension* (vol. 1). Norwood, NJ: Ablex.

Clark, H.H., & Sengul, C.J. (1979). In search of referents for nouns and pronouns. *Memory and Cognition, 7,* 35-41.

Cooper, C.R. (1983). Procedures for describing written texts. In P. Mosenthal, L. Tabor, & S.A. Walmsley (Eds.), *Research on writing: Principles and methods.* White Plains, NY: Longman.

Cox, B., & Sulzby, E. (1984). Children's use of reference in told, dictated, and handwritten stories. *Research in the Teaching of English, 18,* 345-366.

Crothers, E.J. (1979). *Paragraph structure inference.* Norwood, NJ: Ablex.

Crowhurst, M. (1987). Cohesion in argument and narration at three grade levels. *Research in the Teaching of English, 21,* 185-201.

de Beaugrande, R. (1980). *Text, discourse, and process: Toward a multidisciplinary science of texts.* Norwood, NJ: Ablex.

Doyle, A.E. (1982). The limitations of cohesion. *Research in the Teaching of English, 16,* 390-393.

Duffy, G.G., Roehler, L.R., Sivan, E., Rackliffe, G., Book, C., Meloth, M.S., Vavrus, L.G., Weeselman, R., Putnam, J., & Bassiri, D. (1987). Effects of explaining the reasoning associated with using reading strategies. *Reading Research Quarterly, 22*(3), 347-368.

Fahnestock, J. (1983). Semantic and lexical coherence. *College Composition and Communication, 34,* 400-416.

Fishman, A.S. (1978). The effects of anaphoric references and noun phrase organizers on paragraph comprehension. *Journal of Reading Behavior, 10,* 159-170.

Fitzgerald, J., & Spiegel, D.L. (1986). Textual cohesion and coherence in children's writing. *Research in the Teaching of English, 20,* 263-280.

Freebody, P., & Anderson, R.C. (1983). Effects of vocabulary difficulty, text cohesion, and schema availability on reading comprehension. *Reading Research Quarterly, 18,* 277-294.

Friedman, L.B., & Sulzby, E. (1987). Cohesive harmony analysis: Issues of text pragmatics and macrostructure. In J.E. Readence & R.S. Baldwin (Eds.), *Research in literacy: Merging perspectives.* Rochester, NY: National Reading Conference.

Geva, E., & Ryan, E.B. (1985). Use of conjunctions in expository texts by skilled and less skilled readers. *Journal of Reading Behaviour, 17,* 331-346.

Golden, J. (1987). *Coherence in children's written narratives.* Paper presented at the annual meeting of the National Reading Conference, St. Petersburg, FL.

Goodin, G., & Perkins, K. (1982). Discourse analysis and the art of coherence. *College English, 44,* 57-63.

Gottsdanker-Willekens, A.E. (1986). Anaphoric reference instruction: Current instructional practices. In J.W. Irwin (Ed.), *Understanding and teaching cohesion comprehension.* Newark, DE: International Reading Association.

Gutwinski, W. (1976). *Cohesion in literary texts: A study of some grammatical and lexical features of English discourse.* Paris: Mouton.

Hagen, L. (1971). An analysis of transitional devices in student writing. *Research in the Teaching of English, 5,* 190-201.

Halliday, M.A.K., & Hasan, R. (1976). *Cohesion in English.* London: Longman.

Hartnett, C.G. (1984). *Cohesion and rhetorical development: Thus, it more resembles pizza.* Paper presented at the annual conference on College Composition and Communication, New York.

Hasan, R. (1984). Coherence and cohesive harmony. In J. Flood (Ed.), *Understanding reading comprehension.* Newark, DE: International Reading Association.

Haslett, B.J. (1983). Children's strategies for maintaining cohesion in their written and oral stories. *Communication Education, 32,* 91-105.

Henderson, I. (1980). The use of connectives by fluent and not-so-fluent readers. *Dissertation Abstracts International, 40,* 5345A.

Holloway, D.W. (1981). Semantic grammars: How they can help us teach writing. *College Composition and Communication, 32,* 205-218.

Hottel-Burkhart, N. (1980). Cohesion in writing: A review for teachers. *English Record, 31,* 19-22.

Irwin, J.W. (1979). Fifth graders' comprehension of explicit and implicit connective propositions. *Journal of Reading Behavior, 11,* 261-271.

Irwin, J.W. (1980a). The effect of linguistic cohesion on prose comprehension. *Journal of Reading Behavior, 12,* 325-332.

Irwin, J.W. (1980b). The effects of explicitness and clause order on the comprehension of reversible causal relationships. *Reading Research Quarterly, 15,* 477-488.

Irwin, J.W. (1982). The effects of coherence explicitness on readers' comprehension. *Journal of Reading Behavior, 14,* 275-284.

Irwin, J.W. (1986). Cohesion and comprehension: A research review. In J.W. Irwin (Ed.), *Understanding and teaching cohesion comprehension.* Newark, DE: International Reading Association.

Irwin, J.W., & Pulver, C.J. (1984). The effects of explicitness, clause order, and reversability on children's comprehension of causal relationships. *Journal of Educational Psychology, 76,* 399-407.

Kameenui, E.J., & Carnine, D.W. (1982). An investigation of fourth graders' comprehension of pronoun constructions in ecologically valid texts. *Reading Research Quarterly, 17,* 556-580.

Keenan, J.M., Baillet, S.D., & Brown, P. (1984). The effects of causal cohesion on comprehension and memory. *Journal of Verbal Learning and Verbal Behavior, 23,* 115-126.

King, M.L. (1989). Speech to writing: Children's growth in writing potential. In J.M. Mason (Ed.), *Reading and writing connections.* Needham Heights, MA: Allyn & Bacon.

King, M.L., & Rentel, V.M. (1981). *How children learn to write: A longitudinal study.* Columbus, OH: Ohio State University Research Foundation.

Kintsch, W., & van Dijk, T.A. (1978). Toward a model of text comprehension and production. *Psychological Review, 85,* 363-394.

Klecan-Acker, J.S., & Lopez, B. (1985). A comparison of t-units and cohesive ties used by first and third grade children. *Language and Speech, 28,* 307-315.

Lesgold, A.M. (1972). Pronominalization: A device for unifying sentences in memory. *Journal of Verbal Learning and Verbal Behavior, 11,* 316-323.

Lybbert, E.K., & Cummings, D.W. (1969). On repetition and coherence. *College Composition and Communication, 20,* 35-38.

Markels, R.B. (1983). Cohesion paradigms in paragraphs. *College English, 45,* 450-464.

Markels, R.B. (1984). *A new perspective on cohesion in expository paragraphs.* Carbondale, IL: Southern Illinois University Press.

Marshall, N., & Glock, M.D. (1978). Comprehension of connected discourse: A study into the relationships between the structure of text and information recalled. *Reading Research Quarterly, 14,* 10-56.

Matsuhashi, A., & Quinn, K. (1984). Cognitive questions from discourse analysis. *Written Communication, 1,* 307-339.

McClure, E., & Geva, E. (1983). The development of cohesive use of adversative conjunctions in discourse. *Discourse Processes, 6,* 411-432.

McClure, E., Mason, J., & Barnitz, J. (1979). An exploratory study of story structure and age effects on children's ability to sequence stories. *Discourse Processes, 2,* 213-249.

McClure, E., & Steffensen, M.S. (1985). A study of the use of conjunctions across grades and ethnic groups. *Research in the Teaching of English, 19,* 217-236.

McCulley, G.A. (1985). Writing quality, coherence, and cohesion. *Research in the Teaching of English, 19,* 269-282.

McCutchen, D., & Perfetti, C.A. (1982). Coherence and connectedness in the development of discourse production. *Text, 2,* 113-139.

McCutchen, D., & Perfetti, C.A. (1984). *The development of knowledge-dependent and knowledge-independent writing skills.* Paper presented at the annual meeting of the American Educational Research Association, New Orleans, LA.

McCutchen, D., Perfetti, C.A., & Basick, C. (1983). *Young writers' sensitivity to local coherence.* Paper presented at the annual meeting of the American Educational Research Association, Montreal, Quebec.

McKoon, G., & Ratcliff, R. (1980). The comprehension processes and memory structures involved in anaphoric reference. *Journal of Verbal Learning and Verbal Behavior, 19,* 668-682.

Meyer, B.J.F., Brandt, D.M., & Bluth, G.J. (1980). Use of top-level structure in text: Key for reading comprehension of ninth-grade students. *Reading Research Quarterly, 16,* 72-103.

Moberly, P.C. (1978). *Elementary children's understanding of anaphoric relationships in connected discourse.* Unpublished doctoral dissertation, Northwestern University, Evanston, IL.

Moe, A.J. (1979). Cohesion, coherence, and the comprehension of text. *Journal of Reading, 23,* 16-20.

Moe, A.J., & Irwin, J.W. (1986). Cohesion, coherence, and comprehension. In J.W. Irwin (Ed.), *Understanding and teaching cohesion comprehension.* Newark, DE: International Reading Association.

Monson, D. (1982). *Effect of type and direction on comprehension of anaphoric relationships.* Paper presented at the International Reading Association WORD Research Conference, Seattle, WA.

Monson, D., & Gonzales, P. (1984). *Control of cohesive devices in writing, grades two through six.* Paper presented at the annual meeting of the American Educational Research Association, New Orleans, LA.

Morgan, J.L., & Sellner, M.B. (1980). Discourse and linguistic theory. In R.J. Spiro, B.C. Bruce, & W.F. Brewer (Eds.), *Theoretical issues in reading comprehension.* Hillsdale, NJ: Erlbaum.

Mosenthal, J.H., & Tierney, R.J. (1984). Cohesion: Problems with talking about text. *Reading Research Quarterly, 19,* 240-244.

Norris, J.A., & Bruning, R.H. (1988). Cohesion in the narratives of good and poor readers. *Journal of Speech and Hearing Disorders, 53,* 416-424.

Odell, L. (1981). Defining and assessing competence in writing. In C.R. Cooper (Ed.), *The nature and amount of competency in English.* Urbana, IL: National Council of Teachers of English.

Odell, L., & Goswami, D. (1980). *Writing in a nonacademic setting.* Photographic copy, State University of New York, Albany, NY.

Pritchard, R.J. (1986). *Cohesion and composition: A research study.* Paper presented at the fourth international conference on the Teaching of English, Ottawa, Ontario.

Pulver, C.J. (1986). Teaching students to understand explicit and implicit connectives. In J.W. Irwin (Ed.), *Understanding and teaching cohesion comprehension.* Newark, DE: International Reading Association.

Rentel, V.M., & King, M.L. (1983). Present at the beginning. In P. Mosenthal, L. Tabor, & S.A. Walmsley (Eds.), *Research on writing: Principles and methods.* White Plains, NY: Longman.

Richek, M.A. (1976). Reading comprehension of anaphoric forms in varying linguistic contexts. *Reading Research Quarterly, 12,* 145-165.

Roen, D.H. (1981). The effects of selected text forming structures on college freshmen's comprehension of expository prose. *Dissertation Abstracts International, 42,* 4210A-4380.

Scardamalia, M., Bereiter, C., & Goelman, H. (1982). The role of production factors in writing ability. In M. Nystrand (Ed.), *What writers know: The language process and structure of written discourse.* San Diego, CA: Academic.

Sloan, G. (1984). The frequency of transitional markers in discursive prose. *College English, 46,* 158, 165-179.

Smith, J., & Elkins, J. (1985). The use of cohesion by underachieving readers. *Reading Psychology, 6,* 13-25.

Smith, R. (1984). Paragraphing for coherence: Writing as implied dialogue. *College English, 46,* 8-21.

Spiegel, D.L., & Fitzgerald, J. (1990). Textual cohesion and coherence in children's writing revisited. *Research in the Teaching of English, 24,* 48-66.

Squire, J.R. (1984). Composing and comprehending: Two sides of the same basic process. In J.M. Jensen (Ed.), *Composing and comprehending.* Urbana, IL: National Council of Teachers of English.

Stotsky, S. (1983). Types of lexical cohesion in expository writing: Implications for developing the vocabulary of academic discourse. *College Composition and Communication, 34,* 430-446.

Tierney, R.J., & Mosenthal, J.H. (1983). Cohesion and textual coherence. *Research in the Teaching of English, 17,* 215-229.

Tierney, R.J., & Pearson, P.D. (1983). Toward a composing model of reading. *Language Arts, 60,* 568-580.

Trabasso, T., Secco, T., & Van Den Brock, P. (1984). Causal cohesion and story coherence. In H. Mandl, N.L. Stein, & T. Trabasso (Eds.), *Learning and comprehension of text.* Hillsdale, NJ: Erlbaum.

van Dijk, T.A. (1980). *Macrostructures: An interdisciplinary study of global structures in discourse, interaction, and cognition.* Hillsdale, NJ: Erlbaum.

van Dijk, T.A., & Kintsch, W. (1983). *Strategies of discourse comprehension.* San Diego, CA: Academic.

Webber, B.L. (1980). Syntax beyond the sentence: Anaphora. In R. Spiro, B. Bruce, & W. Brewer (Eds.), *Theoretical issues in reading comprehension.* Hillsdale, NJ: Erlbaum.

Winterowd, W.R. (1970). The grammar of coherence. *College English, 31,* 828-835.

Winterowd, W.R. (1985). Counterstatement: Response to Gary Sloan. Transitions: Relationships among t-units. *College Composition and Communication, 36,* 100-104.

Witte, S.P., & Faigley, L. (1981). Coherence, cohesion, and writing quality. *College Composition and Communication, 32,* 189-204.

Jill Fitzgerald

— **F O U R** —

Reading and Writing Stories

*T*his chapter begins with an exploration of what makes a story, focusing on its affective character. Next, results of research are presented on story writing and the relationship between reading and writing stories. The chapter closes with recommendations for classroom teachers and a brief critique of the questions addressed to date in the research on stories.

What Is a Story?

The simple, central question "What *is* a story?" can't be answered in an easy way. I have not yet seen a single verbal description of the term *story* that completely reflects the essence of what a story is. Here is the best definition of story I can offer:

> A story is a particular form of a narrative which sometimes has content that differs from the type of content found in other discourse types. It has a structure or structures distinct from description and exposition. It has plots, characters who interact socially, and themes; it can have inside view, vary in point of view, and have foreshadowing. It contains a problem or a conflict or both, revolves around characters' goals, and has some sort of action and resolution, with various elements related temporally and causally. A story is often characterized by stylistic words and phrases such as "Once upon a time," has an entertainment or literary aesthetic force, and often evokes affective feelings such as interest, surprise, and suspense (Fitzgerald, 1989, p. 9).

What's lacking in this definition is the "feel" of stories. And if the feel of stories isn't there, the words don't fully convey "storiness." Perhaps only a definition that uses poetry can fully delineate the idea.

Here are brief descriptions of story aspects included in the above definition:

Narrative is "discourse that attempts to embody in linguistic form a series of events that occur in time...[and that has] a causal or thematic coherence" (Brewer, 1980, p. 223). Brewer supplies the following as an example of narrative text: "The boy saw a dandelion. He picked the dandelion. He gave the dandelion to his mother." Narrative is distinct from description—"discourse that attempts to embody in linguistic form a stationary perceptual scene"—and exposition—"discourse that attempts to represent in linguistic form the underlying abstract logical processes...[such as] induction, classification, and comparison."

Content is the "stuff" of the story—"the chain of events...[and] existents (characters and settings), the objects and persons performing" (Chatman, 1975, p. 295).

Structure is like a container for the "stuff" of the story. It is "the expression, the means by which the content is communicated [in narratives], the set of actual narrative 'statements' " (Chatman, 1975, p. 295). It is the parts and the connections between the parts.

Plot is a particular configuration of goals, actions, and affective states (Chatman, 1975, 1978; Lehnert, 1981, 1982; Propp, 1968).

Theme is a concept or idea that relates or unifies chunks of story information (Bisanz et al., 1978).

Inside view means seeing inside a character; *point of view* is the perspective provided by the narrator (Bruce, 1984).

Now that we've attended to what might be called a denotative definition of stories, let's turn to the notion of the "feel" of stories. The feel of stories is intimately linked with the reasons we have stories. Why do these things called "stories" exist? Stories are stories and not something else because they do something or fill some need or because they represent ourselves and our lives in some important way. Stories exist because they are ways of thinking and knowing, of learning, organizing, exploring, seducing, manipulating, and controlling others—and more.

What can be said about the belief that stories exist for such reasons?

First, what is the "thought" that is captured in the language of stories? What do we "know" when we create or hear or read stories, and how do we know it?

In an intriguing account of what constitutes "storiness," Bruner (1985) suggests that only two modes of thinking exist, each of which is "natural" and provides a way of ordering experience and constructing reality. One mode is paradigmatic or logico-scientific. It deals in the relationships of connection and argumentation, in general causes and their establishment. It "is defined not only by observables to which its basic statements relate, but also by the set of possible worlds that can be logically generated and tested against observables, that is, it is driven by principled hypotheses" (p. 98).

The other way of thinking, the narrative mode, "deals in human or human-like intention and action and the vicissitudes and consequences that mark their course.... It operates by constructing two landscapes simultaneously. One is the landscape of action.... [The other] is the landscape of consciousness: what those involved in the action know, think, or feel" (pp. 98-99).

So the thinking and knowing that occur in or through stories express primarily the emotive, affective, visceral face of being human. We have stories because we have emotions and feelings, and we have a need to experience and order these emotions and feelings. The story satisfies because it meets these needs.

Second, stories don't just capture and freeze human intentions, emotions, and actions, they reach out. We have stories because they express our emotions to others and help to bond the human community: "A story is a communication [that] beckons towards somebody rather than anybody.... If a story is to be communicated, it must engage the willing attention of others" (Rosen, 1986, p. 231).

Because stories connect people, they "are used to manipulate, advertise, control, above all to soothe, to massage us" (Rosen, 1986, p. 236). And stories can only do these things through seduction. The reader/listener must be willing to allow the storyteller to go on. "Seduction is the means by which the storyteller acquires the right to narrate, displaying a capacity to occupy the conversational space of others without possessing it. It recruits the desires of the other in the interests of maintaining narrative authority" (Rosen, 1986, p. 236).

Results of Research

Studies that used stories to explore a different main interest are not included in this review. For example, a study of deaf and hearing students who read a story and then wrote recalls was left out because the investigators' principal interest was in the amount of information retained; there was no particular interest in stories themselves. Similarly, studies that used writing but showed no central interest in it are not included. For example, studies that happened to use written recalls but did not analyze anything about the writing were not reviewed. Finally, because chapter six in this book addresses emergent literacy, studies involving preschoolers' reading and writing of stories were excluded.

As you read the following sections, it is important to understand that this review and my comments about it are clearly linked to my own professional background as a literacy specialist. My own world of research and knowledge has limited vision. My world is not the world that English scholars and English education specialists have created and know well; nor is it the world of anthropologists and sociologists. Rather, I bring with me a tradition of investigation that is primarily linked to psychology, one that has been dominated recently by the thinking of cognitive psychologists and traditionally by "experimental" paradigms of research.

Reading Stories

A lot of research has been done on stories, especially since the late 1970s. Most of it involves reading or listening. Because research focusing on reading stories has been reviewed elsewhere in detail (Fitzgerald, 1989), it is summarized more generally here.

Knowledge about story structure.   Most of the research on stories has focused narrowly on story structure and, even more specifically, on the structure of stories from a folk- or fairy-tale tradition. Because so much of the research has centered on this topic, I'll start by describing the way many recent researchers have characterized structure.

Story structure, sometimes called story schema, is "an idealized internal [mental] representation of the parts of a typical story and the relationships among those parts" (Mandler & Johnson, 1977, p. 111). The structure is often represented through a story grammar, which defines the important parts of a story and the way they are ordered. Four major story grammars have been used in research. These were developed by Mandler and Johnson and Johnson and Mandler (1980); Rumelhart (1978); Stein and Glenn (1979); and Thorndyke (1977). The four grammars have many common features. Mandler and Johnson's grammar is typical. In it, they identify six major story parts: setting (introduction of the main character of the first episode, which may have statements about locale, time, or props); beginning (a precipitating event); reaction/goal (the protagonist's internal response to the precipitating event and formation of a goal); attempt (effort to attain the goal); outcome (success or failure of the attempt); and ending (long-range consequence of the action, final response of a character, or an emphatic statement).

Here's an example of a simple story called "Albert and the Fish" (from Stein & Glenn, 1977) showing the major story parts and their order:

Setting: Once there was a big gray fish named Albert who lived in a big icy pond near the edge of a forest.

Beginning: One day, Albert was swimming around the pond when he spotted a big juicy worm on top of the water.

Reaction/goal: Albert knew how delicious worms tasted and wanted to eat that one for his dinner.

Attempt: So he swam very close to the worm and bit into him.

Outcome: Suddenly, Albert was pulled through the water into a boat. He had been caught by a fisherman.

Ending: Albert felt sad and wished he had been more careful.

The grammars can be used to describe more complex stories, too. For example, often story parts are embedded within other story parts. This typically happens when an attempt results in an unsuccessful outcome and the protagonist enlists the aid of another, leading to a whole new episode embedded within an outcome.

Overall, research on people's knowledge of story structure suggests that many people have knowledge about how stories are organized (Applebee, 1977, 1978; Mandler, 1978, 1987; Mandler & Johnson, 1977; Stein & Glenn, 1979; Thorndyke, 1977; Whaley, 1981a). Also, people tend to think certain story parts are more important than others (Mandler & Johnson, 1977; Stein & Glenn, 1979; Whaley, 1981b). Settings, beginnings, attempts, and outcomes are seen as central to stories, but many people feel that complex reactions and endings can be omitted if they're easily inferred from the text.

Knowledge of story content. Research has also examined people's beliefs and perceptions about appropriate content for stories. Major findings include the information that many individuals believe stories contain only certain kinds of content (Fitzgerald & Spiegel, 1983b; Fitzgerald, Spiegel, & Webb, 1985; Spiegel & Fitzgerald, 1982). For example, Steinberg and Bruce (1980) discuss three types of content that can occur as conflicts in stories: environmental, in which achievement of a character's goal is obstructed by nature, society, or fate; interpersonal, in which two or more characters have incompatible goals; and internal, in which a single character has two or more incompatible goals. Furthermore, certain types of content tend to be seen as more important than others. For example, information that is most pertinent to the causal chain of events in a story tends to be judged as more important than other content (Black & Bern, 1981).

Effects of text features. Several key effects of text features have been found. For instance, it seems that people use knowledge of story structure to guide their expectations, understanding, and recall of text (see the previously described work on story grammars; Bereiter & Scardamalia, 1982). When reading and listening, individuals hold a sort of structural outline of the major story categories in their minds to make hypotheses about forthcoming information, to better comprehend time and sequence in stories, and to cue recall of specific information.

Structure of stories may also affect readers' affective states (Brewer, 1985; Brewer & Lichtenstein, 1981, 1982). Stories with no beginning evoke little suspense; stories with an early attention-grabbing beginning, followed by text designed to sustain interest, create rising suspense (which drops at the outcome).

The familiarity of certain types of content can affect recognition and recall (Adams & Worden, 1986; Graesser & Nakamura, 1982; Mandler, 1984). The most unusual content (such as actions, personality characteristics, and locations of action) tends to be best recognized and recalled.

Development of key features of stories. Two important findings about the development of key features of stories are that many young children (perhaps as young as four years) develop knowledge of story structure, which becomes richer and more elaborate as they grow older (Applebee, 1978; Fitzgerald & Spiegel, 1983b; Stein & Glenn, 1979). Some individuals, however, do not easily acquire a rich sense of story (Buss et al., 1983; Chall & Jacobs, 1984).

Findings of special interest to teachers. The following are other selected findings that might be of particular interest to teachers:

- A limited amount of research indicates that many lower level trade books and leading basal readers don't conform to adults' structural expectations—that is, they don't contain expected story parts (Bruce, 1984; Steinberg & Bruce, 1980).
- Knowledge of story structure and reading ability seem to be related—better readers tend to have more fully developed knowledge of story structure (Fitzgerald, 1984; McClure, Mason, & Williams, 1983; Smiley et al., 1977).
- Instruction can increase children's knowledge of story structure which, in turn, can affect comprehension and recall (Buss et al., 1983; Fitzgerald & Spiegel, 1983a; Gordon & Braun, 1982, 1983; Morrow, 1985, 1986; Singer & Donlan, 1982; Varnhagen & Goldman, 1986).

Writing Stories

Research on the writing of stories is sparse and has been conducted primarily with elementary grade students. Several tentative findings emerge from these investigations. First, as we would expect, the ability to write stories others judge to be "good" seems to develop over time (Langer, 1985; Villaume, 1988).

Second, young students tend to have trouble writing stories that adults judge as "good." Although it is clear from research on emergent literacy that even preschoolers have knowledge about story characteristics and include some of these characteristics in their writing (see Sulzby & Barnhart, this volume), the limited research in this area suggests that youngsters have trouble juggling the many facets of story writing. For example, students in grades 2 through 6 seem to have trouble organizing ideas for writing (Chall & Jacobs, 1984). When writing or rewriting, students between grades 3 and 7 have difficulty planning compositions to elicit feelings such as suspense (Bereiter & Scardamalia, 1984). Although first and second graders have tacit knowledge of the range of ways to introduce characters in stories and do make use of this knowledge, it often leads to ambiguous introductions (Villaume, 1988). Such difficulties may be particularly pronounced for learning-disabled and reading-disabled students (Nodine, Barenbaum, & Newcomer, 1985).

Third, in some cases, it seems that individuals have knowledge about essential story features but fail to apply it in their writing. For example, one group of researchers found no significant relationship between what young children know about the essential aspects of story structure and the organization they use in writing stories (McGee et al., 1984). Second and fifth graders in this study who demonstrated knowledge of story structure on a picture unscrambling task wrote stories that did not conform to a story grammar. It appears that the special complexities involved in story writing, as opposed to story telling or story reading, contribute to difficulties in this activity.

Fourth, though scant, the evidence so far suggests that intervention in story writing may help. I located only three studies that investigated the possibilities of enhancing story writing through instruction in story structure. In these studies, fourth and fifth graders were taught about common story parts and the order in which they normally occur. For example, in one study (Fitzgerald & Teasley, 1986) fourth graders began by learning six story parts, one part per lesson, over two weeks. Each lesson had a fixed format containing an overview, a definition of the new story part, examples (from both the teacher and the students), presentation of "nonexamples," and activities designed for application of the specific part. In the second phase of instruction, during lessons spread out over two months, students participated in activities that required them to use knowledge of all of the story parts together (Fitzgerald, Spiegel, & Teasley, 1987).

Results of the three studies were mixed. In one (Braun & Gordon, 1984), there were no significant effects of intervention on writing; in the others there were. Students included more text structure categories in their stories (Gordon & Braun, 1982, 1983), and wrote stories that were better organized and higher in quality than students in a control group (Fitzgerald & Teasley, 1986).

Relationships between Reading and Writing Stories

There is minimal evidence of either similarities or differences in the processes involved in reading versus writing stories. Langer (1986) points out that for both activities, individuals focus on constructing meaning and use the same knowledge to formulate ideas and build or extract schemata or content. However, she notes that the two activities can invoke somewhat different mental processes. For instance, story writers tend to be slightly more concerned than story readers with bottom-up issues such as mechanics, syntax, and lexical choice. In addition, story writers tend to be more aware of and concerned with the mental strategies they use to create meaning.

Very few studies have investigated the possibilities of using story reading to affect story writing and vice versa. Of the two studies I found, both indicated positive effects of one on the other, although in one case the effects were minimal. In a study conducted by Bereiter and Scardamalia (1984), third through seventh graders who first wrote suspense stories and then read model suspense stories used more principles for creating suspense when revising their first attempts. However, the same effect was achieved by teaching five principles for suspense without having students read model stories.

In another study (Eckhoff, 1984), second graders' story writing was markedly influenced by the basals they read. Children who read a basal with a sophisticated and complex style wrote with more elaborate structures than did children who read a basal with a simplified style.

Furthermore, it seems that the *kind* of writing that takes place affects the interpretation of what is read. In one study (Newell, Suszynski, & Weingart, 1989) tenth grade students were asked to read and write about two short stories. For the first story, they were asked to write pieces explaining and elaborating on their personal interpretation, using their own experiences as well as elements of the text; for the other story, they were asked to write "formal" pieces interpreting the story by drawing their references from the text alone. When they wrote formal, "text-based" responses, they reviewed more elements of the stories and interpreted the stories more objectively; when they wrote more personal, "reader-based" responses, they tended to review fewer story elements, while subjectively interpreting text elements and exploring the meaning of the text in light of prior experience. Similarly, in another study (Marshall, 1987), eleventh graders who worked on extended writing assignments requiring explanation, elaboration, and interpretation of short stories they had read had fuller understandings of these stories than did students who were assigned more restricted writing projects or no writing at all.

Implications for Teachers

The current research has several implications for the classroom. First, even when students have the knowledge necessary for writing well-structured stories, they don't always use it. This suggests that certain procedural aspects of writing are very difficult for youngsters. To help children overcome such difficulties, teachers can provide many opportunities for practice in writing, with the idea that fluency may develop through repetition. They can also discuss procedural aspects such as note-making methods for planning and the technicalities of revision. Some techniques for teaching story structure that are likely to be successful include asking students questions that pertain specifically to story grammar categories; teaching children about the story parts directly by defining, demonstrating, and eliciting examples; and completing story maps (flowcharts or outlines) to highlight important information.

Second, some children, especially reading-disabled and learning-disabled children, may need tutorials in selected story characteristics, although more research needs to be conducted to determine appropriate methods and overall effectiveness.

Third, it is not safe to assume that the mental processes used in reading and writing stories are identical. Teachers may want to keep this in mind in order to prompt children to use their knowledge of story characteristics during story reading and writing. For example, suppose the teacher asks, "What happened to get the story going?" and no response is given. A follow-up question such as "What part of the story would give us the information about what happened to get the whole story going?" should prompt students to use their knowledge of story parts to search for and identify relevant information.

Fourth, since story reading may influence story writing, wide reading of good literature is likely to be beneficial.

Fifth, having various opportunities for extended writing in response to reading stories is likely to enrich students' interpretations of what they read.

What's Needed?

For the most part, the research on reading and writing stories has addressed something other than the "feel" of stories. I do not in any way want to imply that the research done to date is not valuable or useful or informative; it has given us many insights. But this research (and some of it has been my own) informs us only about limited aspects of "storiness." We have no research that I know of that touches the heart or the exquisiteness of stories.

Why have we explored certain aspects of stories and not others? One reason may be that we have, for the most part, been approaching the study of storiness using what Bruner (1985) calls paradigmatic or logico-scientific thinking. As Bruner says, literary scholars and linguists, cognitive psychologists, folklorists, and anthropologists "have studied not the process, but the product, the tales rather than the tellers" (p. 103). Our questions and our methodologies have shaped, and perhaps limited, our understanding. To state the case boldly, we have used logico-scientific thinking to investigate its opposite—narrative thought.

What kinds of questions would get at the heart of storiness? Let me suggest a few: What is the thought that is captured in the language of stories? How does the mind create stories? Why does the mind create stories? What does it mean to be compelled to read or write a story? The answer(s) to such questions may lead to instructional approaches vastly different from those currently undertaken in educational/psychological research and may entice students to seek the satisfaction of constructing meaning through reading and creating stories.

Finally, how, when, and why does the mysterious attraction in reading and writing stories happen? Worthwhile reading and writing of stories are related to the power of the narrative to attract and engage the reader and writer. And attraction and engagement primarily result from feelings and thought about content and secondarily from feelings and thought produced by the interaction of content and form. Can we learn more about what compels one to write or read stories and about how this seduction takes place? Can we, in turn, learn more about how to enhance in our students these feelings of being compelled to write and read stories?

I wish I could suggest a paradigm for studying stories that would lead us into more research on narrative thought. I'm convinced that we must push ourselves in this direction if we are to come to a fuller understanding of the sense, the thoughts, and the feel of stories, as well as the relationships between reading them and writing them.

References

Adams, L.T., & Worden, P.E. (1986). Script development and memory organization in preschool and elementary school children. *Discourse Processes, 9*(2),149-166.

Applebee, A.N. (1977). A sense of story. *Theory into Practice, 16*(5), 342-347.

Applebee, A.N. (1978). *Child's concept of story: Ages 2-17.* Chicago, IL: University of Chicago Press.

Bereiter, C., & Scardamalia, M. (1982). From conversation to composition: The role of instruction in a developmental process. In R. Glaser (Ed.), *Advances in instructional psychology* (Vol. 2). Hillsdale, NJ: Erlbaum.

Bereiter, C., & Scardamalia, M. (1984). Learning about writing from reading. *Written Communication, 1,* 163-188.

Bisanz, G.L., LaPorte, R.E., Vesonder, G.T., & Voss, J.F. (1978). On the representation of prose: New dimensions. *Journal of Verbal Learning and Verbal Behavior, 17*(3), 337-357.

Black, J.B., & Bern, H. (1981). Causal coherence and memory for events in narratives. *Journal of Verbal Learning and Verbal Behavior, 20,* 267-275.

Braun, C., & Gordon, C.J. (1984). Writing instruction as a metatextual aid to story schema applications. In J.A. Niles & L.A. Harris (Eds.), *Changing perspectives on research in reading/language processing and instruction.* Rochester, NY: National Reading Conference.

Brewer, W.F. (1980). Literary theory, rhetoric, and stylistics: Implications for psychology. In R.J. Spiro, B.C. Bruce, & W.F. Brewer (Eds.), *Theoretical issues in reading comprehension* (pp.221- 239). Hillsdale, NJ: Erlbaum.

Brewer, W.F. (1985). The story schema: Universal and culture-specific properties. In D.R. Olson, N. Torrance, & A. Hildyard (Eds.), *The nature and consequences of reading and writing* (pp. 167-194). New York: Cambridge University Press.

Brewer, W.F., & Lichtenstein, E.H. (1981). Event schemas, story schemas, and story grammars. In J. Long & A. Baddeley (Eds.), *Attention and performance* (pp. 363-379). Hillsdale, NJ: Erlbaum.

Brewer, W.F., & Lichtenstein, E.H. (1982). Stories are to entertain: A structural-affect theory of stories. *Journal of Pragmatics, 6,* 473-486.

Bruce, B. (1984). A new point of view on children's stories. In R.C. Anderson, J. Osborn, & R.J. Tierney (Eds.), *Learning to read in American schools: Basal readers and content texts* (pp. 153-174). Hillsdale, NJ: Erlbaum.

Bruner, J. (1985). Narrative and paradigmatic modes of thought. In E. Eisner (Ed.), *Learning and teaching the ways of knowing* (part II, pp. 97-115). Chicago, IL: National Society for the Study of Education.

Buss, R.R., Yussen, S.R., Mathews, S.R., Miller, G.E., & Rembold, K.L. (1983). Development of children's use of a story schema to retrieve information. *Developmental Psychology, 19*(1), 20-30.

Chall, J., & Jacobs, V.A. (1984). Writing and reading in the elementary grades: Developmental trends among low SES children. In J.M. Jensen (Ed.), *Composing and comprehending.* Urbana, IL: National Conference on Research in English and ERIC /RCS.

Chatman, S. (1975). Toward a theory of narrative. *New Literary History, 6*(2), 295-318.

Chatman, S. (1978). *Story and discourse.* Ithaca, NY: Cornell University Press.

Eckhoff, B. (1984). How reading affects children's writing. In J.M. Jensen (Ed.), *Composing and comprehending.* Urbana, IL: National Conference on Research in English and ERIC /RCS.

Fitzgerald, J. (1984). The relationship between reading ability and expectation for story structures. *Discourse Processes, 7,* 21-42.

Fitzgerald, J. (1989). Research on stories: Implications for teachers. In K.D. Muth (Ed.), *Children's comprehension of text.* Newark, DE: International Reading Association.

Fitzgerald, J., & Spiegel, D.L. (1983a). Enhancing children's reading comprehension through instruction in narrative structure. *Journal of Reading Behavior, 15*(2), 1-17.

Fitzgerald, J., & Spiegel, D.L. (1983b). The development of knowledge of social intentions, plans, and resolutions as reflected in story productions and recall of scrambled stories. In J.A. Niles & L.A. Harris (Eds.), *Searches for meaning in reading/language processing and instruction* (pp. 192-198). Rochester, NY: National Reading Conference.

Fitzgerald, J., Spiegel, D.L., & Teasley, A.B. (1987). Story structure and writing. *Academic Therapy, 22*(3), 255-262.

Fitzgerald, J., Spiegel, D.L., & Webb, T.B. (1985). Development of children's knowledge of story structure and content. *Journal of Educational Research, 79*(2), 101-108.

Fitzgerald, J., & Teasley, A. (1986). Effects of instruction in narrative structure on children's writing. *Journal of Educational Psychology, 78,* 424-433.

Gordon, C.J., & Braun, C. (1982). Story schemata: Metatextual aid to reading and writing. In J.A. Niles & L.A. Harris (Eds.), *New inquiries in reading research and instruction.* Rochester, NY: National Reading Conference.

Gordon, C.J., & Braun, C. (1983). *Teaching story schema: Metatextual aid to reading and writing.* Paper presented at the annual meeting of the American Educational Research Association, Montreal, P.Q., Canada.

Graesser, A.C., & Nakamura, G.V. (1982). The impact of a schema on comprehension and memory. In G.II. Bower (Ed.), *The psychology of learning and motivation* (Vol. 16, pp. 59-109). San Diego, CA: Academic.

Johnson, N.S., & Mandler, J.M. (1980). A tale of two structures: Underlying and surface forms in stories. *Poetics, 9,* 51-68.

Langer, J.A. (1985). Children's sense of genre: A study of performance on parallel reading and writing tasks. *Written Communication, 2,* 157-187.

Langer, J.A. (1986). Reading, writing, and understanding: An analysis of the construction of meaning. *Written Communication, 3,* 219-267.

Lehnert, W.G. (1981). Plot units and narrative summarization. *Cognitive Science, 5,* 293-331.

Lehnert, W.G. (1982). Plot units: A narrative summarization strategy. In W.G. Lehnert & M.R. Ringle (Eds.), *Strategies for natural language processing* (pp. 375-412). Hillsdale, NJ: Erlbaum.

Mandler, J.M. (1978). A code in the node: The use of a story schema in retrieval. *Discourse Processes, 1,* 14-35.

Mandler, J.M. (1984). *Stories, scripts, and scenes: Aspects of schema theory.* Hillsdale, NJ: Erlbaum.

Mandler, J.M. (1987). On the psychological reality of story structure. *Discourse Processes, 10*(1), 1-29.

Mandler, J.M., & Johnson, N.S. (1977). Remembrance of things parsed: Story structure and recall. *Cognitive Psychology, 9,* 111-115.

Marshall, J.D. (1987). The effects of writing on students' understanding of literary texts. *Research in the Teaching of English, 21,* 30-63.

McClure, E., Mason, J., & Williams, J. (1983). Sociocultural variables in children's sequencing of stories. *Disclosure Processes, 6,* 131-143.

McGee, L.M., Ratliff, J.L., Sinex, A., Head, M., & LaCroix, K. (1984). Influence of story schema and concept of story on children's story compositions. In J.A. Niles & L.A. Harris (Eds.), *Changing perspectives on research in reading/language processing and instruction.* Rochester, NY: National Reading Conference.

Morrow, L.M. (1985). Reading and retelling stories: Strategies for emergent readers. *The Reading Teacher, 35*(9), 870-875.

Morrow, L.M. (1986). Effects of structural guidance in story retelling on children's dictation of original stories. *Journal of Reading Behavior, 18*(2), 135-152.

Newell, G.E., Suszynski, K., & Weingart, R. (1989). The effects of writing in a reader-based and text-based mode on students' understanding of two short stories. *Journal of Reading Behavior, 21,* 37-57.

Nodine, B., Barenbaum, E., & Newcomer, P. (1985). Story composition by learning disabled, reading disabled, and normal children. *Learning Disability Quarterly, 8,* 167-169.

Propp, V. (1968). *Morphology of the folktale* (2nd ed.). Translated by L. Scott. Baltimore, MD: Port City Press. (Original work published in 1928.)

Rosen, H. (1986). The importance of story. *Language Arts, 63,* 226-237.

Rumelhart, D.E. (1978). Understanding and summarizing brief stories. In D. LaBerge & S.J. Samuels (Eds.), *Basic processes in reading: Perception and comprehension* (pp. 265-303). Hillsdale, NJ: Erlbaum.

Singer, H., & Donlan, D. (1982). Active comprehension: Problem solving schema with question generation for comprehension of complex short stories. *Reading Research Quarterly, 17*(2), 166-186.

Smiley, S.S., Oakley, D.D., Worthen, D., Campione, J.C., & Brown, D.L. (1977). Recall of thematically relevant materials by adolescent good and poor readers as a function of written versus oral presentation. *Journal of Educational Psychology, 69,* 381-387.

Spiegel, D.L., & Fitzgerald, J. (1982). Conflict and conflict structures in stories told by children. In J.A. Niles & L.A. Harris (Eds.), *New inquiries in reading research and instruction* (pp. 282-286). Rochester, NY: National Reading Conference.

Stein, N.L., & Glenn, C. (1977). *The role of structural variation in children's recall of simple stories.* Paper presented at the annual meeting of the Society for Research in Child Development, New Orleans, LA.

Stein, N.L., & Glenn, C. (1979). An analysis of story comprehension in elementary school children. In R.O. Freedle (Ed.), *New directions in discourse processing* (Vol. 2, pp. 53-120). Norwood, NJ: Ablex.

Steinberg, C., & Bruce, B. (1980). Higher level features in children's stories: Rhetorical structure and conflict. In M.L. Kamil & A.J. Moe (Eds.), *Perspectives on reading research and instruction* (pp. 117-125). Washington, DC: National Reading Conference.

Thorndyke, P. (1977). Cognitive structures in comprehension and memory of narrative discourse. *Cognitive Psychology, 9,* 97-110.

Varnhagen, C.K., & Goldman, S.R. (1986). Improving comprehension: Causal relations instruction for learning handicapped learners. *The Reading Teacher, 39*(9), 896-904.

Villaume, S.K. (1988). Creating context within text: An investigation of primary-grade children's character introductions in original stories. *Research in the Teaching of English, 22,* 161-182.

Whaley, J.F. (1981a). Readers' expectations for story structure. *Reading Research Quarterly, 16,* 90-114.

Whaley, J.F. (1981b). Story grammars and reading instruction. *The Reading Teacher, 34*(7), 762-771.

— F I V E —

Summarizing Text

*E*xamining the process involved in summarizing provides an opportunity for studying a unique relationship between reading and writing. We typically think of readers as constructing a summary, or "macrostructure," from a text and writers as constructing a text from a macrostructure (Slater et al., 1988). While both activities involve construction, reader-summarizers are much more restricted in their construction than writers are. Writers can solicit a number of sources for the starting points of their macrostructures; readers can only solicit the material to be summarized. Authors can elaborate and embellish to their hearts' content; summarizers are prohibited from elaborating on the text's basic macrostructure.

Because summarizing is supposed to preserve the meaning of the material to be summarized, it is unlike other writing activities that treasure original ideas. Being true to the original material is not a simple matter, in part because things can go awry during both reading and summary writing. Garner (1982, p. 279) reminds us that "We cannot...look at a model summary and a less desirable one, and infer with confidence that the student submitting the former has understood and remembered more than the student submitting the latter."

This chapter offers an outline of recent research on summarizing. In the first section, I link three definitions of summaries to their corresponding summarizing processes. Discussed here is whether summarizing is predominantly a reading or a writing activity. In the second section, I show how researchers studying summarizing are continually reminded that their object of study shifts with changes in person, text, and task. Shown here are ways such variables may subvert or enhance the summarizing process. In the final section, I examine recent instruction on summarizing. I also speculate about why telling students to shorten their summaries seems to work equally well as macrorule instruction and I offer several suggestions for teachers.

Definitions and Processes

Discussions about summarizing are less than fruitful when jargon gets in the way. Hidi and Anderson (1986, p. 480) complained that the biggest problem they met in trying to identify summarizing processes was that "different investigators tend to use different terminology to describe fundamentally similar processes." For instance, some researchers call summarizing "macrostructure abstraction" and others call it "main idea comprehension." Johnson (1983) described an opposite problem: researchers use "summary" to describe constructs requiring different processes.

Some Working Definitions

In talking about stories, Johnson (1983) has differentiated among three types of summaries. The first kind is essentially recall output—what a student is able to remember of a story. Recall nearly always involves some reduction of the original text (Brown & Smiley, 1977) and so can be considered a kind of summary, although most of the literature on recall does not identify it in this way.

The second type of story summary is probably the most familiar. It describes the main story events, or plot. Johnson (1983) noted that when her subjects were asked to write a summary, they naturally wrote this kind. Van Dijk and Kintsch's (1983) subjects, however, yielded summaries more like recall output—in essence, a "dump" of memory contents—regardless of whether their instructions were to summarize or to recall.

An expository counterpart for the second kind of story summary is hard to find. We don't have a single, well-known structure for exposition the way we do for traditional stories, and the available structures for exposition (e.g., cause-effect, label-list) aren't as familiar as the story structure is. This may account for researchers' findings that expository summarizing skill develops late (Brown & Day, 1983; Hare & Borchardt, 1984).

The third type of story summary supplies the "point" or "essence" of a story, something akin to the moral of a fable. Some stories have obvious points; others do not (Johnson, 1983). In exposition, when texts are very brief, we search for a main idea; with longer texts, we seek a thesis statement. The literature on main ideas in reading tackles this kind of point-driven summary.

Knowing how researchers define a summary informs us of their positions on summarizing processes, the topic I turn to next.

Summarizing during Comprehension

At a minimum, theorists agree that summarizers start their activity by comprehending individual propositions in a text and the relationships between them—that is, by constructing a text microstructure (Johnson, 1983). After this point, theorists differ in emphasis on where the primary work of summarizing takes place. One camp emphasizes macrostructure building during comprehension; the other believes this happens subsequent to comprehension. The distinction is important because summarizing during comprehension can be conceptualized as a reading task, whereas summarizing after comprehension might be conceived of as a writing task.

Van Dijk and Kintsch fall into the first camp. In several versions of their work (van Dijk, 1979; van Dijk & Kintsch, 1978, 1983), they theorize that comprehending is a summarizing process. They view summaries as expressions of text macrostructure that are constructed during reading, once the text microstructure has been established. Readers in their experiments consistently abstracted higher-level summary statements when asked either to summarize or to recall text. From van Dijk and Kintsch's description, we can safely assume that "summary" denotes recall output.

Van Dijk and Kintsch suggest that readers apply a set of macrorules as they read. These macrorules systematically condense text until it is reduced to its macropropositions. Macrorules include rules of *deletion, generalization,* and *construction.* Readers apply a deletion rule to eliminate irrelevant or redundant propositions that don't presuppose another proposition in a sequence of propositions. Readers apply a generalization rule to substitute one umbrella proposition for a sequence of propositions. For instance, propositions relating to hamsters, guinea pigs, and gerbils may be generalized to one statement about domesticated rodents. Finally, a construction rule replaces a sequence of propositions with a single proposition implied by the sequence. For instance, a macroproposition may be constructed to replace several sentences describing the building of the first trans-North American railroad, even though the "meat" of each individual sentence does not share similar attributes in the way that hamsters, guinea pigs, and gerbils do.

In this summarizing model, then, readers asked to supply a summary of a text need only "read out" their abstracted macrostructure from memory. No further cognitive operations are necessary. In both recall protocols and summaries, the propositions generated are those predicted by the actions of the macrorules; the propositions that are forgotten or not included are not predicted by the macrorules (van Dijk, 1979). Others, too, have found that the likelihood of a reader recalling a proposition is directly related to the relative importance of that proposition in the text (Gomulicki, 1956; Meyer, 1975). This is not to say that lower-level propositions are not stored in memory, only that at least some hierarchical structuring of text ideas occurs during comprehension.

Summarizing after Comprehension

Other researchers contend that retrieval is merely the precursor to two primary summarizing activities: selecting important ideas and condensing them (Brown & Day, 1983; Johnson, 1983). Often these postreading processes lead to a written summary, so in some cases they could be classified as writing processes as well.

Selecting important ideas entails determining the relative value of text portions in light of the whole text. It requires making decisions about what to exclude and what to include. Winograd (1984) found that sensitivity to importance explained variance in both comprehending and summarizing. Sensitivity to importance is a slippery construct, however. Its correlation to comprehending and summarizing may vary as a function of how each construct is measured (Roller, 1985; Swoope & Johnson, 1988). Hare and Borchardt (1984) speculated that students are more or less able to handle summarizing tasks according to their sensitivity to importance.

Summarizing entails more than simply identifying important ideas and laying them out in order. It also demands condensing these ideas in some coherent fashion, especially when writing the summary. This means providing superordinate labels for lower-level propositions and ideas, as well as integrating higher-order text portions and ideas. Johnson (1983) points out that one thorny task is deciding which important ideas need to be stated explicitly and which can be left to inference. When condensing, interpretations or elaborations are inappropriate. As previously stated, the author of a summary has license only to reproduce the original text in a more concise form, all the while keeping in mind the coherence of the new text being constructed.

Brown and her colleagues (Brown & Day, 1983; Brown, Day, & Jones, 1983) have argued that selection and condensation are critical to the summarizing enterprise. Interestingly, though, their set of summarizing macrorules is taken directly from van Dijk and Kintsch's (1978) macrorules—rules van Dijk and Kintsch claim are applied *during* comprehension. Most summarization instructional researchers have in turn used some version of Brown and Day's list (Hare & Borchardt, 1984; McNeil & Donant, 1982). Day (1980) turned van Dijk and Kintsch's deletion rule into two rules, one for deleting unnecessary or trivial information and one for deleting redundant information. She translated their generalization rule into two rules as well, one for generalizing lists of items and one for generalizing lists of actions. She turned their construction rule into rules for selecting and inventing topic sentences.

In making a case for the processing differences between comprehending and summarizing, several researchers have pointed to differences between comprehending and summarizing performance on various measures. Winograd (1984) showed that use of the summarizing rules he developed (drawing heavily from van Dijk and Kintsch) explained variance in summarizing scores but not in comprehension scores. This makes sense when one considers that a written summarizing task and the comprehending tasks used by Winograd (multiple-choice questions and standardized reading comprehension tests) are likely to require dissimilar processing.

Children in Johnson's (1983) study were asked to summarize a story under two conditions. For the recall summarizing condition, they were told they had plenty of time to tell a hypothetical friend all they could remember about the story. For the plot summarizing condition, they were told they had limited time and had to make the story shorter. Johnson found that the children had more trouble summarizing than recalling story information. Child summarizers deleted information randomly, unlike adults, who make deletion decisions based on importance. Johnson suggested that comprehension does not automatically result in the ability to summarize; it only guarantees input for the summarizing processes of selection and condensation. She acknowledged, however, that neither selecting ideas nor condensing them is completely absent from comprehension and recall.

Johnson's work may help explain the processing distinction between creating recall output summaries and plot summaries. Johnson's data clearly describe processing for plot summaries, whereas van Dijk and Kintsch's data describe processing for recall output. Selecting and condensing important ideas are in both cases crucial to the summarizing enterprise; the processing differences may be a matter of degree, not of nature. As we shall see later, whether a summary is largely constructed during reading (as implied by van Dijk and Kintsch's work) or after reading (as implied by Johnson's work) depends on a wide variety of factors.

Rapprochement

The truth about summarizing may lie somewhere in between the perception that it is either a reading or a writing activity. It may be useful to conceptualize summarizing as a recursive process that begins at the time of encoding and ends when the desired summary is complete. Around the time of encoding, summarizers may construct a product that looks pretty much like a retelling or a recounting. At this time, the key selection and condensation processes may be largely automatic. In such instances, comprehending may well be summarizing, and summaries can be "read out" from memory.

Hidi and Anderson (1986) acknowledge that skills may overlap in comprehension/recall and summarizing, although they argue that summarizing entails much more deliberation at the selection and condensing stages. I would suggest simply that recursion of the summarizing process may continue well beyond the automatic, subconscious level, depending on the kind of summary end-product desired. To gain a more succinct summary, especially a written one, would-be summarizers need to become more conscious and strategic about their processing. Nevertheless, the rules for summarizing remain the same. Continued, deliberate application of selecting and condensing strategies will eventually yield the "point." The recursive nature of summarizing makes it difficult to judge precisely when "reading" ends and "writing" begins.

Theoretical definitions of summaries are not the only determinants of processing, however. Hidi and Anderson (1986) suggest that further processing differences may be explained by variations in reader and text. These variations will be the subject of the following section.

Variables That Affect Summarizing

Still to be fully described in the literature is the extent to which person, text, and task variables affect summarizers' activities. The process of summarizing is especially vulnerable to these influences because summarizing is tied up with fuzzy notions of centrality or importance. This section briefly reviews person, text, and task variables and suggests how such variables, either alone or in interaction with one another, might affect selection and condensation strategies in summarizing.

Person Variables

Summarizers come to their task with different views of its nature, different levels of summarizing skill, and different levels of content knowledge relating to the text to be summarized. Each variable affects summarizing differently.

Views of the task. The summarizer's mental representation of a summary has been studied from a variety of perspectives. Generally, students are aware that summarizing entails shortening the original material, and they readily produce summaries that are shorter than the original texts. Brown and Day (1983) called attention to students who seemed to employ a "copy-delete" strategy in writing a summary. In part, this meant students knew enough to delete low-level information in their summaries. In the same vein, young children's summaries tend to be shorter than their recalls (Johnson, 1983; See, 1989).

Students don't seem to have a well-developed internal monitor for optimum summary length, or perhaps they don't care to impose their own sense of appropriate length on the maximum space they are told to use. Some students may see summarizing as just a generic school writing task, one to be dispensed with as quickly as possible. Once Brown and Day's (1983) subjects had deleted low-level information, they merely copied the text into their summaries. Winograd (1984), too, noted that students copied text until they ran out of room. Students apparently are happy to accommodate space restrictions when writing summaries but are unwilling to go beyond the space provided. If given three lines, they write two or three lines; if given a page, they write a page.

In addition, while children know that summaries should be shorter than the original text, they are much less aware of what information to include. See (1989) observed that first graders produced essentially the same proportions of key plot events to total story events in both recalls and summaries of the same stories, a finding much like van Dijk and Kintsch (1983) reported for adults. It seems clear that many or most students are unaware of a key aspect of summarizing: the role of textual importance, or what the author of the original material has signaled to be important. From students' responses, we may deduce that some think "interesting" material ought to be included in a summary (Garner, Gillingham, & White, 1989; Garner & McCaleb, 1985; Hidi & Anderson, 1986; Hidi & Baird, 1986; Taylor, 1986; Winograd, 1984). Hare, Rabinowitz, and Schieble (1989), for instance, noted that summarizers favored including information that was different from, yet related to, their own life experience. Taylor's (1986) fourth and fifth grade subjects apparently thought summaries ought to include unusual and unfamiliar ideas that an audience might be interested in. (Given the oral presentation that often accompanies written reports in schools, students' decisions about including such material may be quite savvy.)

Even when students do pay attention to textual importance in their summaries, the communal notion of the "point" seems at best indeterminate. From groups of sixth graders, prospective teachers, and teachers, Cunningham and Moore (1986) counted nine different ways of representing the main idea of a paragraph, among them an intepretation, a key word, a theme, and a topic.

As a final word on the topic of students' notion of "summary," it is important to note that production deficiencies do not necessarily indicate awareness deficiences (Garner, 1985). Garner et al. (1985) had fifth graders watch videotaped interviews with three summarizers and decide which summarizer did the best job. Based on their ability to place the "bad" summary in the last rating slot, below-grade to average readers showed reasonable awareness of what good summaries needed to include and exclude. Nevertheless, they were unable to transfer this knowledge to their own summarizing activity. Winograd (1984) found a similar discrepancy between awareness and production among eighth graders.

Different views of the nature of summaries have consequences for processing. Students with inadequate or incorrect representations of summaries understandably skip over the tough selecting and condensing activities. Students who think summaries need to be shorter versions of the original can get by with deleting low-level information. Those who are playing to an audience can concern themselves with incorporating interesting ideas in their summaries. Getting down enough words to fill the page may be a higher priority than choosing and condensing the words themselves.

Skill levels. Summarizers also possess different levels of skill at selecting and condensing ideas. Selecting important ideas—juggling the relative values of information at several levels of the text hierarchy—is possibly the most daunting activity in the summarizing enterprise. Yet it is the activity that lies at the heart of the act (Garner, 1982; Hare & Borchardt, 1984).

Students at all age levels have an especially difficult time identifying implicit important ideas (Baumann, 1984; Brown & Day, 1983; Hare & Borchardt, 1984). Even "expert" readers can experience tremendous frustration when attempting to identify implicit important ideas. Johnston and Afflerbach (1985) reported that expert adult readers relied on three sources for cues to textual importance in unfamiliar, difficult text: context or knowledge, text, and personal beliefs about the author. They assigned importance to familiar words or phrases in a sea of unfamiliar text, found cues to importance in repeated mentions of concepts, and judged importance on the basis of their beliefs about the author's intent. The researchers noted that their adult expert readers sometimes assigned conditional importance to a piece of text and sought confirming or refuting evidence for their judgment.

In addition to selecting important ideas, condensing information is a challenging activity. Important ideas in the original text must be transformed for the summary to be successful without sacrificing brevity. Texts can often be reconfigured in more than one way, which complicates the matter. With age and schooling, students improve in their ability to generalize information (Brown & Day, 1983; Hare & Borchardt, 1984; Winograd, 1984). However, even older students are more inclined to leave propositions in their original form and order than to synthesize ideas within and across paragraphs (Brown & Day, 1983; Hare & Borchardt, 1984; Hidi, 1984). Possibly it is riskier to transform text than it is to copy-delete on a piecemeal, sentence-by-sentence or paragraph-by-paragraph basis.

An additional writing skill is required for condensing text, making it doubly difficult. In the act of shrinking a text, local coherence ties are often lost and need to be recovered through rewriting to make ideas "fit" smoothly once again. The greater the condensing needed, the greater the rewriting job. Students frequently ignore this aspect of the summarizing task (Hare & Borchardt, 1984; Taylor, 1986).

Thus, even when students are aware they need to identify and synthesize key ideas, they may be ill equipped to do so. Their level of summarizing skill, embodied in the selecting and condensing strategies, has direct consequences for processing. Those with few resources for evaluating a text for importance will be more bound to explicitly stated text information and more distracted by irrelevant (but possibly interesting) information (Johnston & Afflerbach, 1985; Kintsch, 1989). Those with condensing problems will sacrifice summarizing efficiency. Generalizing ideas within paragraph boundaries reduces text somewhat, but only major transformations across structural boundaries (like paragraphs) really suffice if long and complex texts are to be condensed significantly (Hidi, 1984).

Level of content knowledge. Last among the person variables is content knowledge relating to the text to be summarized (Head & Buss, 1987; Johnston & Afflerbach, 1985). It is a truism in our field that prior knowledge strongly biases the comprehension/summarizing activity. Without sufficient knowledge, important ideas can seem unimportant (or vice versa), particularly in texts with few structural clues to importance. Unfamiliar texts cause even expert adult readers to "deautomatize" their main idea processes (Johnston & Afflerbach). Where prior knowledge is unavailable or inaccessible, then, the processes of selecting and condensing are virtually impossible to undertake.

A word about prior knowledge is in order here. While we assume content knowledge interacts with summarizing prowess, the precise mechanisms of this interaction are unclear. For example, Hare, Rabinowitz, and Schieble (1989) noted that sixth and eleventh grade students in their study invoked recent curricular learning experiences in their main idea constructions and failed to stick to the content of the original third grade text. The researchers speculated that inappropriate constructions may be generated as a function of the distance between one's personal content schemata and those embodied in the material to be summarized.

Text Variables

Text variables are the most studied of the variables that affect summarizing. Hidi and Anderson (1986) identified three, which I will take as a framework for this discussion: length, genre, and complexity of the material to be summarized. Each has predictable consequences for summarizing.

Length. The length of the material to be summarized greatly affects ease of summarizing. All other things being equal, short texts are basically easier to summarize than long texts. When texts consist of only a paragraph, summarizing is a matter of inspecting a few sentences and either selecting an available topic sentence or generating a main idea. Students can do the former with relative ease; the latter comes more slowly (Hare & Chesla,

1986; Hare, Rabinowitz, & Schieble, 1989; Williams, 1986). When the main idea is explicit and unambiguous, a summary may be an outcome of comprehension.

With longer texts come greater comprehension demands: local micropropositions require more attention, and macrostructure building during comprehension may be severely taxed. When texts are longer, summarizers also must exercise greater discretion in choosing ideas to include, all the while juggling more ideas in their memories. What may appear relevant when a single paragraph is considered may be unimportant when a trio of paragraphs is evaluated. What may appear relevant in a trio of paragraphs may be excludable when an entire chapter is considered. Furthermore, important ideas that were once isolated may now demand merging with other important ideas. Rather than face the challenge of consolidating ideas over a long stretch of text, many students choose the more piecemeal method of processing shorter sections (Hare & Borchardt, 1984). Indeed, when a text is very long, students' summaries may resemble undifferentiated recall output, regardless of whether the summarizing occurred during or after comprehension.

In short texts, an irrelevant detail mixed in with the relevant sentences is fairly easy to spot and has a less disruptive effect on summarizing—indeed, adults can efficiently condense the detail into a higher-order proposition (Williams, 1986). When selection and condensing occur recursively over a longer text, students' attention is more likely to wander to juicy, novel, or personally relevant propositions (Hidi & Baird, 1985)—what Garner, Gillingham, and White (1989) term "seductive details." Numerous types of such details have been identified (Garner & McCaleb, 1985; Hidi & Baird, 1986; Winograd, 1984), among them traditional story elements, image-evoking information, quantified information (e.g., big numbers), and surprising or novel information. These details are more likely to find their way into students' summaries of longer texts.

Genre.   Genre is another text variable that affects summarizing. Researchers have mainly compared the ease of summarizing a narrative with the difficulty of summarizing an expository text, and have offered several reasons that narratives are easier to summarize (Baumann, 1982; Hidi & Anderson, 1986). First, young students generally have more experience with stories, so story structures are more familiar to them. Subjects in Kintsch, Mandel, and Kozminsky's (1977) study easily used their knowledge of story structure to reorder scrambled stories in summaries. Second, important and interesting ideas tend to overlap in stories, but not in expositions (Hidi & Baird, 1986). Picking an interesting idea for a story summary may be a more successful strategy than picking one for exposition. Third, exposition deals with more complex, abstract ideas. Last, expository structure is often less linear and less well organized than narrative structure.

The last explanation bears elaboration. Exposition comes in many forms—listing texts, sequence texts, cause-effect texts, comparison-contrast texts, and the like. Indeed, exposition does not necessarily exhibit any clear structure at all (Hare & Chesla, 1986). Summarizing different expository structures is hard in different ways (Hare, Rabinowitz, & Schieble, 1989). Linear sequence texts, like stories, are relatively easy to summarize, as are listing texts that require only a generalization strategy. Nonlinear cause-effect texts that require construction are more difficult to summarize, as are comparison-contrast texts that require two generalizations and an inference to bridge them.

Texts with unfamiliar or unclear structure are also likely to place heavier burdens on the selecting and condensing processes. Summarizers might not find important ideas in their usual places (e.g., first sentences). Even those familiar with out-of-the-ordinary text structures have trouble trying to determine what is essential in a summary (Geiselman & Samet, 1980). Moreover, without a familiar, straightforward structure on which to base a summary, summarizers may have to perform many transformations before a coherent and succinct summary can be produced.

Complexity.   This category bundles together such text characteristics as "low-frequency vocabulary, elaborate sentence structure, abstractness, unfamiliarity of concepts and ideas, and inappropriate or vague organization" (Hidi & Anderson, 1986, p. 476). The effects of complexity on summarizing are themselves complex. Kintsch (1989) studied the effects of macro- and microstructure manipulations on students' summarizing. In her study, good macrostructure was represented by three tiers of important ideas and a single tier of details. Only the topmost tier possessed topic sentences. Poor macrostructure was achieved by reorganizing the content to create unexplained topic shifts. Poor microstructure was achieved by manipulating vocabulary and sentence structure, and by dropping explicit connectives.

Generally, the youngest summarizers produced "shallow interpretations," summaries including only a topic statement from the text and a collection of details. Those students failed to integrate other implicit macropropositions (tiers 2 and 3) into the summary. Older summarizers integrated macropropositions from both explicit and implicit levels, in line with the original text's macrostructure. Moreover, in summarizing well-organized texts, students reduced elaborations and increased generalizations. Tenth graders failed to sustain this exemplary behavior with poorly organized texts, however, including instead more elaborations. Their summaries therefore reflected poor memory retrieval paths. Only the college students knew how to generalize ideas in these texts. Kintsch (1989) suggested that younger subjects may have expended their attention on local coherence processes at the expense of higher-order summarizing inferences.

A subsidiary body of literature on relevance cues also reveals some text effects on summarizing performance (Garner & McCaleb, 1985; Hare & Chesla, 1986; Hare, Rabinowitz, & Schieble, 1989). Positive effects for semantic cues (e.g., explicit topic sentences) and lexical cues (e.g., use of the word "significant"), especially within paragraphs, are predictable and reliable. Obviously, appropriate cuing could lighten the selection task considerably. Initial topic sentences, for instance, may be processed and reprocessed each time a subordinate proposition is encountered. The more frequently a topic sentence is processed, the easier it will be to access during summarizing (Miller & Kintsch, 1980). Indeed, it is possible that the reader's sensitivity to importance becomes an insignificant factor when texts possess many relevance cues (Reder & Anderson, 1980). Interestingly, students persist in seeking main ideas in first-sentence positions even when they appear elsewhere (Donlan, 1980; Hare & Chesla, 1986).

Task Variables

Task variables have received attention of late from researchers who suggest that these variables affect summarizing processing profoundly (Kintsch, 1989; Hidi & Anderson, 1986), although empirical studies are scarce. Here I discuss three variables: access to the text, purpose for summarizing, and restrictions on summary length.

Access. When students summarize from memory, the quality of the summary is constrained by the quality of the original encoding of the text. Actually, students are summarizing their memory's representation of the text, not the text itself (provided they didn't summarize during reading). The quality of comprehension, then, sets a ceiling on summarizing performance. Furthermore, retrieving ideas takes time away from selecting and condensing them.

These concerns may not affect summaries of brief, well-organized texts, possibly because summarizing can occur during reading. The longer and more unwieldly the text, however, the greater the memory load and the worse the consequences for summarizing. Hidi and Anderson (1986) do suggest that the deeper, more active processing required when the text is absent may produce better and more stable recall of material.

When summarizers have access to the text during summarizing, they are free to return to it time and again, both to deepen comprehension and to evaluate ideas more deliberately. Accurate selection seems more likely in a situation where ideas can be read, reread, and visually compared. Checking of condensed ideas also seems more likely when one can return to the original and judge directly whether transformations preserve or alter meaning. The downside to having access to the text may be that copying becomes more enticing than active processing (Head et al., 1988). Head, Readence, and Buss (1987) found that the availability of text made for increased copying of ideas in sixth graders' summaries.

Purpose. We know very little about the effects of summarizers' purposes on their processing. Hidi and Anderson (1986) identify a distinction between reader-based summaries (those produced for an audience) and writer-based summaries (those produced for the summarizers themselves). The research literature addressed reader-based summaries almost exclusively; yet writer-based summaries are probably the more useful and common of the two. Because summaries written for an audience require greater faithfulness to the original text, more attention to length constraints, and conformity to fit the standards of the audience (e.g., teachers, students, researchers), they may demand more and deeper processing to get just the right ideas condensed in just so many words. Even the mechanics matter in summaries written for an external audience.

Summaries written for oneself, on the other hand, often serve as abbreviated external records of the text for personal use. Often they are free-form in structure and include personal elaborations and editorial commentary as well as original text macropropositions. They can entail more piecemeal processing and tolerate fewer integrations, since often writers synthesize these memorial records with other summaries.

Kintsch (1989) implies that summaries written for an audience are appropriate if the summarizer's goal is reproducing received knowledge on a test. In that case, a good and accurate record of the original text is necessary. But, she adds:

> [If] students are expected to apply the content to novel situations, to abstract generalizations, and to make judgments that require inferential understanding, then creating a structure of one's own or restructuring the to-be-learned material would result in a memory representation that is more richly integrated into the personal knowledge base, and hence more adaptable to different situations (p. 40).

The dilemma is particularly worth pondering in light of our advising teachers to help readers and writers integrate prior knowledge with new knowledge. Recent summarization instruction, mine included, works hard to eliminate personal knowledge intrusions in summaries. Perhaps this position should be rethought.

Length restrictions. Associated with the purpose for summarizing is the length of summary required. Length goes hand in hand with decisions about important ideas to include and transformations of these ideas. Unrestricted summary length eases processing demands; restricted summary length imposes greater selecting and condensing burdens on the summarizer, sometimes to the detriment of the end-product (Brown, Day, & Jones, 1983; Garner & McCaleb, 1985). When pushed to construct a briefer summary, students with condensing problems will simply drop important ideas rather than synthesize them.

Summary length interacts with text variables to yield the three different kinds of summaries discussed earlier in this chapter. Putting no constraints on length may result in a recall-like outcome. A severe limit on summary length for a short text may yield a "point." A more moderate restriction for a longer text such as seven sentences for a seven-paragraph article may yield a summary between one and seven sentences long. The selecting and condensing processes may thus be inhibited, encouraged, or made unbearably difficult as a function of restrictions set on summary length.

Implications
The list of person, text, and task variables presented here is by no means exhaustive. Some predictions about interactions among variables are

substantiated; others are a mystery and await research efforts. Based on what we already know, though, we can make some generalizations with relative confidence. To begin, would-be summarizers who are not knowledgeable about what the activity of summarizing involves are unlikely to engage in selecting and condensing strategies. Those who don't know how to select important ideas or condense them will turn to less mature, less effective strategies. Those who aren't familiar with the content of the text to be summarized won't be able to select important ideas.

We can generate additional predictions about summarizers who are knowledgeable about the need to select and condense ideas. For these people, summarizing *during* comprehension is afforded when texts are familiar and brief (or when recalls are acceptable for longer texts), when text structure is well known and macropropositions are clearly cued, and when no length restrictions are placed on the summary. Summarizing *after* comprehension, often a writing task, becomes necessary when texts are longer and less familiar, when macrostructure is disrupted or poorly cued, when local coherence is lacking, and when summary length is extremely restricted. Without doubt, an intricate web of interrelationships among person, text, and task affects the summarizing process.

One question that comes to mind in considering the work of a would-be summarizer relates to the role of instruction. If, in fact, readers do automatically abstract the gist of a text as they read, then instruction on how to summarize is superfluous. The preceding literature review suggests that students can summarize very brief texts with obvious macropropositions with minimal instruction. Fortunately, basal reader series already include this minimal instruction (Hare & Milligan, 1984). For other situations, some kind of summarizing instruction may be warranted. In the final section, I discuss the pros and cons of existing instructional models and make a number of suggestions for instruction.

Instructional Issues

Quite a number of studies focusing on instruction in summarizing have been published in the past decade, Day's (1980, 1986) dissertation work being the earliest among them. Approximately two-thirds of the studies couple direct instruction with a set of summarizing rules. In most of these cases, the rules are adapted from Brown and Day's (1983) adaptation of van Dijk and Kintsch's (1978) macrorules (Bean & Steenwyk, 1984; Hare & Borchardt,

1984; McNeil & Donant, 1982; Palincsar & Brown, 1984; Rinehart, Stahl, & Erickson, 1986). Some studies that fall under the rubric of "main idea instruction" also use rule-governed approaches (Baumann, 1984; Sjostrom & Hare, 1984). On the surface, these studies show favorable effects for a rule-governed approach to summarizing, particularly when the effects of lower-level rules such as deletion and generalization are isolated. It seems, too, that lower-level rules can be taught.

Direct instruction of rules is not an unqualified success, however. The construction rule, with its counterparts in identifying explicit and implicit important ideas, has proved resistant to instruction. Students trained in this rule learn to summarize more efficiently (Sjostrom & Hare, 1984)—that is, they use fewer words to express key ideas—but they do not necessarily increase the number of key ideas expressed. It seems that their ability to select important ideas remains impaired. Students demonstrate significant improvement in their use of the construction rule (Baumann, 1984; Hare & Borchardt, 1984), but this improvement seems to be limited to brief or well-organized texts. A good many instructional studies use as texts Boning's (1970) *Specific Skills Series* paragraphs, whose brevity may facilitate success with the construction rule. With more complex, less well-organized texts, however, identifying implicit main ideas can be harder than consolidating them (Hare & Borchardt, 1984).

The suspicion that the construction rule may be "unteachable" gains strength when one compares the effects of intuitive approaches to summarizing with the effects of rule-governed approaches. Cunningham (1982) developed the GIST procedure to improve fourth graders' comprehension of the gist of paragraphs. Essentially, GIST asks students to summarize the first sentence of the paragraph in 15 words, then the first and second sentences together, and so on until the entire paragraph has been reduced to 15 words.

Bean and Steenwyk (1984) compared rule-governed instruction with GIST instruction, weighting summary scores by the importance of the ideas included. Sixth graders in both rule-governed and GIST groups scored significantly higher than those in a control group, but no significant difference emerged between the two experimental groups. Unfortunately, the studies looking at the GIST procedure used *Specific Skills Series* (Boning, 1970) paragraphs for their dependent measures, so we can't tell whether the rule-governed group would have had an advantage on longer, more complex texts. In the absence of these data, one might speculate that teaching students to invent topic sentences is not worthwhile and that simply telling students to keep shortening their summaries would suffice. Indeed, with "instruction" like the following, taken from Hare and Borchardt (1984) and adapted from Day (1980), students receive little guidance on how to construct an important idea:

> Often authors write a sentence that summarizes a whole paragraph. It is called a topic sentence. If the author gives you one, you can use it in your summary. Unfortunately, not all paragraphs contain topic sentences. That means you may have to make up one for yourself. If you don't see a topic sentence, make up one of your own (p. 66).

Palincsar and Brown (1984) incorporated summarizing instruction in their reciprocal teaching procedure. Students learned a set of strategies, one of which was summarizing, and then applied the strategies to brief texts. Teachers initially provided "expert scaffolding" for students' responses, and then students took turns playing teacher. It may well be that in cases where processes resist explanation, extended modeling and opportunities to practice—to fumble, to take risks, and to receive feedback—are a worthwhile alternative for teachers to consider.

Several recommendations for teachers follow from the preceding discussion. One is that teachers as well as researchers of summarizing processes think about their own definitions of summarizing. Does the definition entail recall, essence, or something in between? Because how one thinks about summarizing has (or ought to have) direct consequences for subsequent instruction, it is very important to be aware of one's personal definition.

Next, I advocate acquainting students with basic summarizing rules. Full and explicit summarizing instruction is not commonly found in textbooks; instead, simple directives to summarize brief chunks of text prevail. As a result, summarizing processes are usually inferred by students. Some students make appropriate inferences, but many others will resort to "copy-delete" and other inappropriate strategies.

Specifically, students should be knowledgeable about how to condense lists (generalization rule), seek or invent topic sentences (construction rule), and eliminate unnecessary detail (deletion rule). They should also understand how to synthesize ideas across paragraphs (a "macro" version of the construction rule). Finally, they should apprehend the role of polishing or rewriting summary prose to improve it.

Teachers can convey these rules either by explaining them directly or by providing "expert scaffolding," such as that found in Palincsar and Brown's (1984) approach. Students practice the rules first on specially created sample texts and later on naturally occurring texts (Hare & Borchardt, 1984). Practicing summarizing rules on naturally occurring texts enables students to learn how text variations affect their manipulation of these rules. To take a simple example, lists are not always available in texts to be summarized; in such circumstances, the "collapse lists" rule is irrelevant.

Note, as mentioned earlier, that these summarizing activities presume some prior knowledge of the content of the text to be summarized. It is difficult—if not impossible—to summarize text content that is completely novel because all ideas may seem equally important or unimportant. The summarizer cannot tell which information to include and which to delete, except by conscientious attention to lexical signals and to text structure patterns (e.g., cause-effect, comparison-contrast); in poorly written, inconsiderate texts, these clues may not be present. Without these structural clues, a summarizer confronted with unfamiliar material may be totally at sea.

As should now be clear, mastering basic summarizing rules is not in itself sufficient for writing good summaries, nor is it all that easy. Students need help in understanding the influences of various person, text, and task variables on the summarizing activity. Teachers can best supply this help by providing a good deal of practice with different texts and in different milieus. Students need to know the difference between interesting and important text material. They need to practice selecting and condensing important ideas to hone their skills. They need to experiment with summarizing texts of different lengths, genres, and levels of complexity. They need to see what happens to their summarizing proficiency when the text is absent and when it is present. And last, but perhaps most important, they need to contrast reader-versus writer-based summaries. The purpose for summarizing seems to affect the summarizing enterprise more than most other person, text, and task variables.

Summing Up

It goes without saying that summarizing is a very complex endeavor. This foray into recent research on summarizing highlights several important ideas about the nature of reading/writing relationships in summarizing.

One is that summarizing can be viewed as either a reading or a writing process. Summarizing itself is a recursive process of selecting and condensing important ideas. When comprehension "clicks" or when summaries are defined as recall output, summarizing is a largely automatic, subconscious process. Under these circumstances, we think of a summary as a product of reading. On the other hand, when comprehension "clunks" or when summaries are defined more restrictively, summarizing becomes a more conscious and deliberate process. Under these circumstances, we may think of a summary as a product of writing. The line between summarizing as a reading activity and summarizing as a writing activity blurs easily, however, since selection and condensation occur recursively from the moment of encoding to completion of the summary.

Considered alone, the dual reading/writing nature of summarizing presents certain challenges in terms of identifying where summarizing processing may go awry. Couple this with the evidence that summarizing is affected by a host of person, text, and task variables, and we begin to understand that our past instructional interventions may have erred by treating summarizing as an undifferentiated whole. It is true that both direct instruction and more intuitive approaches have been shown to improve students' summaries, although only reciprocal teaching seems to offer some promise of assisting students with the resistant construction rule. However, it strikes me that many efforts so far have failed to take into careful account the effects of the different variables on summarizing. When we better understand the interplay among these variables, we should be able to pass on new insights to our students. In this chapter, I extended Hidi and Anderson's (1986) list of variables, but the list can (and should) go on. By no means have we learned all we need to learn about reading/writing relationships in summarizing.

References

Baumann, J.F. (1982). Research on children's main idea comprehension: A problem of ecological validity. *Reading Psychology, 3*, 167-177.

Baumann, J.F. (1984). The effectiveness of a direct instruction paradigm for teaching main idea comprehension. *Reading Research Quarterly, 20*, 93-115.

Bean, T.W., & Steenwyk, F.L. (1984). The effect of three forms of summarization instruction on sixth graders' summary writing and comprehension. *Journal of Reading Behavior, 16*, 297-306.

Boning, R. (1970). *Specific skills series.* Baldwin, NY: Barnell-Loft.

Brown, A.L., & Day, J.D. (1983). Macrorules for summarizing texts: The development of expertise. *Journal of Verbal Learning and Verbal Behavior, 22,* 1-14.

Brown, A.L., Day, J.D., & Jones, R.S. (1983). The development of plans for summarizing texts. *Child Development, 54,* 968-979.

Brown, A.L., & Smiley, S.S. (1977). Rating the importance of structural units of prose passages: A problem of metacognitive development. *Child Development, 48,* 1-8.

Cunningham, J.W. (1982). Generating interactions between schemata and text. In J.A. Niles & L.A. Harris (Eds.), *New inquiries in reading research and instruction* (pp. 42-47). Rochester, NY: National Reading Conference.

Cunningham, J.W., & Moore, D.W. (1986). The confused world of main idea. In J.F. Baumann (Ed.), *Teaching main idea comprehension* (pp. 1-17). Newark, DE: International Reading Association.

Day, J.D. (1980). *Teaching summarization skills: A comparison of training methods.* Unpublished doctoral dissertation, University of Illinois, Urbana, IL.

Day, J.D. (1986). Teaching summarization skills: Influences of student ability level and strategy difficulty. *Cognition and Instruction, 3,* 193-210.

Donlan, D. (1980). Locating main ideas in history textbooks. *Journal of Reading, 24,* 135-140.

Garner, R. (1982). Efficient text summarization: Costs and benefits. *Journal of Educational Research, 75,* 275-279.

Garner, R. (1985). Text summarization deficiencies among older students: Awareness or production ability? *American Educational Research Journal, 22,* 549-560.

Garner, R., Belcher, V., Winfield, E., & Smith, T. (1985). Multiple measures of text summarization proficiency: What can fifth-grade students do? *Research in the Teaching of English, 19,* 140-153.

Garner, R., Gillingham, M.G., & White, C.S. (1989). Effects of "seductive details" on macroprocessing and microprocessing in adults and children. *Cognition and Instruction, 6,* 1-40.

Garner, R., & McCaleb, J.L. (1985). Effects of text manipulations on quality of written summaries. *Contemporary Educational Psychology, 10,* 139-149.

Geiselman, R.E., & Samet, M.G. (1980). Summarizing military information: An application of schema theory. *Human Factors, 22,* 693-705.

Gomulicki, B.R. (1956). Recall as an abstractive process. *Acta Psychologica, 12,* 77-94.

Hare, V.C., & Borchardt, K.M. (1984). Direct instruction of summarization skills. *Reading Research Quarterly, 20,* 62-78.

Hare, V.C., & Chesla, L.G. (1986). When main idea identification fails. In J.A. Niles & R.V. Lalik (Eds.), *Solving problems in literacy: Learners, teachers, and researchers* (pp. 316-325). Rochester, NY: National Reading Conference.

Hare, V.C., & Milligan, B. (1984). Main idea identification: Instructional explanations in four basal reader series. *Journal of Reading Behavior, 16,* 189-204.

Hare, V.C., Rabinowitz, M., & Schieble, K.M. (1989). Text effects on main idea comprehension. *Reading Research Quarterly, 24,* 72-88.

Head, M., Arceneaux, L.S., Readence, J.E., & Willis, E.L. (1988, December). *Effects of instruction and text availability on quality of science text summarization.* Paper presented at the annual meeting of the National Reading Conference, Tucson, AZ.

Head, M., & Buss, R.R. (1987). Factors affecting summary writing and their impact on reading comprehension assessment. In J.E. Readence & R.S. Baldwin (Eds.), *Research in literacy: Merging perspectives* (pp. 25-33). Rochester, NY: National Reading Conference.

Head, M., Readence, J.E., & Buss, R.R. (1987, December). *Effects of instruction and text availability on summarization.* Paper presented at the annual meeting of the National Reading Conference, St. Petersburg Beach, FL.

Hidi, S. (1984). *Summarization of complex texts* (Occasional Paper No. 4). Toronto, Ont.: Centre for Applied Cognitive Science.

Hidi, S., & Anderson, V. (1986). Producing written summaries: Task demands, cognitive operations, and implications for instruction. *Review of Educational Research, 56,* 473-493.

Hidi, S., & Baird, W. (1985, April). *The effect of structural revisions on learning from school texts.* Paper presented at the meeting of the American Educational Research Association, Chicago, IL.

Hidi, S., & Baird, W. (1986). Interestingness—A neglected variable in discourse processing. *Cognitive Science, 10,* 179-184.

Johnson, N.S. (1983). What do you do if you can't tell the whole story? The development of summarization skills. In K.E. Nelson (Ed.), *Children's language* (vol. 4, pp. 315-383). Hillsdale, NJ: Erlbaum.

Johnston, P., & Afflerbach, P. (1985). The process of constructing main ideas from text. *Cognition and Instruction, 2,* 207-232.

Kintsch, E. (1989). *Macroprocesses and microprocesses in the development of summarization skill* (ICS Technical Report No. 89-5). Boulder, CO: Institute of Cognitive Science.

Kintsch, W., Mandel, T.S., & Kozminsky, E. (1977). Summarizing scrambled stories. *Memory and Cognition, 5,* 547-552.

McNeil, J., & Donant, L. (1982). Summarization strategy for improving reading comprehension. In J.A. Niles & L.A. Harris (Eds.), *New inquiries in reading research and instruction* (pp. 215-219). Rochester, NY: National Reading Conference.

Meyer, B.J.F. (1975). *The organization of prose and its effects on memory.* Amsterdam: North Holland.

Miller, J.R., & Kintsch, W. (1980). Readability and recall of short prose passages: A theoretical analysis. *Journal of Experimental Psychology: Human Learning and Memory, 6,* 335-354.

Palincsar, A.S., & Brown, A.L. (1984). Reciprocal teaching of comprehension-fostering and comprehension-monitoring activities. *Cognition and Instruction, 1,* 117-175.

Reder, L.M., & Anderson, J.R. (1980). A comparison of texts and their summaries: Memorial consequences. *Journal of Verbal Learning and Verbal Behavior, 19,* 121-134.

Rinehart, S.D., Stahl, S.A., & Erickson, L.G. (1986). Some effects of summarization on reading and studying. *Reading Research Quarterly, 21,* 422-438.

Roller, C.M. (1985). The effects of reader- and text-based factors on writers' and readers' perceptions of the importance of information in expository prose. *Reading Research Quarterly, 20*, 437-457.

See, C. (1989). *Young readers' knowledge of recall and summarization.* Unpublished master's thesis, University of Illinois, Chicago.

Sjostrom, C.L., & Hare, V.C. (1984). Teaching high school students to identify main ideas in expository texts. *Journal of Educational Research, 78*, 114-118.

Slater, W.H., Graves, M.F., Scott, S.B., & Redd-Boyd, T.M. (1988). Discourse structure and college freshmen's recall and production of expository text. *Research in the Teaching of English, 22*, 45-61.

Swoope, K.F., & Johnson, C.S. (1988). A reexamination of effects of reader- and text-based factors on priority judgments in expository prose. *Journal of Educational Research, 82*, 5-9.

Taylor, K.K. (1986). Summary writing by young children. *Reading Research Quarterly, 21*, 193-208.

van Dijk, T.A. (1979). Recalling and summarizing complex discourse. In W. Burghardt & K. Holker (Eds.), *Text processing: Papers in text analysis and text description* (pp. 49-118). Berlin: Walter de Gruyter.

van Dijk, T.A., & Kintsch, W. (1978). Cognitive psychology and discourse: Recalling and summarizing stories. In W.U. Dressler (Ed.), *Current trends in text linguistics* (pp. 61-80). Berlin: Walter de Gruyter.

van Dijk, T.A., & Kintsch, W. (1983). *Strategies of discourse comprehension.* San Diego, CA: Academic.

Williams, J.P. (1986). Research and instructional development on main idea skills. In J.F. Baumann (Ed.), *Teaching main idea comprehension* (pp. 73-95). Newark, DE: International Reading Association.

Winograd, P.N. (1984). Strategic difficulties in summarizing text. *Reading Research Quarterly, 19*, 404-425.

Instructional
Issues

Elizabeth Sulzby
June Barnhart

— S I X —

The Development of Academic Competence: All Our Children Emerge as Writers and Readers*

*M*uch has been written recently about a new perspective toward young children's reading and writing development—the perspective of emergent literacy. We believe that the emergent literacy perspective points to developmentally appropriate practices for all children in our kindergartens. In this chapter, we discuss some implications such a perspective seems to have for kindergarten children, kindergarten classrooms, and kindergarten teachers. We stress, however, that the leap from research and theory to practice is just that—a leap of faith and belief. Research cannot tell teachers what to do, but it can provide a framework for understanding what goes on in teaching and learning; it cannot provide the *oughts* of practice, but it often helps us understand the *whats* and *whys* of children's behavior.

In this chapter, we will respond to some questions that teachers frequently raise about emergent literacy. In addressing these questions, we will discuss relevant research and theory. We have also borrowed some of the basis for our answers from excellent teaching practices that we see in kinder-

---

*This chapter first appeared in *The Developing Kindergarten: Programs, Children, and Teachers,* edited by Judy Spitler McKee and published by the Michigan Association for the Education of Young Children. It is reprinted here by permission of the Michigan Association for the Education of Young Children.

gartens around the United States. We also want to stress that research in emergent literacy has grown from practice, good practice by thoughtful, scholarly, caring teachers over many decades and perhaps centuries of teaching (see Spodek, 1982). It has also grown from research roots of many people long before the term emergent literacy became popular. Particularly important in our own educational history have been Edmund Burke Huey, Jean Piaget, Lev Vygotsky, Emmet Betts, and John Dewey.

What Is Emergent Literacy?

Reading has often been a controversial topic for kindergartens: Should the kindergartener be taught to read? When? How? Emergent literacy implies that this question is inappropriate. First of all, we should be concerned about writing, and not just reading. Second, reading and writing are interrelated; hence, we can refer to the child as becoming literate, meaning both reading and writing. Third, while various definitions of emergent literacy have been proposed (Mason & Allen, 1986; Morrow, 1989; Teale, 1987; Teale & Sulzby, 1986), all agree that young children know a great deal about reading and writing well before kindergarten, so any argument about when to begin teaching literacy is moot. Much literacy learning and teaching has already gone on in the home setting (Taylor, 1983), even in homes of low income children (Heath, 1983; Sulzby & Teale, 1987; Teale, 1986).

Sulzby (1983, 1988) has defined emergent literacy as "the reading and writing behaviors of young children that precede and develop into conventional literacy." She claims that these behaviors are legitimate parts of literacy, that they are conceptual in nature, and that they are developmental. Since children's emergent reading and writing behaviors are developmental, teachers can begin to explain to an anxious parent what a given behavior (such as scribbling) may mean and illustrate a child's progress by comparing work samples taken from across the year. However, literacy development does not imply hierarchical stages such as those in the Piagetian analysis of cognitive development. Instead, literacy development is partially determined by how literacy is embedded in the culture of the society the child lives in. While the patterns of literacy described in this chapter are qualitatively different from adult patterns, children's development seems to be one of an ever increasing and organized repertoire of linguistic knowledge, rather than a leaving-behind of previous stages of thinking. Sulzby (1985b, 1989) claims that children show patterns of growth and change in literacy that converge, after a long developmental process, at conventional reading and writing, but that children may take different paths to conventional literacy. As with other areas of child development, often when children are progressing in literacy, they may appear to be standing still or even regressing.

While we do not feel that Piagetian stages explain children's literacy development fully, we do find Piagetian ways of thinking extremely helpful (especially Piaget, 1926; see also Ferreiro, 1986). We know that when we examine children's reading and writing behaviors, we have to look below the surface of the behavior to children's concepts and understandings. Recently, one of us visited a kindergarten classroom and invited the children to write stories, using a procedure developed by Sulzby (Sulzby, 1989; Sulzby, Teale, & Kamberelis, 1989). The children were asked to write individual stories: "Write a story," and prompted, when needed, "It doesn't have to be like grown-up writing. Just do it your own way." All of the children in the classroom attempted to write, using typical kindergarten writing forms. Two children illustrate the contrast between the appearance of the behavior and the underlying concepts; these examples illustrate how the appearance and the underlying concepts comprise the total behavior. The first child drew a picture of a boy and girl holding hands. Between them, beneath their clasped hands, were lines of scribble. This child read from the scribble, pointing to each line and reciting a written language-like story. She made her voice, finger, and scribble all end at the same point. A second child drew a picture of a girl in a ballgown on one page and a Valentine heart on the second page. Inside the Valentine were a drawing of a flower and the words "I love you." This child declared that she did not write, "I just draw pictures." When quizzed about whether she had written anything in the Valentine heart, she said that she had written "a flower" and "I love you." The first child's immature-appearing scribble seemed to be used for a much more mature-appearing compositional purpose, whereas the second child's concepts appeared to be far less sophisticated than the conventional-appearing words she had produced.

Which Students Are We Talking About?

All children are becoming literate—all are emerging as writers and readers. It is clear that some children come from backgrounds in which they have been included in home literacy events from birth forward as a matter of course. Other children have had few such experiences. In our research and that of other researchers (Anderson & Stokes, 1984; Clay, 1975; Goodman, 1986; Harste, Woodward, & Burke, 1984; Sulzby & Teale, 1987; Teale, 1986), we note that the kinds of behaviors we describe in this chapter are shown by children from low- as well as middle- and high-income families and by children from all the ethnic and cultural backgrounds that have been studied.

Teale and Sulzby (1986) have reviewed the history of research and practice concerning kindergarten reading and writing. They noted, of course, that writing has been ignored until recently and thus concentrated their historical review upon research in reading. Early in the century, it was almost unheard of to think about teaching reading to kindergarten-aged children in the bulk of U.S. schools. Instead, children were taken lock-step through reading and other instructional materials once they entered first grade, with the outcome that many children were retained in grade. These children were instructed— but without developmental considerations.

The next major step forward in research and related practice was to consider children's readiness for reading. The idea of reading readiness in itself was an important and positive step (see, for example, Betts, 1946), but it was often misapplied—and continues to be today, in many classrooms (see Meisels, 1987, 1989). At first readiness was conceived of as maturity. Development was considered something that teachers had to wait for—to be seen in characteristics such as mental age. During the midcentury, some researchers suggested that reading might be necessarily tied to major, general developmental characteristics such as concrete operations (or its manifestations, such as conservation of number, seriation, or classification) or other measures of maturity, such as those used in the Gesell screening (Meisels, 1987, 1989). (Concepts such as part-whole relationships are particularly difficult to apply with language processing. Conventional or adult concepts about language are multilevel, with fuzzy boundaries between parts, and overlapping parts. This issue becomes more crucial with young children who are constructing every part of every level of language.)

The treatment of readiness as maturity seemed to imply that teachers should withhold instruction until developmental indicators were observed; thus, at any given time, only some children—those who are "ready" by one of these indicators—would profit from instruction. It was certainly a step forward from treating all children as needing the same instruction at the same time and toward not penalizing children for failing to master that instruction at that time, yet a new inequality was created: the "ready" versus the "nonready" child. Unfortunately, this concept is still being misapplied in kindergarten practice currently with children being held out of kindergarten until they are ready rather than providing kindergartens with developmentally appropriate activities, materials, environments, and teaching practices.

The move toward treating reading readiness as something that could be hastened by instruction was in general another positive move forward. Now the idea was that all children should be instructed and that kindergarten was the key time and place for this instruction. The problem, however, was how readiness was defined. Instead of recognizing that children are already becoming literate, proponents of reading readiness searched for predictors of subsequent reading achievement that could be taught. Lists of supposed readiness abilities—such as letter recognition, auditory and visual discrimination, comprehension of orally read stories, maze completion, or sound blending—appeared on tests, in curriculum guides, and in readiness books and workbooks, as well as in the research literature.

Now researchers and practitioners are increasingly viewing reading and writing as emerging within all children, to greater or lesser degree, depending upon the literacy exposure of the child prior to school and upon the environment and instruction in the classroom. The research points to one major characteristic of the classroom—that it should be a literacy-rich environment—and to activities and conditions that support children's emergent literacy in the classroom (see Hiebert, 1986). We offer only a few of the many possibilities and invite other teachers and researchers to expand on our discussion through sharing with each other.

What Does It Mean to Have a Literacy-Rich Environment in My Classroom?

Literacy-rich environments do not necessarily mean that every inch of your room is covered with letters and text. It means that your classroom has opportunities for children to interact with reading and writing throughout the day and in many different ways.

Literacy-rich classrooms do not all look the same. In one district in which we worked, every kindergarten classroom looked very much the same, with lots of print all around the rooms: there were charts, there were books, there was paper and pencil; there were mobiles with words hanging down from the ceiling; there were labels everywhere.

When you went into those similar-appearing, attractive classrooms, however, you found that they were very different. In some of the classrooms, children were constantly enjoying books, writing their own way, incorporating their artwork in their writing, and having time to share books spontaneously as well as listen to the teachers read. Bookcases were low and had many book covers displayed so the children could see them. Some had Story Reenactment and Writing Centers. These children were doing reading and writing throughout the day—during social studies, science, math, choice, and play-activity times. In other classrooms, children were seated at their desks doing worksheets and almost never interacting with the print around the room. Many were copying models of the teachers' writing.

In some of the classrooms, the print that the teacher so carefully had labored over at the beginning of the year to set up as models soon became displaced by children's writing, so that not only were the teacher's conventional models around the room but also examples of the children's writing—all the way from scribble to drawing to letter strings to readable, invented spelling. Soon these rooms did not look so uniform and perfect, but showed more evidence of how the children were using reading and writing functionally.

In literacy-rich classrooms, materials are at children's reach and there is sufficient time during the day for children to interact with those materials. Reading and writing tend to become less visible as separate activities and to become more deeply embedded in other aspects of classroom life. Children's play in the block or doll areas may make it almost unnoticeable that there are note pads by the toy telephone, grocery lists on chalk or bulletin boards, play with discarded computer keyboards, or signs taped on the sides of the block trucks. Other ideas that we have picked up from literacy-rich classrooms are covered in other sections of the chapter, such as the section on classroom libraries, bringing favorite books from home, and displaying children's writing.

How Can I Get My Kindergarteners to Write in School?

Is it possible to get children started writing in the kindergarten as easily as they are reported to write in literacy-rich homes? Many people are still shocked at the ease with which children at kindergarten age (or younger) write, when we invite them and if we accept the forms of writing they prefer. From working with and observing hundreds of classrooms, we can say confidently that all kindergarteners reared in a literate culture like our own can and will write. Sulzby (1989) offers some very simple tips. First and most important, accept the forms of writing and reading that children use. Second and almost as important, make your request simple and straightforward. If you want a child to write, say: "Write a story," or "Write a letter to your mother." Then ask the child to read what she or he has written: "Read me your story," or "Read us your letter." A third guideline is to use the reassurance, "It doesn't have to be like grown-up writing. Just do it your own way."

Sometimes teachers model forms of writing by asking children, "How do kindergarteners write?" or "How could a kindergartener write 'Once upon a time, I saw a monster,' " using a child's suggested story starter. The most common forms of writing in kindergarten are scribble, drawing, non-phonetic letter strings, phonetic (invented) spelling, and conventional spelling. Children read from these forms in many different ways, however, and you need to compare the way the child composes and rereads with the forms of writing to judge how sophisticated the writing is. The forms of rereading can be judged by using the classification scheme in the section on reading favorite storybooks (for more detailed checklists see Sulzby, 1985b, 1989; Sulzby, Barnhart, & Hieshima, 1989).

In a recent first story-writing session, one kindergarten girl scribbled and drew a story about the Letter People in her class's phonics program. Jeremy drew a picture (Figure 1) that included lines that seem to show motion and a random letter string, made up of a series of vowels followed by consonants. His monologue was about a witch who was flying up in the air for a "witchly" dinner. Michael's story was about a witch who only came out on Halloween. His drawing (Figure 2) shows a witch with a broom and a crossed out letter string. Michael explained that the crossed out letters were where he had "made a mistake of this."

Should I Display Children's Writing or Send It Home?

We have found that when children write, they like to share their writing with other people. They share it during writing, but they also like to share it after writing. Taking writing home is a way of displaying it, just as is having displays in the classroom. Under any circumstances, the idea is for the children to see and take part in having significant others experience their

Sulzby and Barnhart

Figure 1

Figure 2

All Our Children Emerge as Writers and Readers   127

writing (Dyson, 1988). And some others are more significant—particularly parents. In one study of gifted preschoolers, Otto and Sulzby (in preparation) found that three-, four-, and five-year-old children wrote very skimpy stories when the researchers were collecting their stories and keeping them, but when the researchers told them that the stories were to take home to show to their parents afterward, they began to write multipage stories with illustrations. These were all, of course, in emergent writing and not in conventional writing. At the end of another two-year longitudinal study in which researchers and children became close friends (Sulzby, 1983), children wrote long, complex, illustrated stories for the researchers in response to an invitation "to write a story for me to remember you by."

In Michigan one teacher created a unit on hospitals in which the children were filling out medical forms. In many classrooms we have seen children filling out grocery lists, filling out order forms for restaurants, and incorporating writing and reading into their fantasy play. In Boston, Schickedanz (1986) has created many of these kinds of activities in the preschool setting. In San Antonio (Martinez & Teale, 1987; Teale & Martinez, 1989), children's writing is displayed everywhere, even hung up on clotheslines across the room. Children in the morning and afternoon kindergarten sessions write back and forth as pen pals and have their own postal service.

At the Hull House Center in Chicago and other kindergartens associated with that project, McNamee and her colleagues (1987; Paley, 1981, 1984) have encouraged children to create dramas that teachers take down as dictation. Children read back from their dictation as notations to remind them of how the fantasy play is to go, but they create their fantasy play as spontaneous improvisation from that text. The script becomes a display of their written composition.

All of these are ways of sharing writing because children are interacting and using writing as the basis for what Teale (1984) and Heath (1983) call "literacy events." These activities are important because they engage children in communicative acts with writing, in real contexts—(*real* includes play for children, of course). They enable children to face real conflicts, such as whether another child can read their scribble, how both Keisha and Kelly can have a K (Ferreiro, 1986), or why another child might have trouble reading a text without spaces.

What's the Relationship between Emergent Literacy and the Language Experience Approach?

There's a very close tie between emergent literacy and language experience. We have noticed a resurgence of interest in language experience and in the use of dictation of children's stories as ways of beginning reading and writing instruction in kindergartens. Much of this increased interest has come about as people have realized that children do indeed come to kindergartens with much knowledge about reading and writing and that we should continue their functional growth in reading and writing rather than act as if they have to begin all over again.

The language experience approach was explored by many pioneers (see Stauffer, 1980) long before psychology and linguistics became sophisticated enough to provide them with the tools that they needed for their forward-looking ideas. One notion from language experience was that writing is "talk written down," and we know from recent research that that is not exactly the case.

Writing is a particular kind of speaking, using the wording and cues of written language. Children shift their speech from conversation and oral storytelling to written language-like form in tasks in which they are asked to write or read and as their knowledge about the relationships between oral and written language develop (Sulzby, 1985a).

We believe that dictation has important purposes in kindergarten classrooms but that it is helpful if we can convey to children how dictation fits together with their own writing. Some of this can be done quite indirectly, by simply taking dictation silently and letting the child see the scribe's struggle to keep up with dictation (Sulzby, 1987). Children's development in dictation can be judged in many ways. Pausing is one of those ways. Early in development children dictate in an oral language-like manner, rushing along without paying attention to the scribe. When stopped, they typically do not retrace their speech or restate it in other words. Later, they begin to slow down after being prompted. Later still, they begin to pause, often in very exaggerated fashion, for the scribe. Some teachers describe this style of dictating with a groan! Finally, children seem to watch (either directly or by listening to the pencil or chalk) the scribe so closely that they gauge the speech of their dictation quite comfortably to that of the scribe. Similar patterns can be seen in children's ability to track dictation in rereading (Sulzby, 1985b).

Children develop in writing by creating their own writing forms, as we have discussed earlier. Children explore these writing forms for a long time before reaching conventional orthography. However, children are abstracting these forms from conventional orthography in the environment around them, so we believe in having a mix of conventional spelling and the child's own writing in the classroom. The explanation to give children is quite simple. Teachers don't need to make much of the differences between conventional orthography and children's emerging forms, but they can refer to "grown-up writing" and "children's writing," "kindergarten writing," "the way grown-ups write," "the way children write," "writing it your own way," etc.

For dictation, the teacher can announce something such as this: "Today when you create a story, I will write it for you in grown-up writing. We call it dictation when you create the story, say it to me, and I write it down for you. When you do your own writing, it doesn't have to be grown-up writing, but for today I will put yours in grown-up writing." Then, while taking dictation, we suggest that the teacher simply write without saying words after the child and certainly without saying letter names or asking for sounds. If the child is talking too fast, the teacher can say: "I can't keep up—here's where I am," and read back the dictation up to that point. Then the teacher can observe how attentive the child is to rephrasing the dictation, pausing long enough for the adult, etc. We have found that this is a teaching as well as an assessment technique and that children learn to pay attention to the print and how the adult does it. Perhaps they pay more attention to this functional feedback than to previous attempts to turn dictation into a lesson in phonics or sentence structure.

What's the Relationship between Emergent Literacy and Process Writing?

The relationship between emergent literacy and process writing (Graves, 1983) is extremely close; in fact, when we ask children to write stories their own way, we are asking them to engage in the process of writing. Process writing is an abbreviated way of denoting a teaching situation in which children engage in all of the processes of creative, proficient writing. They plan, they create, they reread, they revise, all recursively; and finally, when they feel their draft is final, they proofread and edit and produce a clean, readable, conventionally correct copy—as if for publication commer-

Sulzby and Barnhart

cially. In many classrooms, children actually "publish" their final drafts and enter them into classroom libraries. Unfortunately, process writing in some classrooms has become almost a formula of taking children through specific stages of the writing process with specific activities to induce those stages. We think that this is an artificial way of dealing with the writing process, but even that can often be quite effective.

For example, brainstorming and webbing are used as ways to initiate writing. Such activities are simply ways of getting children involved in planning. When we are sitting in circle time with children, discussing what they are going to write about, that is part of planning. When we ask a child to write a story and we see the child look off at the wall intently for a period of time and then suddenly pick up the pencil and begin to scribble, we have just witnessed the child engaged in planning. When the child says to us, "I want to write about...," and then begins to do it, we have just seen the child engaged in planning. So our purpose throughout writing is to engage the child authentically in the writing process.

When we see children look back over what they have written, stop and scratch something out, and fix it, we are seeing them engaged in monitoring and revising their writing. When we ask them later if there is anything in their story that they would like to change, and they help us create a new section in the story or fix a part of the story, they are involved in revision.

A step that is very critical in children's early writing, we think, is how one deals with proofreading. Proofreading means taking your writing and turning it into conventional orthography; however, if children are writing with scribble, it is not appropriate to ask them to make that big step. It would only be when children were writing very fluently with a mix of invented spelling and conventional orthography that you might want to ask them to work with you to help proofread the paper and turn it into conventional orthography.

Some teachers, however, like to take children's writing produced in whatever form and, for some pieces of that writing, to ask the children if they would like to turn it into a book for other people to read. At that point, they may take the child's writing and write it down in conventional orthography. We find that this presents a philosophical dilemma for teachers that many solve in their own ways. Some teachers start out wanting to turn every piece of the child's writing into a transcription of conventional orthography, so that parents can read it and so that the child has a model. Many of these teachers begin to realize that this extreme reaction to children's writing is not necessary, but instead that they need to bring that step of conversion to conventional orthography into some balance for the children.

How Can I Set Up a Writing Center?

Many kindergarten teachers use Play-Activity and Interest Centers. Kindergarten children are drawn to Writing Centers, particularly if they are set up with attractive implements for writing and if the teachers encourage writing. At a minimum, writing centers provide a special place for writing to be done and materials for writing. If budgets are tight and materials are scarce, a center can be set up with just paper and pencil. If possible, however, provide lots of choices of writing implements and paper. Unlined paper allows children to explore the space on the page, to use all emergent forms of writing, and later to put conventional writing and illustration where the child chooses. Many children, however, like to use lined paper. Many teachers provide choices of large and small paper, lined and unlined, white and colored. Similarly, it is good to provide all sizes of pencils, pens, and markers. Having tape, staplers, and other fastening materials available may also encourage multimedia composition and "publishing." Many teachers provide envelopes or encourage children to make their own envelopes.

Topic stimulation is another important feature to think about in center design. Some teachers allow children to choose their own topics and motivations for writing. Others provide story starters, pictures, or other stimulus materials in the centers. We think that in centers, just as in whole-group writing activities, children need many times in which they choose their own topics and other times in which topics are suggested.

Some classrooms are fortunate enough to have typewriters or computers in the Writing Center. Setting up typewriters and computers with desk-like space beside them invites children's role playing. They "go to work," "fill out orders," and "send letters." Figure 3 shows a four-year-old's first composition on a computer, using a mouse and graphics program.

It is a good idea to have Art and Writing Centers close together, so that children can easily use all kinds of creation materials. This can encourage children to write and "publish" their own books. If bookcases are close by and children see books written and published by other children, this too can serve as a motivation for their own writing.

Figure 3

Why Do Children Sometimes Seem to Regress in Writing?

Just as in other parts of development, a step forward may sometimes seem to be a regression. Many children write in invented spelling for isolated words but use scribble for a story. Or they may be writing in invented spelling for a while and suddenly use scribble or drawing. Often this will accompany a step forward in composition. Some children use invented spelling for brief pieces (two to four sentences) but scribble for multipage books. One child used pictures and scribble, with the scribble laid out around the pictures so that the multipage book looked like a printer's mockup (Sulzby & Teale, 1985). Kamberelis and Sulzby (1988) found that children who show indications of imbalance such as this appear to be at periods of transition or growth. One critically important pattern in this research was with invented spelling; children who begin to write in invented spelling often do not use it to decode from for a fairly long period of time. When we observe such children, they often look confused or as if they are regressing; as we learn more about interpreting their development, we can begin to know when apparent regression is actually a sign of progress.

What Is Emergent Storybook Reading and How Can I Use It in My Classroom?

Children begin to read storybooks emergently quite naturally in a home setting. This phenomenon has been described anecdotally for a long time. In recent years, researchers have been studying this process by observing in homes (Sulzby & Teale, 1987; Teale, 1984), interviewing parents (Mason & Allen, 1986; Robinson & Sulzby, 1984), and asking children to read "favorite books" in a research setting (Sulzby, 1985a).

Children read emergently from favorite storybooks or books that have been read to them repeatedly. These are books that children like enough to ask for them to be read over and over. Typically, children attend to these books closely, sometimes chiming in with the parent's reading or finishing sentences or phrases by themselves. Often they correct the parent's reading if a mistake is made or a part is skipped. Sometimes, they pick up the books and begin "reading" them voluntarily. One parent, who had read a counting book to her child repeatedly, noticed the child beginning to read to her doll (Teale & Sulzby, 1988). Quickly the mother grabbed a tape recorder and documented how the child read. Even though this book was not a storybook, the child's language and intonation were similar to one type of language children use for storybook reading and to the interaction which the mother and she had been taking part in during earlier readings.

We will first describe how a teacher can get children reading storybooks emergently in a classroom. Then we will describe the kind of language and intonation that children use and how teachers can assess the emergent storybook reading of children in the classroom.

Some general guidelines are helpful. The classroom should have bookcases of children's books in easy reach of children. Space for reading is also critical—rugs, small chairs, lounges, even cushioned bathtubs are inviting to little ones. Time is the next important element. There needs to be time, preferably a regular time, for the teacher to read to children and time for children to read books on their own.

It is important for teachers to let children know what their beliefs and expectations are. It is also important for teachers to become involved in the books that they read to the children. Good literature is a wonderful bridge between past and present, teacher and child, emotion and cognition (Cullinan, 1989). The following activity is based upon storybooks—that is, books that have a story plot with characters. Such books typically involve the children in thinking about what the problems of the characters are and how they react to them. Such books typically relate to problems or emotions that children themselves experience.

Begin the school year by reading a number of books that you have found to be interesting to children in other years. Read some of these books a second time on the introduction day, stopping at predictable points to invite the children to finish the sentence for or with you.

Then, begin one week's reading quite dramatically. Gather the children around you on the rug. Have lots of inviting books close at hand. Announce to the children that during this week, you and they are going to read lots of old favorites over and over. Ask them which book they want to begin with today. Read straight through if the children seem attentive. If not, pause for them to chime in or stop to ask involving questions. Then ask what book they want you to read next. Stop at two books this first time. Stop quite dramatically, in fact, and announce that today is a special day: "Today, I am going to put all these old favorites down here on the rug for you." (You might want to say in the bookcase or any other spot where children can get to the books easily without traffic problems.) Then say, "We are going to have reading time for all of us. You can each get a book and read it to yourself. As soon as you have read it to yourself, go over and put your name on the sheet of blue paper on my desk. [Any special paper will do.] Then copy the name of your book just after your name. When we are done, we will do something special with that blue paper."

Give the children ten minutes or so to read. You may notice that most of the children "read" out loud. Some may just page through the book and grab a new one. Encourage them to read their books carefully and then write their names and book titles on the special paper. Tell them they can get another book after they have written their names and titles.

End the session as children begin to get restless, telling them that you know that not all children are finished but that they will have storytime again later. Then, later in the morning, group children in pairs of "buddies," and ask them to get their special books from the morning. Now they will share their books with each other. For the first day, do not stress reading the books to each other; instead stress sharing.

Each day this week, begin with storybook time with old favorites. Allow the children to request the books that you read and read at least two books in each session before breaking into individual reading time. On the second, third, or fourth day, invite the children to read to their buddies. Tell them, "You don't have to read like a grown-up. Just read it your own way. Your buddy will enjoy hearing you read it your own way." Monitor the buddies, encouraging them to take turns. If a given book is too long, you might want to encourage the reader to stop after "just a little bit more, so [name of buddy] can read some to you." It's preferable, of course, for children to read whole books, but you do not want children to be left out or sessions to drag on too long.

As soon as you notice that most of the children are willingly taking part in emergent reading behavior with each other, you can relax the structure and simply provide them with "reading time." This technique fits beautifully with Sustained Silent Reading or Drop Everything and Read projects. Some teachers will find that they do not need the heavy structure to begin with their children, but get started by simply providing reading time. Soon reading should become an option during Choice Time.

Storybook reading plays a very important role in literacy development (see Teale, 1984, for an excellent review). Reading to children prior to schooling correlates with later reading achievement and produces a "literacy set" (Holdaway, 1979) in which children know what books are for, what language to expect in books, and that books are for enjoyment and enlightenment. Children begin to "read" emergently when they are read to repeatedly in their homes (Sulzby & Teale, 1987), and emergent storybook reading attempts, like writing attempts, are developmentally ordered (Sulzby, 1985a). A number of children begin to read conventionally from storybooks after or even before beginning kindergarten. Sulzby (1985a) has discovered ten levels of emergent storybook reading that precede conventional reading. These levels can be collapsed into five levels for broad assessment in the classroom or as teachers first begin to assess children's storybook reading behavior. Figure 4 contains the simplified version of Sulzby's Classification Scheme for Children's Emergent Reading of Favorite Storybooks. These categories can also be used to assess children's reading from their own writing by making some extrapolations, but they are drawn from and best apply to reading attempts from storybooks that the child has reread repeatedly.

Figure 4
Classification Scheme for Children's Emergent Reading of Favorite Storybooks (simplified version)

Broad Categories	Brief Explanation
1. Attending to pictures, not forming stories	The child is "reading" by looking at the storybook's pictures. The child's speech is *just* about the picture in view: the child is not "weaving a story" across the pages. (Subcategories are "labeling and commenting" and "following the action.")
2. Attending to pictures, forming *oral* stories	The child is "reading" by looking at the storybook's pictures. The child's speech weaves a story across the pages but the wording and the intonation are like that of someone telling a story, either like a conversation about the pictures or like a fully recited story, in which the listener can see the pictures (and often *must* see them to understand the child's story). (Subcategories are "dialogic storytelling" and "monologic storytelling.")
3. Attending to pictures, reading, and storytelling mixed	This category for the simplified version was originally the first subcategory of category 4. It fits between 2 and 4 and is easier to understand if it is treated separately. The child is "reading" by looking at the storybook's pictures. The child's speech fluctuates between sounding like a storyteller, with oral intonation, and sounding like a reader, with reading intonation. To fit this category, the majority of the reading attempt must show fluctuations between storytelling and reading.
4. Attending to pictures, forming *written* stories	The child is "reading" by looking at the storybook's pictures. The child's speech sounds as if the child is reading, both in the wording and intonation. The listener does not need to look at the pictures (or rarely does) in order to understand the story. If the listener closes his/her eyes, most of the time he or she would think the child is reading from print. (Subcategories are "reading similar-to-original story," and "reading verbatim-like story.")

(continued)

Figure 4 (continued)
Classification Scheme for Children's Emergent Reading
of Favorite Storybooks (simplified version)

5. Attending to print	There are four subcategories of attending to print. Only the *final* one is what is typically called "real reading." In the others the child is exploring the print with such strategies as refusing to read based on print-related reasons, or using only some of the aspects of print. (Subcategories are "refusing to read based on print awareness," "reading aspectually," "reading with strategies imbalanced," and "reading independently" or "conventional reading.")

Adapted from Sulzby (1985a).

Teachers need to read to children often, interactively, and with pleasure. Reread books freely at the children's request or at your own initiative. While rereading is important, also continue to introduce new books and authors, with lots of discussion and pleasure. Some teachers set one day aside for rereading old favorites and the next for introducing a new book. Some of the new books can be introduced in groups, with sets of multiple copies ready for the children to share during their free reading time. Books need to be at easy reach of children, with time provided for children to read to themselves, to other children, or to the teacher, and for teachers to do "lap reading" at children's request. When children read emergently, praise reading, in whatever form you observe it ("What a great story!" "You really read that with lots of excitement," "Wow, you really put a lot into your reading!" and so forth).

Sometimes Big Books with predictable stories and rhymes are used. When these are good literature that children like, they can be quite useful. However, often the teacher's guides that accompany such books or workshops given about Big Books stress pointing at print and explicitly calling children's attention to print. This is important when children are ready for it. We do not think that there is any particular value in pointing to print excessively before children are attentive to it. We think that the research in emergent storybook reading has implications for how Big Books can be selected and used. Pointing to print and having children chant seems to be developmentally rather advanced and is probably used most profitably after children are beginning to use reading intonation and recite stories rather stably. Chanting from rhymes and overly predictable texts has a somewhat different developmental pattern from emergent storybook reading, however; children sometimes give a rote recitation that does not reveal children's growing concepts. So, we urge teachers to select Big Books with care about their content and how they are used.

Teachers can observe emergent storybook reading patterns informally with regular storybooks by eavesdropping when young children read to themselves or other children, or they can elicit children's emergent readings. To elicit storybook reading, ask the child to get a favorite storybook (or pick one that you have read to the children a lot, one that seems to be a favorite of this child). Then say, "Please read me your book." Do not say, "Tell me your book," or "Tell us about your book," if you really want the child to show you his or her concepts about reading. Very young children use speech differently for telling and for reading, even when not reading from print. (If the child does not make such a distinction, that child needs lots of opportunities to tell stories and to read emergently.)

Some schools have Sustained Silent Reading or Drop Everything and Read time. Kindergarteners can take part along with everyone else. The difference is that most kindergarteners will be reading emergently—and most younger students will be reading aloud or in a stage whisper instead of privately. Many kindergarten teachers loosen the rules and allow pairs of children to read to each other. It's a good idea to have comfortable places for children to read, such as lounges, pillows, or rugs. Story Reenactment Centers can be made into special, inviting places to share stories! In one classroom that we visited, the teacher encourages children to bring in their favorite storybooks at the beginning of the week and put them in a common box; then, any time there is transition time or free-reading time, the children go to get their favorite books, reading them alone or reading with each other.

Classroom and School Libraries

In many emergent literacy classrooms, children not only go to the school library for books but have classroom libraries for easy and ongoing access to books (Morrow, 1982; Martinez & Teale, 1988). In such libraries, of course, the children write their own names. However, library activities are extended into broad-ranging ways of sharing books, and these usually involve writing as well as other media. Children may respond to books that they have read by writing and illustrating a poster, by building a shoebox mural, or by creating a dramatic recreation of the book. In one classroom a teacher was hesitantly trying out emergent literacy ideas; she had been sending home children's books from the classroom library nightly but wanted a record of all the books children were reading. The teacher and aide were falling behind in writing the book names on the large Manila envelopes that children used to carry the books home, when it suddenly dawned on them that children who could write stories could surely copy their own book titles! Soon they found the children reading these inventories of all the books they had read during the year. They were amazed to see that the same kind of emergent reading behaviors that they had seen with storybooks and story writing were used by the children in responding to complex titles like *Marvin K. Mooney Will You Please Go Now* or *There's a Nightmare in My Closet* or *Harry and the Terrible Whatzit*.

In addition to wide reading of many authors or rereadings of specific books, we have been impressed with teachers who have explored specific authors (and illustrators) with their children. Then, in their writing, children often reflect their love for and acquaintance with these authors' styles by imitating them. Having a classroom library and school library with ready access for children to read and reread books many times is essential for this kind of literary effect upon literacy development.

Working with Parents to Encourage Children's Emergent Literacy

Establishing an emergent literacy classroom requires much working with parents to help them understand what you are trying to do and help them support it. It is a good idea to have a meeting early in the year, when you are explaining your entire curriculum, to make a point of talking about what you are doing with children's emergent reading and writing. The goal to set up with parents is that you want to help bring their child along as a reader and writer, that you know the child is already reading and writing in some way, and that what you will do is help support that child's growth by providing instruction that will help the child come along.

Stress with the parents what they have already done to help the child become a reader and writer (Marzollo & Sulzby, 1988). Of course, with some parents you may make the judgment that they have not done very much, but

Sulzby and Barnhart

it is always a good idea to talk as if they have or as if they will. Encourage them to read books to their children every day, perhaps encouraging a bedtime-story ritual if that is not apparent in the home. Let them know a little bit about what research says about the importance of reading to children repeatedly. You may want to have a few samples of good books available, because some parents choose books that are not very appropriate for engaging young children. You may even want to model some storybook reading behavior. It would be a nice introduction to a group classroom visit of parents for you to read a book to the children in front of them, engaging the children in the reading and letting them see how you stop and encourage children to make predictions about the story, talk about key parts of the story, or finish sentences for you.

Also talk with the parents about the importance of children's writing. Let them know that children continue to use scribble and drawing and random letter strings even after they are beginning to use invented spelling. You will also need to explain invented spelling to the parents and let them know that what the children are doing when they use invented spelling is practicing phonics, if that is a term that is a catchy phrase in your neighborhood. Give them an idea of the developmental patterns of writing and children's use of writing in composition, stressing that children continue to use many writing forms such as scribble even while they are actually moving ahead to quite sophisticated levels of development. Assure them that you are guiding their children toward conventional reading and writing. Sometimes it is helpful to assure them that you are teaching the sounds and correct spelling through these techniques and that you are monitoring their child's progress and will share work samples with them throughout the year.

How Can I Feel Comfortable Using Emergent Literacy in My Classroom?

This is a complicated question that can be approached from many avenues. Teachers will feel comfortable as they become convinced that what they are doing is for the good of children. However, research in teacher education and teacher development is showing the outside world more of what teachers have always known—teaching is a complex and intellectually challenging profession. When teachers begin to use a complex new set of understandings such as emergent literacy (or process writing, cooperative learning, or manipulative process mathematics), they may take up to about three years actually to internalize the new understandings so that they become part of their teaching repertoire.

Teachers, like all learners, are developmental. When teachers first begin to use emergent literacy techniques in their classrooms, they often feel uncomfortable and may even lose control of some parts of classroom management. Then, as they gain experience, they may look quite proficient but still feel somewhat mechanical and uncomfortable. They may be uneasy about interpreting children's development and depend heavily upon outside advice. Finally, often during the third year, they internalize the concepts so that they begin to improvise, throw away unnecessary frills, and reintegrate other parts of their teaching repertoire with emergent literacy. We urge administrators and supervisors to become aware of the complex challenges that teachers face when deciding to teach kindergarteners in developmentally appropriate ways. Teachers need support, assistance, and encouragement when they take on these critically important challenges for the sake of young children.

References
Anderson, A.B., & Stokes, S.J. (1984). Social and institutional influences on the development and practice of literacy. In H. Goelman, A. Oberg, & F. Smith (Eds.), *Awakening to literacy* (pp. 24-37). Portsmouth, NH: Heinemann.

Betts, E.A. (1946). *Foundations of reading instruction*. New York: American Book.

Clay, M.M. (1975). *What did I write?* Portsmouth, NH: Heinemann.

Cullinan, B.E. (1989). *Literature and the child* (2nd ed.). Orlando, FL: Harcourt Brace Jovanovich.

Dyson, A.H. (1988). Negotiating among multiple worlds: The space/time dimensions of young children's composing. *Research in the Teaching of English, 22*(4), 355-390.

Ferreiro, E. (1986). The interplay between information and assimilation in beginning literacy. In W.H. Teale & E. Sulzby (Eds.), *Emergent literacy: Writing and reading* (pp. 15-49). Norwood, NJ: Ablex.

Goodman, Y.M. (1986). Children coming to know literacy. In W.H. Teale & E. Sulzby (Eds.), *Emergent literacy: Writing and reading* (pp. 1-14). Norwood, NJ: Ablex.

Graves, D.H. (1983). *Writing: Teachers and children at work*. Portsmouth, NH: Heinemann.

Harste, J.C., Woodward, V.A., & Burke, C.L. (1984). *Language stories and literacy lessons*. Portsmouth, NH: Heinemann.

Heath, S.B. (1983). *Way with words: Language, life and work in communities and classrooms*. Cambridge, MA: Harvard University Press.

Hiebert, E. (1986). Using environmental print in beginning reading instruction. In M.R. Sampson (Ed.), *The pursuit of literacy: Early reading and writing*. Dubuque, IA: Kendall/Hunt.

Holdaway, D. (1979). *The foundations of literacy*. Sydney, Australia: Ashton Scholastic.

Kamberelis, G., & Sulzby, E. (1988). Transitional knowledge in emergent literacy. In J.E. Readence & R.S. Baldwin (Eds.), *Dialogues in literacy research* (pp. 95-106). Chicago, IL: National Reading Conference.

Martinez, M., & Teale, W.H. (1987). The ins and outs of a kindergarten writing program. *The Reading Teacher, 40,* 444-451.

Martinez, M., & Teale, W.H. (1988). Reading in a kindergarten classroom library. *The Reading Teacher, 41,* 568-572.

Marzollo, J., & Sulzby, E. (1988). See Jane read! See Jane write! *Parents, 63*(7), 80-84.

Mason, J., & Allen, J.B. (1986). A review of emergent literacy with implications for research and practice in reading. In E.Z. Rothkopf (Ed.), *Review of research in education 13.* Washington, DC: American Educational Research Association.

McNamee, G. (1987). The social origins of narrative skills. In M. Hickmann (Ed.), *Social and functional approaches to language and thought.* Orlando, FL: Academic.

Meisels, S.J. (1987). Uses and abuses of developmental screening and school readiness testing. *Young Children, 42,* 68-73.

Meisels, S.J. (1989). High-stakes testing in kindergarten. *Educational Leadership, 46,* 16-22.

Morrow, L.M. (1982). Relationships between literature programs, library corner designs and children's use of literature. *Journal of Educational Research, 75,* 339-344.

Morrow, L.M. (1989). *Literacy development in the early years: Helping children read and write.* Englewood Cliffs, NJ: Prentice Hall.

Otto, B., & Sulzby, E. (in preparation). Emergent writing and rereading by young children identified as "academically able."

Paley, V. (1981). *Wally's stories.* Cambridge, MA: Harvard University Press.

Paley, V. (1984). *Boys and girls: Superheroes in the doll corner.* Chicago, IL: University of Chicago Press.

Piaget, J. (1926). *The language and thought of the child.* New York: Harcourt Brace.

Robinson, F., & Sulzby, E. (1984). Parents, children, and "favorite" books: An interview study. *National Reading Conference Yearbook, 32,* 267-274.

Schickedanz, J. (1986). *More than the ABC's: The early stages of reading and writing.* Washington, DC: National Association for the Education of Young Children.

Spodek, B. (1982). The kindergarten: A retrospective and contemporary view. In L. Katz (Ed.), *Current topics in early childhood education 4* (pp. 173-189). Norwood, NJ: Ablex.

Stauffer, R.G. (1980). *The language-experience approach to the teaching of reading* (2nd ed.). New York: HarperCollins.

Sulzby, E. (1983, September). *Beginning readers' developing knowledge about written language* (Final Report to the National Institute of Education, NIE-G-80-0176). Evanston, IL: Northwestern University.

Sulzby, E. (1985a). Children's emergent reading of favorite storybooks: A developmental study. *Reading Research Quarterly, 20,* 458-481.

Sulzby, E. (1985b). Kindergartners as writers and readers. In M. Farr (Ed.), *Advances in writing research, vol. 1: Children's early writing development* (pp. 127-199). Norwood, NJ: Ablex.

Sulzby, E. (1987). Children's development of prosodic distinctions in telling and dictating modes. In A. Matsuhashi (Ed.), *Writing in real time: Modeling production processes* (pp. 122-160). Norwood, NJ: Ablex.

Sulzby, E. (1988). *Emergent literacy and whole language.* New York: McGraw-Hill.

Sulzby, E. (1989). *Emergent literacy: Kindergartners write and read, including Sulzby coding system* (monograph accompanying videotape by same title, a publication of Computers in Early Literacy [CIEL] Research Project). Ann Arbor, MI: Regents of The University of Michigan/North Central Regional Educational Laboratory.

Sulzby, E., Barnhart, J., & Hieshima, J. (1989). Forms of writing and rereading from writing: A preliminary report. In J. Mason (Ed.), *Reading/writing connections* (pp. 31-63). Needham Heights, MA: Allyn & Bacon.

Sulzby, E., & Teale, W.H. (1985). Writing development in early childhood. *Educational Horizons, 64,* 8-12.

Sulzby, E., & Teale, W.H. (1987, November). *Young children's storybook reading: Longitudinal study of parent-child interaction and children's independent functioning* (Final Report to The Spencer Foundation). Ann Arbor, MI: University of Michigan.

Sulzby, E., Teale, W.H., & Kamberelis, G. (1989). Emergent writing in the classroom: Home and school connections. In D. Strickland & L. Morrow (Eds.), *Emerging literacy: Young children learn to read and write.* Newark, DE: International Reading Association.

Taylor, D. (1983). *Family literacy.* Portsmouth, NH: Heinemann.

Teale, W.H. (1984). Reading to young children: Its significance for literacy development. In H. Goelman, A. Oberg, & F. Smith (Eds.), *Awakening to literacy* (pp. 110-121). Portsmouth, NH: Heinemann.

Teale, W.H. (1986). Home background and young children's literacy development. In W.H. Teale & E. Sulzby (Eds.), *Emergent literacy: Writing and reading* (pp. 173-206). Norwood, NJ: Ablex.

Teale, W.H. (1987). Emergent literacy: Reading and writing development in early childhood. In J.E. Readence & R.S. Baldwin (Eds.), *Research in literacy: Merging perspectives* (pp. 45-74). Rochester, NY: National Reading Conference.

Teale, W.H., & Martinez, M.G. (1989). Connecting writing: Fostering emergent literacy in kindergarten children. In J. Mason (Ed.), *Reading/writing connections* (pp. 177-198). Needham Heights, MA: Allyn & Bacon.

Teale, W.H., & Sulzby, E. (1986). Emergent literacy as a perspective for looking at how children become writers and readers. In W.H. Teale & E. Sulzby (Eds.), *Emergent literacy: Writing and reading* (pp. vii-xxv). Norwood, NJ: Ablex.

Teale, W.H., & Sulzby, E. (1988). Literacy acquisition in early childhood: The roles of access and mediation in storybook reading. In D.A. Wagner (Ed.), *The future of literacy in a changing world* (pp. 111-130). New York: Pergamon.

Sulzby and Barnhart

Richard T. Vacca
Wayne M. Linek

— S E V E N —

Writing to Learn

*T*wo decades of writing-process research have resulted in rich descriptions and understandings of how children and adolescents learn writing. In comparison, few empirically based studies have explored the effects of writing on learning. How children and adolescents use writing to help themselves learn remains largely a matter of conjecture, authoritative opinion, and theorizing. Fortunately, such activity has, in its own right, resulted in compelling arguments and rationales for writing to learn in content areas. Common sense and experience support the role of writing as a powerful tool for making sense of experience and discovering meaning.

To find meaning and purpose in learning, students must be encouraged to think about what they are learning—and therein lies the power of writing. Unfortunately, as Fulwiler (1987) observed, writing isn't generally thought of as basic to thinking and learning about content fields. Often when content area teachers hear the expression "Writing across the curriculum," it confirms their worst suspicions—that they are going to be expected to teach students to write. Yet this is not the case: as Atwell (1990) notes, there are plenty of English teachers for that. Atwell suggests that teachers of every discipline "ask students to think and write as scientists, historians, mathematicians, and literary critics do—to use writing-as-process to discover meaning just as these scholars do when they go about the real, messy business of thinking on paper" (p. xiii).

Britton et al. (1975) distinguish between two modes of language: expressive and transactional. The expressive mode is tied closely to talk, whereas the transactional mode is the language of "getting things done" or participating in the world's affairs. In his model of how writing ability develops in older students, Britton observed that transactional language is the language of schooling—it is used to inform, persuade, or instruct. When students think on paper, however, expressive rather than transactional language is their natural mode of discourse. If students in academic subjects are called on to express themselves primarily, if not exclusively, in the transactional mode, their writing is unnatural and stuffy, and often serves to inhibit thinking.

Learning itself occurs in the expressive mode of everyday talk in which people normally discuss their thoughts, feelings, and opinions. The approach of writing to learn uses the expressive mode so students can easily think about what is being learned. Through the use of expressive language, students are encouraged to interact personally with course content and to use background experiences, personal feelings, and prior knowledge to make sense of concepts and information. No wonder Medway (1976) argued that "in expressive writing the thinking in the writing is the thinking by which a child gets into a relationship with the topic. Such writing is actually very important because the child is generating his commitment as he writes" (pp. 145-146).

Too often, the expressive mode is missing in students' content area writing. They are expected to produce in the transactional mode without first experiencing the kind of internal talk that allows a writer to explore meaning. When thinking on paper occurs in the expressive mode, there is more to reflect on and work with than when this step is completed totally in students' heads or through discussion. Thoughts are often fleeting and lost when they race through one's head; in discussion, participants sometimes get off track or change the focus.

Writing in the expressive mode is a powerful tool for learning in the content areas. What does the research say to teachers who are considering using writing to help students interact personally with important ideas and concepts? Which activities support thinking on paper through the expressive mode?

Research on Writing to Learn

Our review of the research on writing to learn is selective rather than extensive. According to Newell and Winograd (1989), "there is at present only a slender empirical base from which to conceptualize how writing may aid learning about the topic, that is, how the writing process and what writers take from writing are interrelated" (p. 196). As a result, we limit our review to several studies that illuminate some of the problems associated with writing in the content areas and give us a direction for further inquiry and developing instructional practice. What these studies tell us is that the uses of writing in content areas have been narrowly conceived. Recording information rather than thinking about, thinking with, or thinking through ideas has dominated classroom writing time. The studies we will examine look squarely at the nature of writing-to-learn activities in content classrooms. Different types of writing assignments result in different patterns of thinking and learning. Essay writing, loosely defined as extended writing on a topic, holds much promise for involving students in the process of thinking on paper.

According to Yates (1983), who conducted an exhaustive review of the literature on writing in content areas, writing should be reinforced by talking, listening, and reading. In addition, writing to learn requires active involvement in which students have frequent opportunities to write for different kinds of assignments. Yates also concluded that writing is a recursive process consisting of many stages, and that the teacher must help students develop both a sense of writing as a process and strategies for using writing. Finally, Yates suggested that students must develop a sense of purpose and audience and come to view writing as a meaningful act that involves themselves and their classroom or society.

Two important studies have asked the question "How is writing used in content area classrooms?" Their findings are strikingly similar. In an observational study conducted in England, Martin et al. (1976) found that most of the writing done in secondary schools focused on reproducing information learned in class: "On the whole, the function of this writing seemed to be reporting back by pupils...what they had been told, or read in books...to demonstrate what knowledge had been acquired rather than to help the process of converting unfamiliar information into new knowledge" (p. 63). Writing in these classrooms was restricted to learning that had already happened.

As Martin et al. noted, "The research team's impression was that much of what was being written down had no inherent interest for the writer; it was not being put to use by him in any way other than to prove that he had 'done his homework' " (p. 63).

Applebee (1981) observed the writing taking place in content area classrooms in the United States during an academic year. He classified the ways teachers used writing into four categories. In the first category, Mechanical Use of Writing (or "writing without composing"), students are not required to generate ideas, communicate to others, or explore meaning. In the second category, Informational Uses of Writing, students produce textual information about course-related material. The third category, Personal Uses, focuses on students' interests and activities through journal or letter writing. The fourth category, Imaginative Uses, is characterized by writing stories, plays, poems, or other literary forms.

When Applebee pooled his observations, he found that an average of 44 percent of the lessons he watched involved writing in one way or another. Of this writing time, 24 percent was devoted to mechanical uses and 20 percent to informational uses. Only 3 percent of lesson time was devoted to writing activities in which students were required to produce at least a paragraph of coherent text.

Several studies, one of which we will discuss in detail, have examined the effects of different types of writing tasks on students' learning. Langer (1986) found that different types of assignments lead to different thinking patterns and different kinds of learning. For example, taking notes and answering study questions (two activities that Applebee [1981] would classify as informational writing tasks) focus students' thinking on narrow issues and reproduction of information. Essays, on the other hand, enable students to focus on larger issues and concepts: "When writing essays, students seem to step back from the text after reading it—they reconceptualize the content in ways that cut across ideas, focusing on larger issues or topics" (Langer, p. 406).

Marshall (1987) also provided empirical evidence for the role that essay writing plays in student learning, showing that essay writing is connected to better literary understanding over time. Marshall concluded that writing tasks requiring students to answer study questions do not allow them to elaborate on meaning and may even inhibit learning.

In a study of high school students, Newell (1984) contrasted three classroom uses of writing commonly integrated with content area reading assignments. As in the Langer (1986) and Marshall (1987) studies, the three writing tasks were writing answers to comprehension questions, taking notes, and writing essays using information from personal experiences, thoughts, or observations. Students read passages and were given 45 minutes to complete one of the three writing tasks. They were then tested on recall, passage-specific knowledge, and application of concepts.

During a six-month period, Newell found that students spent significantly more time on task when writing essays. Knowledge-gain scores from pretest to posttest showed that when students had little prior knowledge, answering questions was more helpful than taking notes, and that essay writing was better still. For students with a great deal of prior knowledge, writing essays was again better than both taking notes and answering questions. For passage-specific knowledge, essay writing enabled students to produce abstract associations for key concepts and to make a more conscious effort to find an appropriate structure for the ideas they generated.

From Newell's qualitative viewpoint, the writing and learning operations students used when writing essays were quantitatively and qualitatively different from those used for answering questions and taking notes. Essay writing was a more complex and demanding task. It required writers to establish a series of logical proofs to reason out and support their opinions. This in turn required an integration of relevant concepts that was missing in the other forms of writing. Although the amount of time students spent on planning before writing was the same for answering questions as for essay writing, Newell found that students' planning behavior changed from a rather restricted concern for information during a question-answer activity to a concern for explaining the information during essay writing.

Newell and Winograd (1989) extended the analysis of Newell's (1984) study. They concluded that when students write about what they have read in content area texts, the relationship between writing and learning is indeed complex. The nature of the writing task, as well as the difficulty of the text material, influences the kind of learning that takes place. When students have many opportunities to explore meaning and to elaborate on what they have read through essays and other learner-centered writing activities, they extend their thinking about content area concepts.

At present, "we know that writing is rarely used to help students explore and extend content-area information" (Newell & Winograd, 1989, p. 213). How can teachers help students to think on paper, to elaborate, to be reflective, to use expressive language?

Writing to Encourage Thinking on Paper

Learning is inextricably related to language, both oral and written. The relationships between talk and writing hold much promise for content area writing. Talk can stimulate thinking and expose holes in an individual's knowledge. This happens when one talks about what one has read and then draws implications from the new information uncovered by the discussion. During discussion, old information is brought out and looked at in light of new information. It is during this process that inconsistencies and gaps are revealed and new hypotheses begin to take form.

Talking about ideas before writing about them generates motivation that is absent when students are simply directed to produce written answers to study questions. Study questions often require a search for correct answers rather than personal involvement. Talk helps students put thinking into words and ensures that thinking about new ideas actually happens. Many students do well by just thinking, but they are the ones who always do well. When knowledge falls on unthinking ears, however, it can be memorized by rote or quickly forgotten rather than actively related to old ideas and stored. Talking and writing enable students who are not naturally reflective to become involved in the same thinking processes better students use routinely.

We suggest that small-group discussions be used before and during writing to learn. We prefer this type of discussion because each student in a group can be expected to participate actively. There is less hiding in small groups than in whole-class discussions, particularly if the group appoints a leader to include everyone systematically in expressing his or her thinking. Small-group discussion also reduces personal risk. Students who are hesitant to speak out in a large group may feel at ease discussing topics with a few classmates. The beauty of this arrangement is that the entire class can still share the fruits of small-group discussion. Each group appoints a recorder who will let the whole class know about the group's thinking at the end of the discussion period. During the summary or group sharing time, individuals in the small group may support or add to what the recorder has said. For

Vacca and Linek

those who don't work well in groups, provide the option of (or require) an individual brainstorming piece.

Talk, however, can intrude on the thinking process. This is because talk "is evanescent, and this places a severe limit—a limit connected with the duration of short-term memory—on the coherence and organization one can give to an extended passage of thinking" (Medway, 1984, p. 63). Talk will stimulate the process, but when it comes time to reformulate theories and hypotheses, monologues in writing give one the opportunity to look back for control and consistency. Therefore, expressive oral and written language serve as catalysts for reading and studying course material.

Expressive Writing Activities

Writing is used to discover and clarify meaning—to understand—and to communicate meaning to others—to be understood (Vacca & Vacca, 1989). One vital way for students to study and comprehend what they read is through the act of composing. But what does one do to get students to use writing or compose in this way?

To stimulate extended writing, Tchudi and Yates (1983) suggest using a variety of discourse forms to help provide a context for various kinds of writing. They particularly recommend biographical sketches, anecdotes and stories, letters, dialogues and conversations, editorials and commentaries, songs and ballads, scenarios, scripts, responses to literature, observations, and reviews.

In addition to the use of discourse forms to stimulate thinking on paper, Vacca and Vacca (1989) recommend a variety of writing-to-learn activities that allow students to use expressive language. These activities emphasize the process of manipulating and extending ideas to broaden and improve the context for writing in content area classrooms.

Learning logs. The learning log strategy is simple to implement and particularly effective when used regularly. Students keep ongoing records of learning "as it happens" in notebooks or loose-leaf binders. They write in their own language about what they are learning. Although some teachers prefer devoting five to ten minutes at the end of a period for students to make log entries, there is no one correct way to structure this writing time.

Some teachers may ask students to respond to "process questions" similar to the following: What did I like or dislike about class today? What did I understand about today's class work? What is not clear about today's class work? At what point did I get confused? Why did I get confused? Other teachers may start new topics by asking students to write down their expectations and predictions of what might be involved. Still other teachers, after determining that their students have learned their material well, may ask students to use their logs to imagine how they would explain the information to a younger, less well-informed person. The entries in these logs influence learning by generating ideas, revealing problems, clarifying thinking, and generating questions.

But what does a teacher do about the student who sits, stares at the paper, and doesn't write anything? To get around this situation, a teacher can use freewriting in conjunction with learning logs. Draper (1982) advises the following approach:

> Emphasize...[that] the purpose of...free writing is to generate a flow of words and thought without concern for polished phrases or mechanics. The writer is not to worry about spelling, punctuation, grammar, complete sentences, or paragraphs. He is to write, keep writing, and if a block occurs, to repeat the last written word again and again until another thought comes (p. 153).

Freewriting places no restrictions on the student's thinking because whatever comes to mind is put in writing. Over time, freewriting often improves writing fluency while the writer's voice emerges.

Focused freewriting is similar to freewriting and is ideal for content area classrooms. With focused freewriting the teacher directs students to write as much as they can on the topic being studied in five to ten minutes without the pressure of competing or being evaluated. Students are then encouraged to share and react to one another's freewriting in whole-class or small-group discussions. Once again, we suggest small groups because when all students are expected to share, risk-taking is encouraged.

Group discussion should begin by focusing on the positive aspects of the writing's content—that is, on congratulating students for what they do know. Next, the teacher and students ask questions to help writers recognize which ideas need development to clarify their own and their audience's understanding. Advice may be given to help writers focus on a topic or clarify their purpose for writing. This step lets writers know whether they are attempting to do too much or too little.

Learning logs are versatile and can incorporate various types of writing-to-learn tasks. Unfinished writing, which is similar to first-draft writing, is a good example. Gere (1985) explains unfinished writing as "writing that evinces thought but does not merit the careful scrutiny which a finished piece of writing deserves" (p. 4). Unfinished writing activities can also be used as separate learning tasks. Other activities that can be easily incorporated into learning logs or used as separate activities are dialogues, fictitious interviews, and unsent letters.

Dialogues permit writers to think about situations, conflicts, and possible solutions by creating an exchange between two or more persons, possibly characters in a book or historical figures being studied. Writing a dialogue provides an opportunity for students to react to the ideas being presented in class and extend thinking about material being studied.

Fictitious interviews (Myers, 1984) are a special type of dialogue: Students create a discussion between an interviewer and an inanimate or animate object. For students to write such interviews, they must understand the material being studied. Writing the dialogue will help students retain the material. Myers gives the following example:

> When studying the effects of drugs or alcohol on the brain, a student might interview a group of brain cells who relate what happened to them and some of their "gray matter" friends as a result of a drink or two.... Similar interviews could be conducted with the stomach, the lungs, or other parts of the body (p. 28).

With unsent letters, students are asked to write to specific people in response to material under study. This role-play situation directs students' thinking to particular audiences while combining personal and informative writing. In addition to engaging in interpretive and evaluative thinking, students must use a lot of imagination.

Summaries.   Summaries are valuable because they require students to distinguish between important and trivial information. They also require students to organize information in view of their previous knowledge. Reviewing written summaries helps the teacher figure out who is on track and who is lost. In addition, summarizing activities help students prepare for discussion.

Summaries have many different forms. Often a student is asked to read a story or passage, then summarize in writing what has occurred. This simple recall activity can be easily adjusted into a thinking/learning activity. One way to make this adjustment is by using what we call admit and exit slips—the former allow the student to "admit" a difficulty, and the latter provide an opportunity to "exit" class by expressing understanding or confusion about the material covered. Students write their comments anonymously on half sheets of paper at the beginning or end of class. The purpose of these slips is to have students react to what they have read or what has happened in class in an expressive and nonthreatening way, rather than just regurgitating information.

When using admit slips, ask students to respond to questions such as these at the beginning of class: What is confusing you about...? What questions came to mind while you were completing your assignment? What is your reaction to...? What problems came up when you were reading your text? Collect the slips and read them aloud to begin class discussion. Students are often surprised to find that they are not the only one with a problem or question. This anonymous sharing enables even the quietest or shyest students to have a voice in the discussion and builds their trust and self-esteem. It also lets the teacher focus on points that need clarification.

Exit slips, on the other hand, bring closure to learning. At the end of class students react to the questions previously suggested or to questions that require summarizing, synthesizing, evaluating, or projecting. This writing is revealing and can be used to establish direction for the next lesson. Another possibility is for teachers to respond directly to exit slips at the beginning of the next class in order to open students to new connections and clarify the reasoning behind classroom activities.

Process descriptions (Myers, 1984) focus on enhancing learning by having students summarize the steps in carrying out an experiment, performing CPR, changing spark plugs, and so on. Writing descriptions helps students visualize the steps in sequence. In addition to increasing retention, students can exchange papers, compare notes while following one another's written steps, and spot gaps in their own learning. This activity focuses discussion on why specific steps are important while promoting clarity and completeness in future student writing.

Biopoems set up situations for students to summarize their thinking about content information in a specific framework. Students are asked to play with ideas in order to put large amounts of material into precise language within a poetic form. The biopoem follows a pattern that necessitates that students think, reflect on, and synthesize what they have learned in class about a concept, event, person, place, or thing. The following pattern suggested by Gere (1985) is for a person or character:

Line 1. First name

Line 2. Four traits or words that end in "ing" to describe

Line 3. Relative ("brother," "sister," "daughter,") of _____

Line 4. Lover of _____ (list three things or people)

Line 5. Who feels _____ (three items)

Line 6. Who needs _____ (three items)

Line 7. Who fears _____ (three items)

Line 8. Who gives _____ (three items)

Line 9. Who would like to see _____ (three items)

Line 10. Resident of _____

Line 11. Last name

The above pattern can easily be adjusted to meet the requirements of any content area subject matter.

Some Thoughts on Classroom Environment

Regardless of the activity or form, remember that learning logs and other writing-to-learn activities always demand thinking but seldom result in a polished, finished product. The emphasis is on communicating content ideas or problems with content, not with the surface level of writing. Errors in spelling, capitalization, punctuation, and grammar should therefore be ignored. Teachers should work to develop a trusting atmosphere in their classrooms and refrain from making judgmental or evaluative comments when students admit a lack of understanding about what is happening in class.

This does not mean that students should never complete a finished written product. The learning log or writing activity can serve as a resource for the student when a more formal writing project is assigned. Our point is that expressive writing or writing to learn should occupy most of the students' writing time. Ideally, when writing to learn occurs across the curriculum, the English teacher serves as a resource person or coordinator for helping students develop form and surface structure in their writing while content area teachers attend more to the understanding and organization of content and meaning. (Of course, if the content area is literature study, the English teacher must often play both these roles.)

The following summary of principles for writing to learn in the content areas is adapted from Tchudi and Huerta (1983, p. 45):

- Keep content at the center of the writing process, addressing yourself to what the writing says and treating how it says it as incidental.

- Design writing activities that help students structure and synthesize their knowledge, not merely regurgitate it.

- Provide audiences for student writing, real or imaginary, so that students have a sense of writing for someone other than the teacher.

- Look for writing activities that allow the student to play the roles of learner and researcher.

- Attend to the process of writing: (1) Spend time on prewriting, helping students acquire a solid grasp of the material; and (2) provide assistance and support as students write, helping them solve problems as they arise rather than waiting until they turn in a written assignment to be graded.

- Let students revise one another's papers. Provide support through revision checklists and guidelines.

- Don't confuse revising with editing: (1) Approach revision first, having students clarify the content and substance of their work; and (2) focus on editing of spelling, mechanics, usage, etc., only in the final phases of writing, and only when publishing for specific purposes.

- Make a conscious effort to provide pupils with an audience that enables them to write what they really think, an audience that will value and question their writing without debilitating criticism.

- Display or otherwise publicize student writing through shows, demonstrations, book publishings, and oral readings. Don't be the only reader of your students' work.

We believe these principles should guide the use of writing strategies in content area subjects. However, using the suggested strategies and guiding principles will not lead to success unless teachers provide a low-risk environment.

What do we mean by this? We define a low-risk environment as an atmosphere free of pressure to turn in a polished performance in the initial stages. When teachers and peers respond to expressive writing they should focus on thinking, not on the mechanics of writing. A low-risk environment is one in which students feel free to express their thinking. In the expressive stages, thinking should be accepted, valued, questioned, and explored further—not criticized or evaluated. This means that the teacher and other students must act as a supportive learning community.

There are many considerations to keep in mind when attempting to create this sort of atmosphere. The first and most important task for the teacher is to define his or her role in the classroom at all times. The importance of making clear to students when the teacher is acting as a facilitator and when as a judge should not be underestimated. We believe teachers should be facilitators most of the time. This does not mean that no evaluation is required; it means simply that students must know which role has been assumed so they know how to interact at a given moment. For example, students need to know when a teacher is acting as a facilitator so they can relax, bounce ideas around, or admit that they do not understand something without fear of being judged. Likewise, it is only fair that students know exactly what will be graded, when it will be graded, and under what circumstances or conditions it will be graded. One cannot build the high level of trust necessary for a low-risk environment when students are unsure of what to expect when.

The next step is to encourage risk taking. Provide situations in which students do not have to put their own feelings and opinions on the line. Allow writers to take on fictional roles so that situations can be explored from another person's point of view. Have only volunteers publicly share what they have written. Later on, tell students that during the week they will be writing daily and at the end of the week they will select one piece of writing to polish and share with the group.

After the teacher's roles are clearly defined and students have come to trust him or her and each other, the creation of a supportive community of learners is easier. Students should be encouraged to help one another without put-downs, harmful competition, or unnecessary criticism. They should applaud the writing efforts that individuals choose to share with the group.

This type of supportive community opens the door for the discussion and sharing that are crucial to the cooperative learning strategies we have suggested.

But how does one create a supportive community of learners in a classroom? Model the supportive behaviors expected and congratulate students when they use them. De-emphasize competition and reward student efforts at helping one another. Be a good listener rather than a good talker. Instead of astounding students with expert, mature understanding of the subject matter, help them recognize what they already know and how it fits or connects with what they are learning. Ask questions that stimulate their thinking and lead them to find out where their thinking is not clearly reflected in their writing. Be sure to praise the information while questioning the source and reasoning.

If students are not accustomed to being supportive, you should model and develop supportive behaviors in whole-group situations before attempting small-group work or cooperative learning. Patience is essential since this development often takes weeks or months. Once supportive behaviors begin developing, start group work with pairs or triads of students. After students have learned to interact successfully in smaller groups, move to the optimal group size of four or five students.

Remember, students should always be expected to respect and support one another. Any criticism offered should be helpful and constructive. Students who refuse to act in a supportive or cooperative manner should be given the option (or, in extreme cases, required) to work individually until they can behave as expected. Cooperative learning does not mean allowing students to take over the class. The teacher is the conductor of a carefully organized orchestra, and all the players must share responsibility. Hard work and practice yield a symphony of learning whose whole is greater than the sum of the individual scores.

References

Applebee, A.N. (1981). *Writing in the secondary school: English and the content areas.* Urbana, IL: National Council of Teachers of English.

Atwell, N. (1990). *Coming to know: Writing to learn in the intermediate grades.* Portsmouth, NH: Heinemann.

Britton, J.N., Burgess, T., Martin, N., McLeod, A., & Rosen, H. (1975). *The development of writing abilities.* New York: Macmillan.

Draper, V. (1982). Formative writing: Writing to assist learning in all subject areas. In G. Camp (Ed.), *Teaching writing: Essays from the Bay Area Writing Project.* Portsmouth, NH: Boynton/Cook.

Fulwiler, T. (1987). *Teaching with writing.* Portsmouth, NH: Boynton/Cook.

Gere, A. (1985). *Roots in sawdust: Writing to learn across the curriculum.* Urbana, IL: National Council of Teachers of English.

Langer, J.A. (1986). Learning through writing: Study skills in the content areas. *Journal of Reading, 29,* 400-406.

Marshall, J.D. (1987). The effects of writing on students' understanding of literary texts. *Research in the Teaching of English, 21,* 30-63.

Martin, N., D'Arcy, P., Newton, B., & Parker, R. (1976). *Writing and learning across the curriculum 11-16.* Portsmouth, NH: Boynton/Cook.

Medway, P. (1976). Lecture notes. In N. Martin, P. D'Arcy, B. Newton, & R. Parker (Eds.), *Writing and learning across the curriculum 11-16* (pp. 145-146). Portsmouth, NH: Boynton/Cook.

Medway, P. (1984). From talking to writing. In N. Martin (Ed.), *Writing across the curriculum pamphlets* (pp. 60-85). Portsmouth, NH: Boynton/Cook.

Myers, J.W. (1984). *Writing to learn across the curriculum.* Bloomington, IN: Phi Delta Kappa.

Newell, G.E. (1984). Learning from writing in two content areas: A case study/protocol analysis. *Research in the Teaching of English, 18,* 265-287.

Newell, G.E., & Winograd, P. (1989). The effects of writing on learning from expository text. *Written Communication, 6*(2), 196-217.

Tchudi, S.N., & Huerta, M.C. (1983). *Teaching writing in the content areas: Middle school/junior high.* Washington, DC: National Education Association.

Tchudi, S.N., & Yates, J. (1983). *Teaching writing in the content areas: Senior high school.* Washington, DC: National Education Association.

Vacca, R.T., & Vacca, J.L. (1989). *Content area reading* (3rd ed.). Glenview, IL: Scott, Foresman.

Yates, J.M. (1983). *Research implications for writing in the content areas.* Washington, DC: National Education Association.

— E I G H T —

How Reading Model Essays Affects Writers

*I*mitating exemplary models is among the hoariest methods of learning to write, dating back to the Greek academies where students learned rhetoric by memorizing the orations of the masters and practiced and advocated by such luminaries as Ben Franklin:

> [John Collins] took occasion to talk to me about the manner of my writing; observed that, though I had the advantage of my antagonist in correct spelling and point...I fell far short in elegance of expression, in method and in perspicuity, of which he convinced me by several instances. I saw the justice of his remarks, and thence grew more attentive to the manner in writing, and determined to endeavor an improvement.
>
> At about this time I met with an odd volume of the *Spectator*.... I bought it, read it over and over, and was much delighted with it. I thought the writing excellent, and wished, if possible, to imitate it. With this view I took some of the papers, and, making short hints of the sentiment in each sentence, laid them by a few days, and then, without looking at the book, try'd to complete the papers again, by expressing each hinted sentiment at length, and as fully as it had been expressed before, in any suitable words that should come to hand. Then I compared my *Spectator* with the original, discovered some of my faults, and corrected them.... By comparing my work afterwards with the original, I discovered many faults and amended them; but I sometimes had the pleasure of fancying that, in certain particulars of small import, I had been lucky enough to improve the method or the language, and this encouraged me to think I might possibly in time come to be a tolerable English writer, of which I was extremely ambitious [from *The Autobiography of Benjamin Franklin*].

Franklin's experience with the *Spectator* seems to prove this to be an effective learning method: He identified the elegance and articulation of good writing and reproduced these in his own expression. Teachers who employ this method assume that their students can perform in the same way—that they can assimilate production procedures by studying products.

This chapter begins by reviewing historic use of the strategy of reading "model essays" to promote better writing. Next I look at the rationale for this approach and review the use of models to promote learning in other areas. Following sections examine criticisms of and research on the method, including my own research on how it affects the writing process. Finally, I discuss effective ways of using models in composition instruction.

History and Rationale

The practice of reading model essays to learn writing skills can be traced to antiquity. *Progymnasmata* ("writing exercises"), by Hermogenes and Aphthonius, provided both rules for and models of writing forms; it "went through an astounding number of editions, in both Greek and Latin versions" (Corbett, 1965, p. 543). Corbett traces the influence of these texts all the way to 16th-century Europe, labeling the tradition "formulary rhetoric." While other strategies have competed for primacy over the centuries, the imitation of model essays has endured as an instructional approach. Following the decline of the "classical" period in the 19th century, "rhetoric courses in the schools gradually assumed a new orientation—the study of the four forms of discourse: exposition, argumentation, description and narration" (Corbett, p. 566), with instruction focused on studying and imitating masterly renditions of these forms.

This orientation has persisted through to the present irrespective of the recent shift in attention toward the processes involved in writing. A survey by McCann and Smagorinsky (1988) found that although many texts are now starting to present writing as a process—albeit a simplistic one consisting of prewriting, writing, and revision—they do so in a discrete section while retaining an emphasis on the study of model essays. Only a handful of professional books, such as the National Council of Teachers of English TRIP series (Hillocks, 1975; Johannessen, Kahn, & Walter, 1982; Smagorinsky, McCann, & Kern, 1987; Smith, 1984), effectively relate process to form, and these publications tend to reach a limited audience of teachers instead of having widespread use among students.

The field of composition is not unique in its assumptions about the pedagogical soundness of studying models. Psychologists have investigated the effects of this approach in a variety of areas and have found that under certain circumstances studying models can be instructive. Strupp and Bloxom (1973) studied the effects of modeling psychotherapy sessions and found that certain types of clients—those whose expectations about the sessions were different from the reality of them—could benefit from watching a model of a therapy session before participating in one themselves. The researchers caution that the effects of a model depend on the learner's background knowledge and skills. In this case, the learners—patients with no experience in group psychotherapy—were unaware of the sessions' formalities and benefited from observing a film of others involved in therapy.

On the other hand, lack of appropriate background knowledge may prevent learners from being able to follow the model. Bransford (1979) gives the example of a theoretical physicist modeling a mathematical proof that is clear to other physicists but incomprehensible to most of us. Strupp and Bloxom (1973) argue that the problem is far more complex than whether models do or do not promote learning; rather, we must consider individual learners' characteristics and the nature and sophistication of the task we are asking them to perform. Without content knowledge, a study of forms is unhelpful. Modeling seems to work best when learners have the appropriate content knowledge but lack a structure for representing it.

The primary assumption behind using models in writing instruction is that students will see how good writers organize, develop, and express their ideas. This is particularly helpful if students are learning to write forms with distinct features, such as argumentation. Students are then expected to imitate the writing presented in the models. The problem educators face is that few students are blessed with the insights and abilities of Ben Franklin; instead, we must help students with different amounts of skill and motivation. We must, therefore, ask how we can use this approach to benefit the writing of *most* students.

Pros and Cons

Paul Eschholz (1980) is one of the few authorities in recent years to defend the use of models in composition courses:

> Certainly few people will take exception to the general rule that one good way to learn how to write is to follow the example of those who can write

well.... Professional writers have long acknowledged the value of reading; they know that what they read is important to how they eventually write. In reading, writers see the printed word; they develop an eye—and an ear—for language, the shape and order of sentences, and the texture of paragraphs. The prose models approach to the teaching of writing holds that writers can develop and improve their writing skills through directed reading. Teachers who use this approach believe that one of the best ways to learn to write is to analyze and imitate models of good writing systematically. Such study, they feel, exposes students to important new ideas and to the basic patterns of organization in non-fiction prose as well as to other specific strategies or techniques that all good writers use.

Eschholz goes on to describe a three-stage teaching method for one type of writing: (1) Read a "classic" model to learn how to write a comparison/contrast essay; (2) analyze the features of the model, focusing on organization, thesis, paragraph structure, coherence, logic, exactness, and unity (this analysis might include practice at imitation); and (3) write a similar type of essay.

Students benefit from such instruction, says Eschholz, by learning the traditional rhetorical modes, becoming better readers, learning what good writing is and applying this knowledge to their own writing, and learning topic selection by using models as "theme starters." Students who study model essays can eventually improve their own writing:

> When provided with a steady diet of the best contemporary non-fiction, they come to appreciate what all good writing has in common.... If students are doing a good deal of writing while they are reading, it is not long before they are reading like writers.... Consciously or unconsciously students begin to collect their own models of good writing (pp. 28-29).

Criticism of the approach of reading models to improve writing falls into several areas. One blanket criticism is that the study of a product simply cannot *teach* a writing process. According to Murray (1980), "The process of making meaning with written language cannot be understood by looking backward from a printed page. Process cannot be inferred from product any more than a pig can be inferred from a sausage" (p. 3). This curious analogy does little to illuminate *why* Murray feels that models do not work. In an earlier work, Murray (1968) is more specific, charging that models are irrelevant to writers' real needs. A model, he says, "only vaguely illuminates a particular kind of writing problem relevant to the student's own growth in composition" (p. 220).

Other criticisms of form-oriented instruction have echoed this concern. Perhaps the most famous and vituperative attack along these lines comes from Emig (1971), who writes as follows:

> A species of extensive writing that...deserves special mention is the five-paragraph theme.... This mode is so indigenously American that it might be called the Fifty-Star Theme. In fact, the reader might imagine behind this...Kate Smith singing "God Bless America" or the piccolo obligato from "The Stars and Stripes Forever."
>
> Why is the Fifty-Star Theme so tightly lodged in the American composition curriculum? The reason teachers often give is that...this theme somehow fulfills requirements somewhere in the real world.
>
> This fantasy is easy to disprove. If one takes a constellation of writers who current critical judgment would agree are among the best American writers of the sixties, can one find a single example of any variation of the Fifty-Star Theme? (p. 97).

These criticisms come from the early days of the movement toward "process" instruction, when Murray and Emig attacked the notion of any sort of external constraints on writing, particularly those imposed by teachers. In the face of widespread, slavish submission to teacher-prescribed form, their reaction was important, but in retrospect it appears extreme. The five-paragraph theme, while not practiced by the "best" essayists in their mature work, does teach certain organizational principles. Teachers assume (perhaps incorrectly) that students will transfer these principles to more sophisticated writing. The assumption is a logical one, however; after all, the critics themselves use these same organizational principles in the very articles that decry the structure.

Murray argues that writing in established forms does not promote growth in composing ability. This claim seems to deny that writers engage profitably in narration, description, argumentation, and so forth. One might argue convincingly that writers rarely produce compositions in the exact forms of the models, and that modes overlap too frequently to justify their discrete study. It seems odd, however, to reject the study of models altogether on this basis. In this chapter, for example, I have organized my ideas according to a conventional model (without knowledge of which I probably could not publish in this medium), and use "standard" modes of writing such as definition, argument, narration, description, and compare/contrast. In engaging in these processes, I have profited from observing examples—the many research reports and articles I have read—of how others have engaged in them. My study of models is only *one* of the ways in which I have learned to produce academic writing, part of a repertoire of communication strategies for participating in this particular discourse community. If, however, my experience is even roughly representative of what many writers go through in learning particular conventions, then the outright rejection of using models to teach writing is unwarranted.

Other critics have focused more profitably on the relationship between form and content. In the reading models approach, form precedes content. Judy (1980) argues that " 'form' in writing has traditionally been presented as something independent of a writer's content, indeed, as something which exists before content... [Form] grows from content and is inseparable from it. One doesn't simply pick a form and match ideas to it" (p. 41). The flow of ideas can be inhibited by an early emphasis on the form in which they must be expressed, maintain Collins and Gentner (1980):

> One of the most damaging habits for a novice writer to have is that of confusing idea manipulation with text manipulation so that text structure constraints enter into the process of writing at an early stage, before the ideas are ready. When this happens, not only does the writer waste a great deal of time and effort polishing prose that will eventually be discarded but, even worse, the effort to perfect text may cause the writer to lose track of the desired content (p. 53).

These critics object to the position of models in the instructional sequence, maintaining that students need to explore their content knowledge before learning the structure in which they cast it. We see here the seeds of theory about how knowledge affects composing: knowledge of form, both declarative (labeling the parts) and procedural (strategies for producing it), and knowledge of content, both declarative (the writer's factual knowledge base) and procedural (strategies for transforming declarative knowledge into text) (Hillocks, 1986a). These critics contend that procedural knowledge related to content should not be secondary to declarative knowledge of form, as is usually the case when using models to teach writing.

Finally, some critics have raised questions regarding the instructional time and emphasis given to reading models. Gorrell (1977) cautions that reading can become a substitute for writing when teachers focus too intently on the study of literary greats: "The reading-writing course becomes a reading course with a few more or less related theme assignments.... If the reading dominates completely, or is not related to writing, the course ceases to be a composition course" (p. 59). This concern echoes criticisms of other form-related approaches to teaching writing, such as emphasizing grammar: time spent on it takes time away from instruction with other, more effective methods (Hillocks, 1984, 1986b).

In general, experimental research has shown models to have limited value. Models often serve as treatments in control groups along with such well-documented instructional failures as grammar instruction (Hillocks, 1984, 1986b). Even when students study models in experimental groups, their writing rarely improves significantly over the writing of students in control treatments. Models are particularly ineffective when they emphasize a great many features. Vinson (1980), for instance, used models to instruct students in the use of concrete detail, sensory imagery, unnecessary detail, and single impression; the students in this group made no statistically different gains over students in control groups. Only in studies in which models were brief and stressed a few specific features did they improve students' writing to any notable extent (Andreach, 1976; Stefl, 1981). This finding, however, has not been consistently replicated. Even so, the most successful models used in comparative studies have focused on particular features, rather than illustrating the many skills demonstrated by master writers.

Reconciling the Points of View

Much of the criticism of reading models has been as speculative as the justification for using them. My own research on writing processes (Smagorinsky, 1989, 1991) suggests reasons for the uneven effectiveness of models in improving composing. My study was part of a larger piece of research (Hillocks, in progress) contrasting the effects of three instructional treatments on students' skill in writing extended-definition essays. The use of extended definition, one of the traditional writing modes, dates back at least to Aristotle. In learning to write definitions, students acquire a skill that serves them well across a variety of tasks: determining rules or laws, producing criticism, classifying organisms, and distinguishing between items that belong to a set and those that do not. Definitions have clearly accepted elements common to their use in all disciplines: criteria, or rules that distinguish between members and nonmembers; examples that illustrate the criteria; and contrasting examples that seem to illustrate the criteria but lack some essential characteristic. The following segment, used in all treatments in the Hillocks (in progress) study, illustrates the elements in a definition of ethnic prejudice derived from Gordon Allport's *The Nature of Prejudice*:

> *Criterion*: Ethnic prejudice is thinking ill of others without cause but solely on the basis of presumptions spurred by race, heritage, or ethnicity.
>
> *Example*: A few years ago many Americans thought exceedingly ill of Turks—but very few had ever seen a Turk, nor did they know any person who had seen one. Their justification lay exclusively in what they had heard of the Armenian massacres and of the legendary Crusades. On such evidence are all members of a nation condemned.
>
> *Contrasting example*: Take the hostile view of Nazi leaders held by most Americans during World War II. Was it prejudice? The answer is no, because there was abundant available evidence regarding the evil policies and practices accepted as the official code of the party.

Definition is a good form to use for the study of the effects of models since its elements and their relationships can be clearly presented in exemplary essays. Provided that students have content knowledge of the topics, they can use knowledge of form to represent their ideas in essays of this type.

The Research

The three instructional treatments contrasted in the study derived from conflicting theories on the type of knowledge writers need in order to write effectively. One theory states that having students study models of exemplary writing is itself sufficient for them to learn how to write well. The first of the three treatments included extensive study of model definitions with a focus on labeling their elements.

The other two treatments both included a study of model essays, but focused on instruction in a particular type of composing procedure. Instead of assuming that students can extract procedural knowledge from a study of finished products, these treatments assumed that students require explicit instruction in how to write. The types of procedures included in the two treatments represent different views of the nature of knowledge, a conflict with deep roots in cognitive theory.

The first of these treatments included instruction in general procedures. Students in this treatment group combined a study of model essays with instruction in the general composing procedures of brainstorming and freewriting (which is something like brainstorming on paper—an unrestricted, nonlinear procedure designed to help the writer discover topic, purpose, meaning, and so on). For nearly half a century, educational theorists have attempted to identify general heuristics that learners can apply in any problem-solving situation. Polya (1954), for instance, identified general procedures such as breaking a problem into subproblems, representing problems with diagrams, and so on—all of which can be learned and applied to virtually any problem. Ennis (1990) has argued that "it makes sense to talk about significant general critical thinking abilities and dispositions" (p. 16). Some scholars have argued that certain general composing strategies will enable one to be successful with any composing task. Brainstorming and freewriting are frequently advocated general writing procedures. Theorists such as Elbow (1973) and Murray (1980) have claimed that freewriting is an effective all-purpose writing strategy. Murray describes its merits as follows:

> We do not teach our students rules demonstrated by static models; we teach our students to write by allowing them to experience the process of writing. That is a process of discovery, of using written language to find out what we have to say. We believe this process can be adapted by our students to whatever writing tasks face them—the memo, the poem, the textbook, the speech, the consumer complaint, the job application, the story, the essay, the personal letter, the movie script, the accident report, the novel, the scientific paper (p.20).

The remaining treatment was labeled task-specific procedures and combined the study of models with instruction in procedures specific to the task of writing extended definitions. McPeck (1990) has argued that "there are almost as many different kinds of critical thinking as there are different kinds of things to think about" (p. 10) and that therefore general approaches to learning and thinking are inadequate to solve particular types of problems. Rather, different types of tasks require particular knowledge that may not be relevant to other tasks. Writing a complaint about a product, for instance, requires an assessment of how the complaint will be received and the ability

Smagorinsky

to word the complaint in the most effective way; this approach is not effective if the goal is to write a poem.

The task-specific procedures treatment included instruction in a procedure devised to produce a definition: students were given examples related to the word or phrase to be defined. For instance, students defining "freedom of speech" examined seven examples, along these lines:

- A group of college students, unable to obtain tickets for a rock concert, manage to enter the hall where the concert is about to begin. At a signal, they begin to shout "Fire!" as loudly as they can. Everyone in the hall ignores the shouting.

- Same as above, but a panic ensues and several people are injured.

Students were instructed to generate a criterion from each of the seven examples using these procedures: jot down ideas about the topic, generate examples, consider different versions of each example, generate criteria from the examples, test the criteria with additional examples, revise, and repeat these procedures with different examples.

To study the effects of the treatments, I collected pretest and posttest think-aloud protocols from six students in each group. I asked each student to think aloud as he or she composed, tape-recorded their speaking, and then had the tapes transcribed to be segmented and coded. The protocols allowed me to study changes in the students' thinking based on the type of knowledge they had gained from instruction. The protocol analysis revealed treatment effects in two main areas: critical thinking and purposeful composing.

Critical thinking. I mean here the ability to generate precise criteria. As noted earlier, definition aims at distinguishing between members and nonmembers of a set. Recall, for instance, the criterion for ethnic prejudice: "Ethnic prejudice is thinking ill of others *without cause....*" Students would often attempt a criterion without sufficient distinction. A student might say simply, "Ethnic prejudice is thinking ill of other types of people," which is too broad. These "criteria" were categorized in the protocol analyses as *attributes*; that is, statements that describe a characteristic of the concept being defined, but without the contrast necessary to distinguish members from nonmembers.

Another type of generalization was an *incidental statement* which, while often true, is evasive, tangential, or nonessential. Such a statement might be "Ethnic prejudice has caused a great deal of trouble in the world," which is certainly true but does not help define the concept. Students would often support attributes and incidental statements with examples, but the generation of such statements to the exclusion of criteria showed a lack of precise, critical thinking. Students who improved in the area of critical thinking improved their ratio of criteria to attributes and incidental statements.

Purposeful composing. Here I mean the degree to which students improved their ability to link generalizations to supporting evidence. In their pretests, students tended to produce generalizations (criteria, attributes, and incidental statements) and evidence (examples and contrasting examples) without using them in relation to one another, engaging in a process close to brainstorming.

For instance, in her pretest protocol on "friendship," Cindy generated a series of attributes but did not support any with examples. (In all protocol transcripts that follow, each segment is preceded by its category label, which I inserted. Words recorded in the student's essay are italicized; all statements not in italics were thought without being written.)

Attribute: You don't have to like everything about that person.

Elaborate attribute: That's not what's important.

Attribute: You may not even have anything in common,

Attribute: but *they just make you feel good inside yourself.*

Attribute: They don't care how you look or dress.

Attribute: It's someone to tell your good and bad feelings to.

Attribute: *They try and help you when things are going bad or something's wrong, or try and make situations better or not as bad.*

Elaborate attribute: *They always make you try to see the bright side of things,*

Attribute: *and they don't try to change you to what they want.*

In the posttests, generalizations were less common; students were more likely to focus on providing support for their generalizations. Cindy began her posttest protocol on "leadership" by thinking of ideas before writing, and then using them purposefully as she wrote.

Attribute: Leadership is an action of a person who takes charge.

Attribute: They help people?

Elaborate attribute: They take charge of a group.

Search: What is something like leadership but isn't?

Incidental statement: There's different kinds of leadership.

Attribute: There's social leadership—they organize what's going on.

Attribute: A leader takes charge. Leadership is an action that takes charge over...the person takes charge over people.

Example: They lead in a discussion.

Elaborate example: They start, like in a classroom a teacher starts a class.

Warrant: A teacher is a leader because they take charge of a class and organize and lead it.

Example: The president is a leader.

Positive judgment: That would fit my criteria.

Elaborate example: He can raise taxes or whatever.

Warrant: So he's in charge.

She went on to develop the attribute of "taking charge" into a criterion, supporting this with the example of a teacher assigning students to particular seats to control behavior. Instead of writing down a series of unsupported attributes as she had done in the pretest, she thought about the definition before writing and determined which ideas to relate to each other when she began to write.

Results

Students who combined the study of models with instruction in general or task-specific composing procedures improved more on critical thinking measures than did students who studied only models; similarly, students who combined the study of models with task-specific composing procedures improved more in purposeful composing than did students who studied only models. (Although the students in the general procedures group also improved in purposeful composing, the gains were not as dramatic.)

Critical thinking. According to one-tailed t-tests for individual comparisons among the three treatment groups, students in the task-specific procedures group scored significantly higher than students in the models group on both the total (t = 2.588; $p < .025$) and written (t = 2.584; $p < .05$) measurements for improving critical thinking. Students in the general procedures group also scored significantly higher than students in the models group on both the total (t = 2.405; $p < .025$) and written (t = 2.086; $p < .05$) measurements. (Contrasts in these improvement scores are shown more fully in Table 1, which gives the specific results on a one-way ANOVA with three levels. Scores labeled "written" are for final drafts of students' essays; scores labeled "total" are for students' taped think-aloud performances.)

Purposeful composing. According to one-tailed t-tests for individual comparisons among treatments, students in the task-specific procedures treatment group scored significantly higher than students in the models treat-

Table 1
ANOVA Improvement Scores on Critical Thinking

Treatment	Mean	Standard Deviation
Total:		
Models	-.167	5.811
General procedures	7.667	5.465
Task-specific procedures	8.0	5.099
Written:		
Models	0	5.762
General procedures	5.667	3.327
Task-specific procedures	7.167	4.0

Source of Variation	df	Mean Square	F	Significance of F
Total:				
Group	2	128.167	4.29	.034
Error	15	29.878		
Written:				
Group	2	85.722	4.49	.03
Error	15	19.078		

Smagorinsky

ment for both the total ($t = 2.659$; $p < .05$) and written ($t = 1.855$; $p < .05$) measurements. (Contrasts between all three treatment groups, expressed with the results of a one-way ANOVA with three levels, are shown in Table 2.)

Discussion

The results of this study suggest that reliance on reading models alone is insufficient to improve writing. The read-analyze-write sequence described by Eschholz (1980) carries with it an assumption that by studying models students can develop an understanding of appropriate content knowledge, figure out how to structure their content knowledge so that it fits into the form delineated by the model, and render their ideas into coherent prose.

Table 2
ANOVA Improvement Scores on Purposeful Composing

Treatment	Mean	Standard Deviation
Total:		
Models	2.167	6.853
General procedures	8.333	10.132
Task-specific procedures	10.166	2.714
Written:		
Models	3.5	7.064
General procedures	5.5	9.628
Task-specific procedures	9.333	3.077

Source of Variation	df	Mean Square	F	Significance of F
Total:				
Group	2	105.389	2.014	.168
Error	15	52.333		
Written:				
Group	2	52.722	1.04	.378
Error	15	50.689		

The data from this study suggest that the typical student is not up to the formidable task of teaching him- or herself these composing procedures, a conclusion also reached by Eschholz, who advocated combining models with experience in general composing procedures.

Combining instruction in the forms essays take with instruction in procedural knowledge produced far better results. Both procedural treatments helped students think critically about the ideas generated, and students who were taught task-specific procedures made strong gains in relating definition elements. The addition of instruction in composing procedures clearly boosted the power of the models instruction. Other research suggests that the study of models increases the effectiveness of instruction in general composing procedures. Hillocks's (1984, 1986b) meta-analysis of experimental research on writing from 1963 to 1983 found that freewriting (one of the general composing procedures used in this study) is "only about two-thirds as effective as the average experimental treatment" (1986b, p. 249), while treatments involving an "inquiry" focus (the task-specific procedure in this study) "are nearly four times more effective than freewriting and over two-and-a-half times more powerful than the traditional study of model pieces of writing" (p. 249). Composition research over this 20-year period seems to show that instruction with models greatly enhances the effectiveness of instruction in general composing procedures.

This study supports the notion that writers who understand the relationship between form and content can improve their writing. Simply reading a model piece of writing, however, is insufficient to teach young writers how to produce compositions (see, for example, Greene, in press). A model seems to be most beneficial when learners have appropriate content knowledge and need to learn how to transform it into text; the model can illustrate how to relate the bits of knowledge within a coherent structure. While mindful readers like Ben Franklin might learn procedures for good writing through the diligent study of the masters, most novices need more direct instruction in composing strategies. Teachers and students need to understand how models can effectively complement other types of knowledge.

Important in this understanding is an awareness of the appropriate complexity of the models in terms of the students' content knowledge; the number of features stressed in the model and their relationships to other aspects of instruction; the placement of the model in the instructional sequence; and the allocation of instructional time for the study of models and

Smagorinsky

for instruction in other aspects of composing. Instruction that combines procedural knowledge related to content with carefully selected models can lead to substantial improvements in writing proficiency.

References

Andreach, J.R. (1976). The use of models to improve organizational techniques in writing. *Dissertation Abstracts International, 36*, 4980-A.

Bransford, J. (1979). *Human cognition: Learning, understanding, and remembering.* Belmont, CA: Wadsworth.

Collins, A., & Gentner, D. (1980). A framework for a cognitive theory of writing. In L.W. Gregg & E.R. Steinberg (Eds.), *Cognitive processes in writing* (pp. 51-72). Hillsdale, NJ: Erlbaum.

Corbett, E.P.J. (1965). *Classical rhetoric for the modern student.* New York: Oxford University Press.

Elbow, P. (1973). *Writing without teachers.* New York: Oxford University Press.

Emig, J. (1971). *The composing processes of twelfth graders.* Urbana, IL: National Council of Teachers of English.

Ennis, R. (1990). The extent to which critical thinking is subject-specific: Further clarification. *Educational Researcher, 19*(4), 13-16.

Eschholz, P.A. (1980). The prose models approach: Using products in the process. In T. Donovan & B.W. McClelland (Eds.), *Eight approaches to teaching composition* (pp. 21-36). Urbana, IL: National Council of Teachers of English.

Gorrell, R.M. (1977). Question II, 7. In R.B. Shuman, (Ed.), *Questions English teachers ask.* Rochelle Park, NJ: Hayden.

Greene, S. (in press). Mining texts in reading to write. *Journal of Advanced Composition.*

Hillocks, G. (1975). *Observing and writing.* Urbana, IL: ERIC/RCS and National Council of Teachers of English.

Hillocks, G. (1984). What works in teaching composition: A meta-analysis of experimental treatment studies. *American Journal of Education, 93*(1), 133-170.

Hillocks, G. (1986a). The writer's knowledge: Theory, research, and implications for practice. In A.R. Petrosky & D. Bartholamae (Eds.), *The teaching of writing* (pp. 71-94). Chicago, IL: University of Chicago Press and National Society for the Study of Education.

Hillocks, G. (1986b). *Research on written composition: New directions for teaching.* Urbana, IL: National Conference on Research in English and ERIC.

Hillocks, G. (in progress). Acquiring knowledge for writing: The processes and effects of three focuses of instruction.

Johannessen, L.R., Kahn, E., & Walter, C.C. (1982). *Designing and sequencing prewriting activities.* Urbana, IL: ERIC/RCS and National Council of Teachers of English.

Judy, S. (1980). The experiential approach: Inner worlds to outer worlds. In T. Donovan & B.W. McClelland (Eds.), *Eight approaches to teaching composition* (pp. 37-51). Urbana, IL: National Council of Teachers of English.

McCann, T., & Smagorinsky, P. (1988). *Prospectus for composition textbook.* Unpublished manuscript.

McPeck, J. (1990). Critical thinking and subject specificity: A reply to Ennis. *Educational Researcher, 19*(4), 10-12.

Murray, D.M. (1968). *A writer teaches writing.* Boston, MA: Houghton Mifflin.

Murray, D.M. (1980). Writing as process: How writing finds its own meaning. In T. Donovan & B.W. McClelland (Eds.), *Eight approaches to teaching composition* (pp. 3-20). Urbana, IL: National Council of Teachers of English.

Polya, G. (1954). *Mathematics and plausible reasoning.* Princeton, NJ: Princeton University Press.

Smagorinsky, P. (1989). The reliability and validity of protocol analysis. *Written Communication, 6*(4), 463-479.

Smagorinsky, P. (1991). The writer's knowledge and the writing process: A protocol analysis. *Research in the Teaching of English, 25*(3), 339-364.

Smagorinsky, P., McCann, T., & Kern, S. (1987). *Explorations: Introductory activities for literature and composition, grades 7-12.* Urbana, IL: ERIC/RCS and National Council of Teachers of English.

Smith, M.W. (1984). *Reducing writing apprehension.* Urbana, IL: ERIC/RCS and National Council of Teachers of English.

Stefl, L.D. (1981). The effect of a guided discovery approach on the descriptive paragraph writing skills of third grade pupils. *Dissertation Abstracts International, 42*, 2493-A.

Strupp, H.H., & Bloxom, A.L. (1973). Preparing lower-class patients for group psychotherapy: Development and evaluation of a role induction film. *Journal of Consulting and Clinical Psychology, 41*, 373-384.

Vinson, L.L.N. (1980). The effects of two prewriting activities upon the overall quality to ninth graders' descriptive paragraphs. *Dissertation Abstracts International, 41*, 927-A.

Cheryl L. Spaulding

— N I N E —

The Motivation to Read and Write

*D*uring the 1980s, interest in motivational issues surged among researchers and teachers in the fields of reading and writing. No longer was the only goal of reading and writing instruction to teach children *how* to read and write; teachers now encouraged children to *want* to read and write, both in and out of school, for academic and personal reasons. The whole language movement reflects this commitment to promoting student interest in and engagement with the processes of reading and writing (Goodman, 1986).

This attention to increasing students' engagement with reading and writing tasks seems warranted. We don't need specialists to tell us that many people in the United States no longer have much inclination to read and write. More and more, we in this country turn on the television news instead of reading the newspaper, rent a video instead of reading a novel or short story, and dial a phone number instead of writing a letter. We are a society of people who by and large *can* read and write, but who choose not to. To use Hynds's (1990) term, the literacy problem in the United States is to a great extent one of "aliteracy" as well as illiteracy. Hence, the efforts of reading and writing teachers to design instructional environments that will spark students' interest in and engagement with literacy tasks is a positive step.

One of the most obvious outcomes of this concern for the role of motivation in literacy learning is an abundance of articles—especially but not exclusively in the practitioner journals—addressing issues of student interest, engagement, and motivation (see, for example, Barbieri, 1987; Cleary, 1990; Hirschman, 1985; Johannessen, 1989; Lancy & Hayes, 1988; Rensenbrink,

1987; Sanders, 1987; Silver, 1989; Spaulding, 1989; Wepner, 1984). With very few exceptions, however, these articles are based on only a partial understanding of human motivation. In other words, most of the scholars and practitioners in the field of literacy instruction are unaware of what psychologists already understand about motivation. Indeed, Onore (1990) goes so far as to reject instructional practices based on what she and Boomer (1982) refer to as "the motivational model" (p. 65). Ironically, their proposed alternative (the "negotiated curriculum model") seems more consistent with the findings of contemporary work on human motivation than the model they want to replace. Onore and Boomer are typical of scholars in the fields of reading and writing instruction, most of whom seem unaware of motivation theory and its obvious compatibility with contemporary notions of literacy development and instruction.

The purpose of this chapter, therefore, is to illustrate how contemporary theory and research on human motivation can inform theory, research, and practice in reading and writing instruction. First, I present an overview of contemporary motivation theory, focusing especially on what motivation theorists call intrinsic motivation. Then I address three instructional domains—reading, writing, and literature (a special aspect of reading)—showing how scholars and practitioners in each of these domains tend to construe motivational issues in distinct ways. I conclude with a discussion of the need for a more unified concept of students' motivation to engage in literacy tasks, one that recognizes the inherent similarities between reading and writing processes and is consistent with what we know about motivation.

Contemporary Motivation Theory

According to Lepper (1988), there has recently been a resurgence of interest in motivation theory as psychologists try to apply the findings of cognitive psychology to fields such as education. The cognitive psychological models, built around the metaphor of the human brain as a computer, do not always translate well to nonlaboratory settings such as classrooms; they do not account for the influence of affective and social factors on individuals' willingness to expend effort on some endeavors and not others.

In the educational arena, motivation theory is typically used to explain why different students expend different amounts of energy on academic tasks. The underlying assumption of this work is that if we can understand why some students persevere when faced with challenging tasks and spend much time and effort to learn assigned material, then we will have some idea about how to help those students who are less motivated to do the same things. An additional underlying assumption is that if students are motivated to learn they will be more successful learners.

As is the case in many other fields of inquiry, the study of motivation theory is characterized by numerous and competing ideas; to do justice to them all is beyond the scope of this chapter. Instead I will frame the issues in this overview in terms of the theory I consider the most encompassing and inclusive. While some of the other theoretical frames use different terminology for their constructs and processes, they are usually describing the same underlying phenomena and hence have much in common with the discussion I present here. (For competing discussions of motivation theory, see Ames & Ames, 1984, 1985, 1989).

Extrinsic Motivation

Most scholars of human motivation point to two types of motivation: extrinsic and intrinsic (Deci, 1975; Deci & Ryan, 1985; Lepper, 1988; Spaulding, 1992). Extrinsic motivation is the more easily recognized and better understood, primarily because it makes intuitive sense. We can all recognize common extrinsic motivation in our own thought processes. We are extrinsically motivated to engage in an activity when we recognize that by doing so we are likely to experience what we perceive to be a positive or desirable outcome (Atkinson, 1974; Bandura, 1977). The desire to earn money is, for example, a common extrinsic motivation for undertaking an unpleasant task; other extrinsic goals include receiving praise from authority figures, attaining a higher social status, or obtaining good grades in school. Individuals can also be extrinsically motivated to *avoid* negative or undesirable outcomes. For example, students who study to avoid being punished for earning bad grades are also extrinsically motivated.

The point is that our behavior is extrinsically motivated when we are attempting to achieve some goal or outcome that is logically and inherently extrinsic to our behavior. The currently accepted theoretical explanation of extrinsic motivation is a cognitive reinterpretation of traditional reinforcement theory. In other words, the idea of extrinsic motivation is similar to the outcome-response connection posited by reinforcement theorists (Skinner, 1953), with the addition of individuals' cognitive assessment of the value and likelihood of attaining specific outcomes (Atkinson, 1974; Vroom, 1964).

Intrinsic Motivation

Most of the motivational strategies and techniques used in American classrooms today are consistent with our definition of extrinsic motivation, but recent work in reading and writing instruction has focused on a more intrinsic form of motivation. Intrinsic motivation is characterized by a desire to engage in an activity because doing so brings personal satisfaction, regardless of potential extrinsic outcomes: "Intrinsically motivated behavior [is] defined as behavior undertaken for its own sake, for the enjoyment it provides, the learning it permits, or the feelings of accomplishment it provokes" (Lepper, 1988, p. 292).

Essentially, intrinsic motivation is the byproduct of two sets of self-perceptions, those of competence and self-determination (Deci, 1975, 1980; Deci & Ryan, 1985; Lepper & Hoddel, 1989). When individuals perceive themselves as being capable of completing a specific task or engaging in a specific endeavor *and* they perceive themselves as having some degree of control over that task or endeavor, then they are likely to be intrinsically motivated to engage in that task or endeavor. Conversely, if either of these perceptions is not present, intrinsic motivation is also likely to be missing.

Let me give you an example to illustrate the role that each of these self-perceptions plays in directing human behavior. If I were told that I had won a trip for myself and my friends to anyplace in the world as long as I was willing to pilot the airplane, I would not be highly motivated to take advantage of the offer. My reason for refusing the prize would be that I do not believe I am capable of piloting an airplane without doing harm to myself, my fellow passengers, and to someone else's property. My perceptions of competence would be low (or in this case maybe nonexistent), precluding any intrinsic motivation to take the trip. Not everyone, however, would feel the way I do about piloting a plane. Last year when I used this example with a group of teachers, one man in the audience told me that he would simply take flying lessons. Obviously, he believed that with the right help he was capable of learning how to fly; I, however, do not believe I have that capability. Thus, when individuals' perceptions of competence are low, opportunities to be self-determining will be meaningless to them and they are not likely to be motivated, intrinsically or otherwise.

On the other hand, imagine that I have won another trip, this time a month-long drive through New England and down the coast. To accept this offer, all I have to do is agree to take the trip as it has been planned. And planned it has been: my hotel reservations have been made; my meals have been ordered in advance at restaurants already chosen; my route has been mapped out down to the parks, towns, and cities I will visit and how long I can stay at each place. Indeed, none of the decisions travelers usually make for themselves remains to be made. Even though I feel thoroughly capable of taking this trip, I would not be too excited about it because I enjoy discovering things for myself and making my own decisions. My intrinsic interest in this trip would certainly be compromised because my perceptions of personal control have been undermined.

Most theorists who attempt to explain intrinsic motivation deal with perceptions of both competence and control in their theoretical constructions. Some tend to emphasize issues of competence over those of control (Bandura, 1986; Harter & Connell, 1983; Schunk, 1989a), while others emphasize control over competence (deCharms, 1968; Deci, 1975; Deci & Ryan, 1985; Lepper, 1988). What seems evident from a review of this literature is that *both* constructs are necessary to account fully for the psychological state of intrinsic motivation. My own work (Spaulding, 1989, 1990), however, suggests that while both sets of self-perceptions are required for intrinsic motivation, perceptions of competence are more important than perceptions of control when trying to explain individuals' task-related engagement. It is only when a strong self-perception of competence exists that having the opportunity to control decision making is critically important.

By way of illustrating this last point, consider again the two vacations just described. In the car trip through New England, my opportunities to feel as if I were determining the course of events myself were undermined. However, despite the fact that I might not enjoy the trip as much as I would if I were making my own decisions, I still might be willing to make the best of it and go. But in the case of the airplane trip, my perceived inability to pilot a plane would thoroughly preclude my taking advantage of the offer. I am likely to avoid altogether situations that make me feel incompetent unless I receive the assistance I need to perform well in those situations.

To illustrate the importance of receiving needed assistance, consider one more vacation example. If I were going to travel to a land where the people's customs and language were unfamiliar to me, I would very likely want to travel with a guide and have all my travel plans prearranged by a travel agent. In other words, when my perceptions of competence are low, loss of control over the planning process is more welcome, primarily because

I'm more apt to view outside planning as much-needed assistance than an unnecessary hindrance. Again, my perceptions of competence or my chance to get the assistance I need to perform competently are more critical than opportunities to take personal control. Worth reiterating, though, is the common finding in the literature that when perceptions of both competence and self-determination are high, intrinsic motivation is usually high as well (Arlin, 1975; Rodin, Rennert, & Solomon, 1980; Spaulding, 1990).

Perhaps unfortunately for educators, this definition of intrinsic motivation as a byproduct of individuals' perceptions of competence and control makes an uneasy match with the instructional models that have guided educational practice in the United States over the last hundred years. The constructs of competence and self-determination employed by motivation theorists are often in opposition to the views of instructional practice that fill our practitioner journals, methods textbooks, and inservice workshops. Effective instructional programs have been designated as either teacher-centered or student-centered (Cuban, 1982, 1984), and teachers have been prodded either to ensure student competence through highly teacher-directed instruction (Rosenshine, 1987) and minimal competency testing (Popham, 1985) or to foster well-rounded development by encouraging students to make their own curricular decisions based on their interests and future plans (Kohl, 1969; Silberman, 1970). Our tendency to separate instructional practice into teacher-centered and student-centered models means that we help students to feel and be competent or to feel and be self-determining, but rarely both. The result may be that some students' intrinsic motivation to engage in academic endeavors is precluded.

Academic Motivation and Instruction

If we break the larger field of language arts down into subfields of reading, writing, and literature, we will recognize that each subfield tends to reflect only one side of the intrinsic motivation coin. Of the three fields, scholars in reading are the most likely to draw directly on motivation theory and research when addressing issues of student engagement with comprehension tasks.

Reading

The field of reading has been predominately concerned with issues of competence. Some scholars have studied readers' skill at decoding words using phonetic and context clues; others have focused on the role that prior knowledge of discourse structures and topics plays in reading. During the last decade, concepts well established in the motivation literature have made their way into studies of reading processes and instruction. This new interest in motivational psychology parallels a shift in the field away from the more limited view of reading as a collection of cognitive skills and bodies of prior knowledge, and toward a concept of reading as a collection of cognitive skills, bodies of prior knowledge, and the metacognitive strategies needed to manage and monitor the successful use of skills and knowledge (Baker & Brown, 1984). As reading researchers began to consider more carefully the role of metacognition in learning to read, their cognitive variables (e.g., goal setting, self-monitoring, self-verbalization) began to look more and more like the variables that motivation theorists such as Bandura (1986), Rohrkemper (1986), and Schunk (1989a, 1989b) were studying. It was only a matter of time before the two fields came into direct contact (Paris & Oka, 1986; Schunk & Rice, 1987).

Thus, the bulk of research on motivational issues in reading instruction focuses on metacognitive strategies and strategy instruction (Brown, Palincsar, & Armbruster, 1984; Palincsar & Brown, 1984; Paris, Cross, & Lipson, 1984; Paris, Lipson, & Wixson, 1983; Paris & Oka, 1986; Schunk, 1986). Typically, students in strategic reading programs are taught (usually through modeling) a specific set of metacognitive strategies that have been found to improve comprehension. Students are then required to practice the strategies under the guidance of the teacher or a more expert peer, who typically provides feedback about the students' progress in learning the strategies. Ultimately, learners carry out the strategies independently, monitoring and discussing with others their use in real reading situations. The goals of these training studies and programs are to develop readers' declarative, procedural, and conditional knowledge about the metacognitive strategies that characterize effective reading (Paris & Oka, 1986). That is, the readers must know what the strategies are (declarative), how to carry them out (procedural), and when to use them (conditional).

When researchers address motivational issues in these training studies, they are usually attempting to understand why students who have the requisite knowledge to carry out newly learned strategies do not always do so. Researchers have shown that students who believe both that they know how to use the strategies they have learned and that using them is likely to lead to better comprehension of texts are the ones most likely to engage in efforts actually to use them (Brown, 1988; Schunk, 1986; Schunk & Rice, 1987).

One need look no further than Bandura's work on participant modeling—a treatment designed to develop perceptions of efficacy (or competence) by means of performance attainments (Bandura, 1977; Bandura, Jeffery, & Gajdos, 1975; Bandura, Jeffery, & Wright, 1974)—for an example of the similarity between motivation theory and training programs designed to enhance students' use of metacognitive strategies when reading. Although Bandura was focusing on the treatment of phobias, which usually takes place in clinical settings, his description of participant modeling sounds very much like something that would go on in classrooms with strategic reading programs:

> The participant modeling approach...utilizes successful performances as the primary vehicle of psychological change. In implementing participant modeling, therapists...structure the environment so that clients can perform successfully despite their incapacities. This is achieved by enlisting a variety of response induction aids, including preliminary modeling of threatening activities, graduated tasks, enactment over gradual temporal intervals, joint performance with the therapist, protective aids to reduce the likelihood of feared consequences and variation in the severity of the threat itself. As treatment progresses, the supplementary aids are withdrawn so that clients cope effectively unassisted. Self-directed mastery experiences are then arranged to reinforce a sense of personal efficacy (1977, p. 196).

The primary goal of programs such as participant modeling and strategic reading intervention is to produce individuals who are self-regulated and who can successfully and independently cope with the demands of the target situation, whether it be picking up a snake or learning to read. We must be careful here not to confuse self-regulation with self-determination. Self-regulation suggests that a person is able to complete tasks on his or her own, drawing on internalized competencies and strategies. To be self-determining, however, that person must not only be self-regulating, but must also have control over the tasks to be completed.

Consider the following example. If my teacher tells me to read a chapter from a textbook so that I can give a summary to the class, I might be highly self-regulated while working on that assignment, drawing on all of the strategies targeted in reading programs such as Palincsar and Brown's (1984) reciprocal teaching or Paris and Oka's (1986) informed strategies for learning. However, because the task is strictly defined, I will probably not feel self-determining while working on it. My teacher is the one who determined the specifics of the assignment, not me. Thus, reading researchers and practitioners developing and investigating instructional interventions tend to emphasize the competence part of the equation leading to intrinsic motivation, but they do not as often address the issue of students' perceived control.

An important and influential exception to this generalization is the theory behind the whole language approach to reading instruction (Goodman, 1986; Goodman, 1989). According to McGee and Lomax (1990), the major tenets of the whole language movement are "authenticity, risk taking, choice, [and] empowerment" (p. 133). These tenets are obviously more consistent with an emphasis on self-determination than they are with a focus on students' actual and perceived competence.

The incompatibility between whole language and strategic reading can best be explained by examining how the proponents of the former approach view reading instruction. Whole language emphasizes learning to write as a means of learning to read (Butler & Turbill, 1987; Hansen, 1987; Turbill, 1986) and reading real literature rather than basal readers and textbooks (Atwell, 1987; Johnson & Louis, 1987; Stewig & Sebesta, 1989). In other words, many reading specialists who have embraced whole language as an instructional philosophy have actually moved well beyond the field of reading, relying heavily on the work of writing and literary theorists for their justifications for practice. (As the next sections of this chapter illustrate, those in writing and literature instruction tend to view student engagement in terms of self-determination, not competence.) Whole language advocates' concern with student self-direction seems to stem from the extension of their theoretical base into these related fields.

Writing

In contrast to the emphasis on competence so prevalent in the literature on reading processes and instruction, the literature on writing processes and instruction tends to emphasize the importance of students' control over their texts and the writing situation. The term most often used to describe student control is "ownership" (Atwell, 1987; Graves, 1983). All writers, from beginners to professionals, should be allowed and encouraged to take ownership of their work, using their writing to express personal understandings of topics and to pursue their own academic and social purposes. The idea is that when students take ownership of their writing, their level of engagement will be high.

Graves (1983) was one of the first to use "ownership" with reference to writing processes and instruction; Atwell (1987) popularized the term with middle and secondary school English teachers. According to Atwell, "writers need...[the] three basics of time, ownership, and response" (p. 54). That is, they need an extended period of time to write, preferably every day; they need to control the writing situation and task; and they need other people to read (or listen to) what they have written and give them honest responses. Atwell's premise is that if these three conditions are met, students will become active, engaged writers who take pleasure in writing and in sharing their work with others. This goal sounds very much like Lepper's (1988) definition of intrinsic motivation, which emphasizes enjoyment of learning and feelings of accomplishment.

Graves and Atwell are clearly not alone in their belief that ownership is basic to helping students become interested and engaged writers (Jochum, 1989; Kirby, 1988; Schuster, 1983; Susi, 1986). Researchers working on writing processes and instruction have also picked up on this notion (Berkenkotter, 1983; Buddemier, 1983; Freedman, 1987; Goodman & Wilde, 1985; Hudson, 1986; Marshall, 1984, 1987; Wason, 1987; Zuercher, 1989). Unlike many reading researchers and instructors, those in the writing field obviously understand the importance of perceived control in explaining students' task-related engagement. What they give much less attention to, though, is the importance of perceived competence.

I do not mean to suggest here that Graves, Atwell, and their colleagues have been thoroughly unconcerned about students' writing competence. Indeed, a primary goal of most instructional programs is to improve student writing. In their programs, however, competence is not typically construed as a source or cause of students' motivation to write, but rather as an outcome. Their reasoning goes something like this: Students will be highly engaged with writing tasks and assignments that allow them to take control of their writing. They should be involved with selecting their own topics, targeting an audience, choosing a specific genre, finding their own voices, and expressing personal opinions. These opportunities to make choices about writing lead to heightened levels of interest in and commitment to that writing. Once students are committed to writing an effective piece, they will work hard to use or develop the competence to produce a polished piece of writing.

This approach does provide students with numerous opportunities to learn more about how to write well and effectively. My point is simply that Graves, Atwell, and their colleagues do not see this (or any other form of instructional support) as a major contributor to their students' intrinsic motivation to write. Rather, instructional support is made available to the students *after* they have become intrinsically interested in their writing.

My own work on students' writing-task engagement suggests that the contribution of ownership opportunities to students' writing-task engagement may be overestimated and the role of actual and perceived competence underestimated (Spaulding, 1989, 1990). My studies suggest that ownership opportunities lead to increased writing-task engagement only when students already feel *capable* of taking control of their writing assignments. When students perceive themselves as incompetent writers, providing opportunities to take ownership of writing assignments may actually lead to decreases in engagement.

Other researchers have also discussed the combined effect of perceived competence and control on students' writing-task engagement. Kirsch (1988) suggests that students will be successful writers only when they have confidence in themselves as writers *and* when they are knowledgeable about the rhetorical choices available to them. Bos (1988) describes a process-oriented writing program that encourages students to take ownership of their writing while encouraging teachers to model strategic thinking and writing so that students will know how to go about taking ownership. Of special interest is that both Kirsch and Bos were writing about ways to help less able student writers. Perhaps their understanding of the role of competence in promoting students' engagement with writing tasks is explained by the fact that they were working with student populations that traditionally have not had success in writing.

Another major exception to the heavy emphasis on ownership exists in Bereiter and Scardamalia's (1982) work. Like their colleagues studying metacognitive processes in strategic reading (Paris & Oka, 1986; Palincsar & Brown, 1984), Bereiter and Scardamalia focus on how teachers can help students develop competence with new and challenging writing tasks. Their instructional intervention, known as procedural facilitation, "refers to any reduction in the executive demands of a task that permits learners to make fuller use of the knowledge and skills they already have" (p. 52). The emphasis here is not on building new abilities in student writers but rather on helping them use their abilities to address the task at hand successfully.

Finally, Hillocks's (1986) work on writing instruction also emphasizes the role of the teacher in helping students learn to write effectively. His meta-analysis of experimental investigations compared four modes of writing instruction (presentational, natural process, environmental, and individualized) and found the strongest support for the environmental mode. According to Hillocks, this mode has as its characteristics clear and specific objectives, materials and problems selected to engage students in particular processes, and activities, such as small-group discussions. Teachers working in the environmental mode give few lectures and do not rely on teacher-led discussion; they structure activities so that students have opportunities to work on particular tasks in small groups before undertaking similar tasks independently (p. 122).

Although neither Bereiter and Scardamalia nor Hillocks specifically addresses issues of student motivation, Bandura (1986) has shown that the experience of success is the single greatest predictor of high levels of perceived competence for (and subsequent engagement with) similar tasks. Not surprisingly, both procedural facilitation and environmental instruction have much in common with strategic reading interventions, such as reciprocal teaching and informed strategies for learning. They model effective strategies for completing specific tasks, give students opportunities to practice them in collaborative settings, and then encourage students to use them independently in their day-to-day literacy-related activities.

Despite these few exceptions, however, the field of writing instruction stands in contrast to the field of reading instruction, construing issues of student engagement and motivation primarily in terms of students' opportunities to be self-determining rather than in terms of their ability to be self-regulating.

Literature

When I began writing this chapter, my plans were to discuss the implications of motivation theory and research for the fields of reading and writing instruction. Before getting too far, however, I realized that the field of literature instruction warranted attention as well. Surprisingly, even though many types of literary studies are founded on reading processes, the scholars in this field seem to have more in common with writing researchers and theorists than they do with their colleagues in traditional reading departments, at least from a motivational point of view.

In the 1970s, reader response theory—a view of literary response that puts readers at the center of the interpretive process—began to receive considerable attention (Flood & Lapp, 1988; Galda, 1988; Mailloux, 1990). Reader response theorists believe that the meaning of a piece of literature does not exist in the text or in the intentions of the author but instead is the result of each reader's encounter with the text. Some reader response theorists go so far as to say that there are as many meanings of a given text as there are readers of that text. While reader response theorists vary greatly in their specific theoretical configurations of the response process, they share a focus on how the reader creates meaning from text. This emphasis on the reader's construction of meaning tends to align the field of literature instruction with the field of writing instruction. Practitioners and researchers in both fields tend to relate the issues of engagement and motivation to students' opportunities to take personal control of their writing and literary interpretations.

Two reader response theorists who have had an enormous impact on literature instruction are Bleich (1978) and Rosenblatt (1978). Although Bleich attributes the reader with a greater amount of personal control over the text than does Rosenblatt, they both support a pedagogy that encourages readers to make personal sense of literary works and to express their interpretations in their writing about literature, as well as in whole-class and small-group discussions. Articles in the practitioner journals draw on the works of these scholars, either directly or indirectly, in their claims that students should be given the "authority" to interpret texts independently (Beehler, 1988; Martin, 1989; Miall, 1986; Probst, 1986a), that they should learn to view themselves as meaning *makers* rather than *receivers* (McAnulty, 1989; Mitchell, 1989; Musgrave, 1987; Probst, 1986a,b; Smith, 1989; Swaffar, 1986), that they should go beyond mere comprehension of literary works to include their unique affective and aesthetic responses (Eddins, 1989; Gambell, 1986; Hynds, 1990; Probst, 1988), and that they should be encouraged to choose some of the literature they read in school (Dellit, 1984; Lott, 1989). In addition, researchers of students' responses to literature and literature instruction often focused their studies on the issue of student control (Eeds & Wells, 1989; Flood & Lapp, 1988; Marshall, 1987, 1990; Rogers, 1987).

While the versions of reader response theory that have influenced the teaching of literature (especially at the elementary and secondary school levels) have largely been oriented toward student control of the interpretive process, other versions are more related to competence than to control. Fish's (1980) and Mailloux's (1982) work emphasizing interpretive strategies and conventions falls into this category. According to these researchers, individuals interpret literary works with a set of learned strategies or conventions, and differences in interpretations can be traced to differences in these strategies or conventions. Many of the strategies used to interpret a literary work are learned unconsciously as a result of readers' socialization into a community where certain world views are shared; other strategies and conventions are learned in more formal, academic settings, such as literature classrooms. While Fish's and Mailloux's versions of reader response theory account for variation in individuals' responses to literary texts, they tend to support a pedagogy that focuses less on student control than on ways to help students develop competence in their use of specific interpretive strategies and conventions. With a few exceptions, however (see, for example, Athanases, 1988), Fish's and Mailloux's theories have not filtered down to the classrooms of U.S. elementary and secondary schools.

One other exception to the emphasis on student control of literary interpretations exists in Hillocks's (1980; Hillocks & Ludlow, 1984) work on the teaching of literature. While Hillocks and his colleagues (Kahn, Walter, & Johannessen, 1984) do not advocate stripping students of their interpretive authority, they do emphasize the need to teach a hierarchy of skills needed to comprehend and interpret literature. This emphasis on competent use of comprehension and interpretive skills aligns these researchers more clearly with practitioners and theorists of reading instruction.

On the whole, however, the field of literature is much like that of writing, construing issues of student engagement primarily in terms of opportunities to exercise authority over literary interpretations rather than in terms of ability to be self-regulating interpreters.

Motivating Readers and Writers

Intrinsic motivation is a byproduct of feeling both competent and in control, of being self-regulating and self-determining (Deci, 1975, 1980; Deci & Ryan, 1985; Lepper & Hoddel, 1989). Therefore, when reading instruction focuses on students' perceptions of competence at the expense of their perceptions of control, some students' intrinsic motivation is undermined. Similarly, when writing and literature instruction focus on students' perceptions of control at the expense of their perceptions of competence, some students' intrinsic motivation will suffer.

Perhaps we should not be surprised that these three fields emphasize different sides of the motivational coin. The act of writing seems, on the surface, to provide individuals with more opportunities to take control and to pursue their own purposes than does the act of reading. And literature seems to allow readers greater latitude in interpretation than do textbooks because of the greater ambiguity usually found in the former type of writing. Thus, the focus on control in the fields of writing and literature and the focus or competence in the field of reading may seem to fit the inherent nature of the activities themselves.

Recent research into the relationships between reading and writing, however, suggests that these processes are more similar than they might appear (Langer, 1986; Shanahan, 1984; Stotsky, 1983). Like writing and interpreting literature, reading involves constructing meaning. Readers do not simply receive what is written on the page; they use prior knowledge to construct interpretations of texts, even when they are reading strictly for information. And like readers, both writers and interpreters of literature draw on a collection of skills, strategies, and conventions that they must use effectively in order to write and interpret successfully. In fact, the similarities between the reading, writing, and interpreting processes should lead us to adopt the same motivational frameworks for each process, not different ones.

Motivation theory itself argues against adopting distinct frameworks for each subfield. Perceived control and perceived competence have both been found to be important predictors of engagement across widely disparate activities, ranging from academic endeavors (Schunk 1989a, 1989b; Spaulding, 1990) to athletic activities (Feltz, Landers, & Raeder, 1979) and from giving up smoking (DiClemente, 1981) to watching television (Salomon, 1984). There is no reason not to adopt the same motivational theory to explain students' engagement with tasks as similar as reading, writing, and interpreting literature.

Researchers and teachers of language arts must therefore pay attention to students' perceived competence and control—to their ability to self-regulate and their opportunities to be self-determining. One instructional model that addresses both issues is Langer and Applebee's (1986, 1987; Applebee & Langer, 1983) version of instructional scaffolding. This approach consists of five principles of effective language arts instruction. Langer and Applebee do not advocate specific practices but instead assert that a wide range of practices would be consistent with the model and that teachers are the ones who should choose—or even design—specific practices that are consistent with the five principles (Applebee, 1988).

Of the five principles, four focus on competence in much the same way that interventions such as reciprocal teaching (Palincsar & Brown, 1984), Informed Strategies for Learning (Paris & Oka, 1986), procedural facilitation (Bereiter & Scardamalia, 1982), and environmental instruction (Hillocks, 1986) do. These four principles are referred to as "task appropriateness," "instructional support," "collaboration," and "internalization." Task appropriateness means that students should be working on tasks that are moderately challenging. Tasks that are too easy or too hard will do little to develop students' actual or perceived competence. When students successfully complete tasks that pose moderate challenges, they both increase their competence and learn to attribute their success to their ability and effort, resulting in enhanced *perceptions* of competence.

Instructional support means providing students with assistance when they are confronted with moderately challenging tasks. This can be provided by a teacher or a more competent peer. Strategy instruction interventions are excellent examples of how teachers and peers can give this needed support. Collaboration and internalization extend instructional support by providing students with opportunities to collaborate with others who know how to proceed with the task or assignment. Learners develop competence to carry out tasks independently by internalizing the cognitive structures, strategies, conventions, and processes used by the more skilled individual.

A primary goal of instructional scaffolding is obviously to increase students' actual and perceived academic competence. What makes it different from the other competence-enhancing models is its fifth principle: "ownership." In their descriptions of instructional scaffolding, Langer and Applebee actually put the principle of ownership at the top of the list. Teachers using instructional scaffolding to guide their instructional planning and practice encourage students to take personal control of reading and writing tasks, using these tasks to meet their own purposes and satisfy their own interests. Becoming self-regulating is not sufficient; students must use their new abilities to regulate themselves to achieve some personally defined, meaningful goals. Instructional scaffolding is, in other words, a blending of the perspectives seen in the fields of reading, writing, and literature; as such, it is a better framework for thinking through issues of student motivation in language arts classrooms.

Instructional scaffolding has not been widely researched. Because it does not consist of a set of specific practices, it cannot be compared with specific practices in training or intervention studies. As a theoretical construction, it demands studies that test its principles. Numerous questions about the model remain to be investigated: Should ownership opportunities be introduced in a lesson or an activity? Should students always be encouraged to take personal control of their reading, writing, and interpreting tasks? Or should students first develop some minimal level of actual and perceived competence in using the strategies and conventions needed to complete those tasks?

My own work in this area leads me to believe that individuals differ in the degree to which they are willing to take control of their learning. For example, in one study (Spaulding, 1989) I found that high school students reporting low, medium, and high levels of perceived writing competence had different responses to teachers with distinct instructional styles. Students reporting low and high levels of perceived competence were more engaged with writing tasks assigned in highly structured lessons that provided them with few opportunities to take control of their academic work. In contrast, students reporting a middle level of perceived competence were more engaged by less structured lessons offering numerous opportunities to take control of their work.

The results of this study suggest that a moderate level of perceived writing competence is necessary before students will be responsive to opportunities to take control of their writing assignments. For those students reporting high levels of perceived writing competence, however, the less structured and less teacher-controlled classroom situation was not conducive to high levels of task-related engagement. I speculate that these students, who typically have been very successful in school at least in part by meeting their teachers' expectations and conforming to the school rules, were uncomfortable with a teacher who was not specific about his or her expectations and did not require strict conformity.

In another study (Spaulding, 1990), I found that seventh grade students who reported a high level of perceived competence for typical school-based language arts tasks were more highly engaged with a writing assignment that was addressed to an audience other than their teacher, whereas students who reported a low level of perceived competence were more engaged with a writing assignment that did address their teacher. In other words, the frequently touted motivational benefits of having students write to "real" audiences (Atwell, 1987; Cohen & Riel, 1989) held true only for students who were confident of their linguistic competence.

On the basis of my research, I have come to the conclusion that some students will resist direct instruction in specific skills and strategies, while others will want and expect such assistance from their teachers. Some will seek opportunities to take charge of their assignments, pushing those assignments in directions that suit their interests and plans, while others will feel highly uncomfortable with assignments that require them to make choices and decisions.

Because of these individual differences in students' responses to a given instructional context, research investigating the effects of a specific intervention on students' academic motivation and task-related engagement should do more than look for main effects. One study reported by Willinsky (1990) compared a skill-sequence program with an expressive writing program, both of which were designed to teach first graders how to read and write. Contrary to his expectations, Willinsky found that the students in the expressive writing classrooms outperformed their peers in the skill-sequence classroom on only one of his four outcome measures: namely, writing vocabulary. The students in the expressive writing classrooms used a more varied array of words in their writing. No differences were found between the two groups for the three other outcome measures: functions evident in the students' writing; the students' attitudes toward writing; and the students' views of themselves as writers.

Because the design of this study allowed only for analyses of main effects, Willinsky was unable to determine whether students were more responsive to the expressive writing program or to the skill-sequence program. In other words, his conclusion that there were no differences between the programs on three of the outcome variables may be incorrect. Had he categorized the students along some dimension, such as their perceived linguistic competence, and then tested for interactions between the treatment condition and the targeted student characteristic, he may well have found that the two programs operated in different ways for different students.

As professional educators, we need to understand how individual differences in students' motivation interact with the five principles advocated in the instructional scaffolding model. The following areas deserve attention:

- How much instructional support is needed to ensure maximum levels of task-related engagement? Is it possible to provide too much instructional support? Do students differ in their motivational responses to such support?
- What differences are there in students' responses to instructional support provided by peers or teachers?
- How do students' needs and desires for instructional support change as a function of their growing competence with respect to a specific task or endeavor?
- How do students' needs and desires for instructional support change as a function of task difficulty?

As the above questions illustrate, a tension exists in the instructional scaffolding model, a tension between giving students the assistance they need to succeed on challenging tasks and giving them the opportunity to take control of their learning. Rather than falling back into the thinking that has characterized much of educational practice over the last century, this model embraces that tension between ensuring student competence and promoting student control. Truly effective teachers are the ones who learn how to work with this tension, increasing and decreasing instructional support and ownership opportunities as the occasion demands. This approach is highly consistent with theories of intrinsic motivation and should lead to a theory of language arts instruction that can be applied equally well to the subfields of reading, writing, and literature, at the same time as it helps teachers in their attempts to increase students' motivation to read and write.

References

Ames, C., & Ames, R.E. (Eds.). (1985). *Research on motivation in education: Vol. 2, the classroom milieu.* San Diego, CA: Academic.

Ames, C., & Ames, R.E. (Eds.). (1989). *Research on motivation in education: Vol. 3, goals and cognitions.* San Diego, CA: Academic.

Ames, R.E., & Ames, C. (Eds.). (1984). *Research on motivation in education: Vol. 1, student motivation.* San Diego, CA: Academic.

Applebee, A.N. (1988). The enterprise we are part of: Learning to teach. In M. Lightfoot & N. Martin (Eds.), *The word for teaching is learning: Essay for James Britton.* Portsmouth, NH: Heinemann.

Applebee, A.N., & Langer, J.A. (1983). Instructional scaffolding: Reading and writing as natural language activities. *Language Arts, 60,* 168-175.

Arlin, M. (1975). The interaction of locus of control, classroom structure, and pupil satisfaction. *Psychology in the Schools, 12,* 279-286.

Athanases, S. (1988). Developing a classroom community of interpreters. *English Journal, 77,* 45-48.

Atkinson, J.W. (1974). The mainspring of achievement oriented activity. In J.W. Atkinson & J.O. Raynor (Eds.), *Motivation and achievement.* Washington, DC: Winston.

Atwell, N. (1987). *In the middle: Writing, reading, and learning with adolescents.* Upper Montclair, NJ: Boynton/Cook.

Baker, L., & Brown, A.L. (1984). Metacognitive skills and reading. In P.D. Pearson (Ed.), *Handbook of reading research.* White Plains, NY: Longman.

Bandura, A. (1977). *Social learning theory.* Englewood Cliffs, NJ: Prentice Hall.

Bandura, A. (1986). *Social foundations of thought and action: A social cognitive theory.* Englewood Cliffs, NJ: Prentice Hall.

Bandura, A., Jeffery, R.W., & Gajdos, E. (1975). Generalizing change through participant modeling with self-directed mastery. *Behavior Research and Therapy, 13,* 141-152.

Bandura, A., Jeffery, R.W., & Wright, C.L. (1974). Efficacy of participant modeling as a function of response induction aids. *Journal of Abnormal Psychology, 83,* 56-64.

Barbieri, M. (1987). Writing beyond the curriculum: Why seventh grade boys write. *Language Arts, 64,* 497-504.

Beehler, S.A. (1988). Close vs. closed reading: Interpreting the clues. *English Journal, 77*(6), 39-43.

Bereiter, C., & Scardamalia, M. (1982). From conversation to composition: The role of instruction in a developmental process. In R. Glasser (Ed.), *Advances in instructional psychology* (vol. 2). Hillsdale, NJ: Erlbaum.

Berkenkotter, C. (1983). *Student writers and their audiences: Case studies of the revising decisions of three college freshmen.* Paper presented at the annual meeting of the Canadian Council of Teachers of English, Montreal, P.Q., Canada. (ED 236 618)

Bleich, D. (1978). *Subjective criticism.* Baltimore, MD: Johns Hopkins University Press.

Boomer, G. (Ed.). (1982). *Negotiating the curriculum: A teacher-student partnership.* Sydney, Australia: Ashton Scholastic.

Bos, C.S. (1988). Process-oriented writing: Instructional implications for mildly handicapped students. *Exceptional Children, 54,* 521-527.

Brown, A.L. (1988). Motivation to learn and understand: On taking charge of one's own learning. *Cognition and Instruction, 5,* 311-321.

Brown, A.L., Palincsar, A.S., & Armbruster, B.B. (1984). Instructing comprehension-fostering activities in interactive learning situations. In H. Mandl, N.L. Stein, & T. Trabasso (Eds.), *Learning and comprehension of text.* Hillsdale, NJ: Erlbaum.

Buddemier, R.E. (1983). See Tom write: Ownership in writing. *Dissertation Abstracts International, 43*, 2261A.

Butler, A., & Turbill, J. (1987). *Towards a reading-writing classroom.* Portsmouth, NH: Heinemann.

Cleary, L.M. (1990). The fragile inclination to write: Praise and criticism in the classroom. *English Journal, 79*(2), 22-28.

Cohen, M., & Riel, M. (1989). The effect of distant audiences on student writing. *American Educational Research Journal, 26*, 143-159.

Cuban, L. (1982, October). Persistent instruction: The high school classroom, 1900-1980. *Phi Delta Kappan, 64*, 113-118.

Cuban, L. (1984). *How teachers taught: Constancy and change in American classrooms: 1890-1980.* White Plains, NY: Longman.

deCharms, R. (1968). *Personal causation: The internal affective determinants of behavior.* San Diego, CA: Academic.

Deci, E.L. (1975). *Intrinsic motivation.* New York: Plenum.

Deci, E.L. (1980). *The psychology of self-determination.* Lexington, MA: D.C. Heath.

Deci, E.L., & Ryan, R.M. (1985). *Intrinsic motivation and self-determination in human behavior.* New York: Plenum.

Dellit, J. (1984). Literature and the question of choice. *Australian Journal of Reading, 7*, 200-204.

DiClemente, C.C. (1981). Self-efficacy and smoking cessation maintenance: A preliminary report. *Cognitive Therapy and Research, 5*, 175-187.

Eddins, D. (1989). Yellow wood, diverging pedagogies; or, the joy of text. *College English, 51*, 571-576.

Eeds, M., & Wells, D. (1989). Grand conversations: An exploration of meaning construction in literature study groups. *Research in the Teaching of English, 23*, 4-29.

Feltz, D.L., Landers, D.M., & Raeder, U. (1979). Enhancing self-efficacy in high avoidance motor tasks: A comparison of modeling techniques. *Journal of Sport Psychology, 1*, 112-122.

Fish, S. (1980). *Is there a text in this class? The authority of interpretive communities.* Cambridge, MA: Harvard University Press.

Flood, J., & Lapp, D. (1988). A reader response approach to the teaching of literature. *Reading Research and Instruction, 27*, 61-66.

Freedman, S.W. (1987). *Peer response groups in two ninth-grade classrooms* (Technical Report No. 12). Berkeley, CA: Center for the Study of Writing, University of California. (ED 287 171)

Galda, L. (1988). Readers, texts, and contexts: A response-based view of literature in the classroom. *New Advocate, 1*, 92-102.

Gambell, T.J. (1986). The teaching of literature. *English Quarterly, 19*, 142-152.

Goodman, K.S. (1986). *What's whole in whole language?* Portsmouth, NH: Heinemann.

Goodman, Y.M. (1989). Roots of the whole-language movement. *Elementary School Journal, 90*, 113-127.

Goodman, Y.M., & Wilde, S. (1985). *Writing development in third and fourth grade native American students (social context, linguistic systems, and creation of meaning).* A research report. Program in language and literacy, Occasional Paper No. 14. University of Arizona, Tucson, AZ. (ED 278 017)

Graves, D. (1983). *Writing: Children and teachers at work.* Portsmouth, NH: Heinemann.

Hansen, J. (1987). *When writers read.* Portsmouth, NH: Heinemann.

Harter, S., & Connell, J.P. (1983). A structural model of the relationships among children's academic achievement and their self-perceptions of competence, control, and motivational orientations in the cognitive domain. In J. Nicholls (Ed.), *Advances in motivation and achievement: Vol. 3, The development of achievement motivation.* Greenwich, CT: JAI.

Hillocks, G. (1980). Toward a hierarchy of skills in the comprehension of literature. *English Journal, 69,* 54-59.

Hillocks, G. (1986). *Research on written composition. New directions for teaching.* Urbana, IL: ERIC/RCS.

Hillocks, G., & Ludlow, L. (1984). A taxonomy of skills in reading and interpreting fiction. *American Educational Research Journal, 21,* 7-24.

Hirschman, P. (1985). Parents motivate children to read. *The Reading Teacher, 38,* 490-491.

Hudson, S.A. (1986). Context and children's writing. *Research in the Teaching of English, 20,* 294-316.

Hynds, S. (1990). Talking life and literature. In S. Hynds & D.L. Rubin (Eds.), *Perspectives on talk and learning.* Urbana, IL: National Council of Teachers of English.

Jochum, J. (1989). Whole language writing: The critical response. *Minnesota Reading Association Highlights, 11,* 5-7.

Johannessen, L.R. (1989). Teaching writing: Motivating inquiry. *English Journal, 78,* 64-66.

Johnson, T.D., & Louis, D.R. (1987). *Literacy through literature.* Portsmouth, NH: Heinemann.

Kahn, E.A., Walter, C.C., & Johannessen, L.R. (1984). *Writing about literature.* Urbana, IL: National Council of Teachers of English.

Kirby, D. (1988). Beyond interior decorating: Using writing to make meaning in the elementary school. *Phi Delta Kappan, 69,* 718-724.

Kirsch, G. (1988). Students' interpretations of writing tasks: A case study. *Journal of Basic Writing, 7,* 81-90.

Kohl, H.R. (1969). *The open classroom: A practical guide to a new way of teaching.* New York: New York Review.

Lancy, D.F., & Hayes, B.L. (1988). Interactive fiction and the reluctant reader. *English Journal, 77,* 42-45.

Langer, J.A. (1986). *Children reading and writing: Structures and strategies.* Norwood, NJ: Ablex.

Langer, J.A., & Applebee, A.N. (1986). Reading and writing: Toward a theory of teaching and learning. In E. Rothkopf (Ed.), *Review of research in education* (vol. 12). Washington, DC: American Educational Research Association.

Langer, J.A., & Applebee, A.N. (1987). *How writing shapes thinking: A study of teaching and learning.* Urbana, IL: National Council of Teachers of English.

Lepper, M.R. (1988). Motivational considerations in the study of instruction. *Cognition and Instruction, 5,* 289-309.

Lepper, M.R., & Hoddel, M. (1989). Intrinsic motivation in the classroom. In C. Ames & R. Ames (Eds.), *Research on motivation in education: Vol. 3, Goals and cognitions.* San Diego, CA: Academic.

Lott, J.G. (1989). Not teaching poetry. *English Journal, 78,* 66-68.

Mailloux, S. (1982). *Interpretive conventions: The readers in the story of American fiction.* Ithaca, NY: Cornell University Press.

Mailloux, S. (1990). The turns of reader-response criticism. In C. Moran & E.F. Penfield (Eds.), *Conversations: Contemporary critical theory and the teaching of literature.* Urbana, IL: National Council of Teachers of English.

Marshall, J.D. (1984). Schooling and the composing process. In A.N. Applebee (Ed.), *Contexts for learning to write: Studies of secondary school instruction.* Norwood, NJ: Ablex.

Marshall, J.D. (1987). The effects of writing on students' understanding of literary texts. *Research in the Teaching of English, 21,* 30-63.

Marshall, J.D. (1990). *Discussions of literature in inner city schools.* Paper presented at the annual meeting of the American Educational Research Association, Boston, MA.

Martin, B.K. (1989). Teaching literature as experience. *College English, 51,* 377-385.

McAnulty, S.J. (1989). Breaking the barriers: Teaching Martin Jamison's "Rivers." *English Journal, 78,* 75-78.

McGee, L.M., & Lomax, R.G. (1990). On combining apples and oranges: A response to Stahl and Miller. *Review of Educational Research, 60,* 133-140.

Miall, D.S. (1986). Authorizing the reader. *English Quarterly, 19,* 186-195.

Mitchell, S.P. (1989). Before the search: Genuine communication and literary research. *English Journal, 78,* 46-49.

Musgrave, P.W. (1987). Telling gaps: Adolescents making literary meaning. *English in Australia, 81,* 30-35.

Onore, C. (1990). Negotiation, language, and inquiry: Building knowledge collaboratively in the classroom. In S. Hynds & D.L. Rubin (Eds.), *Perspectives on talk and learning.* Urbana, IL: National Council of Teachers of English.

Palincsar, A.S., & Brown, A.L. (1984). Reciprocal teaching of comprehension-fostering and comprehension-monitoring activities. *Cognition and Instruction, 1,* 117-175.

Paris, S.G., Cross, D.R., & Lipson, M.Y. (1984). Informed strategies for learning: A program to improve children's reading awareness and comprehension. *Journal of Educational Psychology, 76,* 1239-1252.

Paris, S.G., Lipson, M.Y., & Wixson, K.K. (1983). Becoming a strategic reader. *Contemporary Educational Psychology, 8,* 293-316.

Paris, S.G., & Oka, E.R. (1986). Children's reading strategies, metacognition, and motivation. *Developmental Review, 6,* 26-56.

Popham, J.W. (1985). Measurement-driven instruction: It's on the road. *Phi Delta Kappan, 66,* 628-634.

Probst, R.E. (1986a). Mom, Wolfgang, and me: Adolescent literature, critical theory, and the English classroom. *English Journal, 75,* 33-39.

Probst, R.E. (1986b). Three relationships in the teaching of literature. *English Journal,* 75, 60-68.

Probst, R.E. (1988). Dialogue with a text. *English Journal,* 77, 32-38.

Rensenbrink, C. (1987). Writing as play. *Language Arts, 64,* 597-602.

Rodin, J., Rennert, K., & Solomon, S. (1980). Intrinsic motivation for control: Fact or fiction. In A. Baum, J.E. Singer, & S. Valios (Eds.), *Advances in environmental psychology II.* Hillsdale, NJ: Erlbaum.

Rogers, T. (1987). Exploring a socio-cognitive perspective on the interpretive processes of junior high school students. *English Quarterly, 20,* 218-230.

Rohrkemper, M. (1986). The functions of inner speech in elementary students' problem solving behavior. *American Educational Research Journal, 23,* 303-313.

Rosenblatt, L.M. (1978). *The reader, the text, the poem: The transactional theory of the literary work.* Carbondale, IL: Southern Illinois University Press.

Rosenshine, B. (1987). Direct instruction. In M.J. Dunkin (Ed.), *International encyclopedia of teaching and teacher education.* New York: Pergamon.

Salomon, G. (1984). Television is "easy" and print is "tough": The differential investment of mental effort in learning as a function of perceptions and attributions. *Journal of Educational Psychology, 76,* 647-658.

Sanders, M. (1987). Literacy as "passionate attention." *Language Arts, 64,* 619-633.

Schunk, D.H. (1986). Verbalization and children's self-regulated learning. *Contemporary Educational Psychology, 11,* 347-369.

Schunk, D.H. (1989a). Self-efficacy and cognitive skill learning. In C. Ames & R. Ames (Eds.), *Research on motivation in education: Vol. 3, goals and cognitions.* San Diego, CA: Academic.

Schunk, D.H. (1989b). Social cognitive theory and self-regulated learning. In B.J. Zimmerman & D.H. Schunk (Eds.), *Self-regulated learning and academic achievement: Theory, research, and practice.* New York: Springer-Verlag.

Schunk, D.H., & Rice, J.M. (1987). Enhancing comprehension skill and self-efficacy with strategy value information. *Journal of Reading Behavior, 19,* 285-302.

Schuster, C.I. (1983). *The un-assignment: Writing groups for advanced expository writers.* Paper presented at the annual meeting of the Wyoming Conference on Freshman and Sophomore English, Laramie, WY. (ED 234 409)

Shanahan, T. (1984). The nature of reading-writing relation: An exploratory multivariate analysis. *Journal of Educational Psychology, 76,* 466-477.

Silberman, C.E. (1970). *Crisis in the classroom: The remaking of American education.* New York: Random House.

Silver, K.O. (1989). The extended conference: A technique to encourage writing. *English Journal, 78,* 24-27.

Skinner, B.F. (1953). *Science and human behavior.* New York: Macmillan.

Smith, C.R. (1989). Walking into the middle of modern poetry: Teaching Byer's "Cornwalking." *English Journal, 78,* 77-79.

Spaulding, C.L. (1989). Understanding ownership and the unmotivated writer. *Language Arts, 66,* 414-422.

Spaulding, C.L. (1990). *Interactive effects of dependency on teacher, self-perceived linguistic competence, and psychological distance of teacher on students' writing task engagement.* Paper presented at the annual meeting of the American Educational Research Association, Boston, MA.

Spaulding, C.L. (1992). *Motivation in the classroom.* New York: McGraw-Hill.

Stewig, V.W., & Sebesta, S.L. (1989). *Using literature in the elementary classroom.* Urbana, IL: National Council of Teachers of English.

Stotsky, S. (1983). Research on reading/writing relationships: A synthesis and suggested directions. *Language Arts, 60,* 627-642.

Susi, G.L. (1986). Christian and the question mark: A story of ownership. *The Reading Teacher, 40,* 132-135.

Swaffar, J.K. (1986). Reading and cultural literacy. *Journal of General Education, 38,* 70-84.

Turbill, J. (1986). *Now we want to write.* Portsmouth, NH: Heinemann.

Vroom, V.H. (1964). *Work and motivation.* New York: Wiley.

Wason, E.L. (1987). Writing across the curriculum. *Canadian Journal of English Language Arts, 11,* 5-23.

Wepner, S.B. (1984). Motivation and computers: A real incentive for teachers. *The Reading Teacher, 38,* 363-364.

Willinsky, J. (1990). *The new literacy: Redefining reading and writing in the schools.* New York: Routledge.

Zuercher, N.T. (1989). *Students' self-assessment.* Paper presented at the annual Conference on Writing Assessment, National Testing Network in Writing, Montreal, P.Q., Canada.

Teacher Research

— T E N —

Children's Book-Selection Strategies

The readers workshop format for teaching reading responds to individual learning styles and accommodates each student's abilities and interests (Atwell, 1987). It mirrors the writing workshop format with which it is integrated. The case study presented in this chapter provides an ethnographic account of how the students in my first grade readers workshop selected their own reading texts, the trade books with which they learned to read. This aspect of the readers workshop was chosen for special examination because during previous years my students had said that choosing the books was the hardest part of learning to read.

This study shows how I set up the readers workshop at the beginning of the school year. As the year progressed I watched the students' book-selection processes and learned ways to facilitate this prereading activity. I also found that for many students, "books" written by other students in the class were the reading material of choice. Evidently, for these students, the reading/writing connection was very clear.

Setting the Stage

Twenty-two apprehensive first graders entered Room 2. Parents craned their necks as they tried to catch one last glimpse of their precious children, who would be away from home for a full day of school for the first time. Inside the classroom, the children waited for me to break the uneasy silence. Another school year was beginning, but there would be nothing mundane about it. I would be addressing my students from a new stance: that of researcher as well as teacher.

I had arranged the desks in one large semicircle with a smaller one inside the first. The desks weren't touching, but the arrangement promoted a feeling of community. I had brought in two cardboard boxes full of books from our town library and had checked out many additional books from our school library. Some of the books focused on our first unit of study in science, others were personal favorites. These books, ranging from picture books and easy readers on up through more difficult texts, were on display throughout the room: standing on top of the bookshelves, on the window sills, and on the science table. Some were neatly tucked into the bookshelves with only their spines showing. Some were still in the boxes and out of sight in my closet.

This was the second year that the students in my first grade classroom would be using trade books for their texts as they evolved into readers. The commercial reading programs had been put on the shelf; the basal readers were used as anthologies. Phonetic and word-decoding skills would be taught to the students in the context of their reading materials rather than in isolation. I also taught skills minilessons frequently throughout the year.

That first morning we talked about what the students expected to learn in the first grade. Most of them thought that they would learn to read. I told the students that we would indeed be learning to read and that they should look at the books that were all around our room because they would be able to choose one of them to read during quiet reading time later in the day. Then I said, "Let's get started with our reading right now."

Some of the students looked at me in disbelief; some tried to tell me that they couldn't read. Undeterred, I moved an easel to the center of the classroom. I then pointed to each word as I read from a big book about a little girl's first day of first grade.

We read this big book several times during that first day of school, and I encouraged the students to join me in saying the words. After lunch I distributed copies of the same book to each student so they could read together as a class. Before they went home we reread the big book, once with me leading and once together as a group. I pointed out that they truly had learned to read this book and sent home copies for them to read to their families. From that first day I referred to my students as readers, just as we refer to them as writers in writers workshops.

We also started our quiet reading time that first day. Each student selected a book. Everyone was to remain at her or his desk during the quiet reading time, and reading was the only activity that was to take place. I, too, read silently during this time. That first day, we sustained the quiet reading for five minutes. At the end of that time, I asked if anyone would like to tell the class what she or he had been reading. Eventually most of the students did volunteer to share something, if nothing more than the title or a favorite illustration from their book. In this way the students got to see or hear about many books. Some of them already had an idea of which one they would like to read the next day.

The second day of school, I took some of the books out of my closet to share with the class. These were favorites of mine and I tried to let my enthusiasm for them rub off on my students. I told a little about each book or read a page or two, just enough to whet the students' desire to read it. I had selected books with repetitive language, in predictable language patterns. Some of the books had no words at all. I set the books on display or allowed a student to take the one I had just finished describing. We had a quiet reading time and talked as a group about the books we were reading. The children seemed to appreciate this opportunity to enjoy books with no interruptions or distractions.

We began to develop a routine. When the students came into the room each morning, they would select their books and have a quiet reading time. Then we would all assemble on the carpet and I would read to the students. Often I would pick a particular author and we'd concentrate on learning about this writer, reading as many of his or her books as we could find. We also started our regular weekly visits to the school library so the students had even more books to choose from when it came time for quiet reading. Later in the fall, I introduced monthly trips to our town library in order to provide even more books for the children to choose from. However, this class was a lively group and our first trip there was almost a disaster. Getting the students to settle down and find two or three books they wanted to check out was not an easy task, especially since they had not yet developed strategies for selecting their books. Also, many of the students were unfamiliar with the layout of the library.

Selecting Books

After just a few weeks of school, the students could recognize quite a few books that we had read as a class. They also recognized books their peers had described when we shared what we'd read during quiet reading time.

From the very beginning, though, each student seemed to have a unique style in selecting books. I began to focus my work as a researcher on how individuals choose their reading materials.

Robert was a chunky 6-year-old with a husky voice and rosy round cheeks. He lived with his parents and a 20-year-old brother; his grandparents lived next door. As the only child in a family of adults, he functioned in an adult world and loved to carry on adult conversations. He had a keen interest in earth-moving equipment and trucks, and he seemed to gravitate toward books on this subject.

Patrick, on the other hand, was about average height and weight for a 6-year-old. He lived with his parents and two brothers, one older and one younger. Patrick functioned very quietly in the classroom and had a wide variety of interests. He found almost any book interesting. He would take more reading materials to his desk than he could possibly read during quiet reading time and then reluctantly put back the unread books at the end of our readers workshop. He excelled in all academic areas of our curriculum.

Toward the end of October I introduced individual reading conferences. I told the students that they were to bring three books they had read to the conference. During the conference, we first discussed the books that the student had brought. Then the student picked one of the books on which to focus the conference. We would talk about the story line, the main character, or the setting. Sometimes we'd talk about whether the story was make believe or real; sometimes we tried to decide if there was a lesson we should learn from the story. I would ask the student to read a favorite page or part to me. These book talks were conducted person to person, not adult to child. It was a most enjoyable part of the school day for me.

My goal was to hold an individual reading conference with each child once a week. When the students figured out that these conferences were taking place on a regular basis, they realized that they needed to keep discovering and reading more books in order to be ready for their next conference. For example, Robert could no longer look only at the pictures in the books about earth-moving equipment because, for the most part, he could not read the text of these books and so could not share with me. I noted a change in the type of reading material he chose. He began to rely heavily on the books that I had read to the class, books with repetitive language. When I asked him why he had picked these books, he would reply that he liked the illustrations. Looking at books and learning from the pictures was not eliminated for

Robert, but a new dimension to his involvement with books had been added: he was now trying to read the text.

Robert was not the only one relying on books I had read to the class; during October and November Patrick, too, chose from these books. In fact, in October 71 percent of the students chose books that I had read to the class for their individual reading conferences.

I had long known that it was important to read to the students, but the extent of the impact my reading appeared to have on these beginning readers took me by surprise. In retrospect, I realize that using the books that I had read to them gave the students a starting point: it allowed them to imitate reading behavior by saying the familiar words they had heard me read.

I also discovered, almost by accident, how much the students liked to hear their favorite stories over and over again. In November, I wrote about this in my teaching log:

> One thing that is interesting to me is the effect that reading a story more than once can have on my students. Many teachers, which in the past included me, think that they have to "spring" a book on kids...take them by surprise.
>
> However, I am discovering what wonderful things happen when kids get to experience a book more than once. Their sense of expectation and anticipation as we approach their favorite part, or a scary or silly part, is something to behold. They focus on favorite phrases, catchy words, repetitive phrases.
>
> Sometimes they begin to giggle before I get to the funny part of a familiar story. I have looked up from my reading to see students clutching each other as a particularly scary passage approaches.
>
> I am also learning to put out books that I will be reading to the class. Just being familiar with the book, looking at the pictures, seems to heighten their involvement in and enjoyment of the story. This must somehow be involved with the important reading skill of making predictions.

During the individual conferences in November, when I asked my students why they had chosen a particular book for the conference, their most frequent response was "because I can read it." Their reading repertoire was not that wide at this point in the school year.

Expanding Options

By December, other aspects of our readers workshop were in place. Our quiet reading time each morning was now extended to 12 minutes and was followed by reading in pairs rather than a discussion. I allowed the students to decide who they would like to work with, and for the most part this procedure went well.

Also in December, we began to take a few minutes each day for "Book Share." An entry in my teaching log from December describes this aspect of the workshop:

> Today we began our Book Share. I invited the students to write their names on the chalkboard if they had read a good book that they would like to tell the rest of the class about. Stephen accepted my invitation. He and Joey had been reading together. Joey, who had been taught how to read the book by another student, was feeling very confident and successful in his role as tutor to Stephen.
>
> Stephen felt that he needed Joey to share the book properly. I asked Stephen why he enjoyed the book enough to want to share it with the class. He said that it was good and the words were easy to read. Then he and Joey proceeded to take turns reading pages of the book. They did a beautiful job and their classmates were impressed.

I could now clearly see the effect that reading in pairs and Book Share were having on the students' book-selection processes. They were exposing each other to books that they had read during quiet reading time. Adults often take the recommendation of a friend when they are looking for something to read. Likewise, my beginning readers were choosing books that they had seen their friends reading, books that their partners had brought for reading in pairs, or books that had been discussed at Book Share.

During the writers workshop portion of our day, the students were writing and "publishing" their own books. These, too, were available for use at quiet reading time as well as for reading in pairs. These were very popular selections; some students would take stacks of these books to their desks. In December, once again my students told me that they picked certain books for their individual reading conferences because they could read them and because they liked the illustrations. But now student-written books began to be prominent at the reading conferences. Several students chose their own published books or those of their classmates for the focal point of their reading conference. Even though these books were not particularly easy to read, the language patterns were familiar. At times the author had served as tutor to the classmate who wanted to read the book.

The students were reading and replacing books from our classroom library every day, and as fall turned to winter, organizing all the books that we had in the classroom was becoming a problem. We needed a system. We developed some ways to categorize the books in our room: we sorted the books by author and by topic. This system for organizing our reading materials also seemed to help the students select books. It eliminated a lot of the aimless wandering among the books that invariably occurred when it was time to make selections. For some students, it seemed to enhance the development of certain strategies for selecting books. Patrick, for example, discovered a favorite author, and would go straight to that author's section in our classroom each morning. Reading books by an author whose work they have enjoyed previously is a book-selection strategy used by many adults. I considered this to be a rather mature strategy for selecting books, but some of my beginning readers had already learned to employ this technique.

Yet with all the options I was giving my students, in November and December the majority of them (some 60 percent, as opposed to the 71 percent in October) continued to tell me that the reason they chose a particular book for their reading conference was simply that they could read it. As I wrote in my teaching log on the first of December:

> I am finding that, across the board, almost all of my students' book selections at this point in their reading careers are made on the basis of the book's readability. The students are simply choosing books because they can read them. It will be interesting to see if this changes as they become more proficient readers.
>
> But this year's class does not seem to be having quite as much trouble as last year's group did in selecting the books they read. I wonder if it is the group of children or the fact that I am becoming more proficient at facilitating this aspect of the readers workshop for my students.

In January we held our first reading incentive program to encourage the students to read at home. The class was divided into two teams. The children earned a point for each page they read at home, and team scores were tallied.

Figure 1
Questionnaire Sent to Parents and Guardians

Please put a checkmark beside the statements that apply to your child.

☐ My child chooses to read books that have been read aloud to her/him.

☐ My child reads books that we already have at home.

☐ My child reads books that we get from the library.
How did your child go about selecting books at the library? _____
_____

☐ My child chooses books that are by an author he/she has previously read (Mercer Mayer, Eric Carle, etc.).

☐ My child chooses books this way: _____
_____

Parents' cooperation for this project was obviously essential. Involving parents in this way made me realize that I needed to get some information from the parents for my study. I wanted to know how each child selected the books she or he read at home. So I wrote a letter to parents and guardians and asked that they answer a few questions (reproduced in Figure 1). From the 22 letters I sent home, I received 19 responses. The overwhelming majority of the parents and guardians indicated that their children read books that they already had at home. The second most frequent response was that children chose to read books by an author whose work they had read previously. A breakdown of the responses is shown in Figure 2.

At this stage in the school year, we began to rate all the books of a certain type that we had read as a class. For example, we listed all the fairy tales that we had read and rated each as "excellent," "good," or "OK." I hoped that this process would encourage the children to think critically about text and to learn that, for instance, they could stop reading a book they weren't enjoying.

By January, the students began to give me more diverse responses to the question "Why did you select this book?" Some responded that they chose the book because they liked the illustrations. Others still chose their own published books or those of their classmates for their reading conferences. The reading/writing connection seemed very clear to these students.

Figure 2
Results of the Questionnaire

My child reads books for this reason

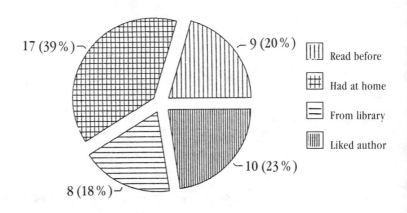

17 (39%)

9 (20%)

10 (23%)

8 (18%)

|||| Read before

⊞ Had at home

☰ From library

||||| Liked author

Note: Percentages reflect multiple answers from 19 households.

But many of my beginning readers seemed to have reached a turning point: they began to develop enough confidence in their reading ability to risk choosing an unfamiliar book.

From January to the end of the school year, only roughly one-third of the students continued to choose books that I had read to the class for their reading conferences. The students seemed to be learning personal strategies for selecting their own reading materials. Adults, too, use personal strategies: I often rely on recommendations from friends; in contrast, one adult I interviewed about her book-selection process said, "I never read a book that someone else tells me about." Others I questioned said that they have a favorite author or read only nonfiction. My students were selecting their books for similar reasons.

Robert still said that he chose certain books because he liked the illustrations. Patrick had branched out from books by his favorite author to student-published books and a book by an author whose other books I had read to the class. Around this time, I wrote in my teaching log:

I am excited about the fact that this method of teaching allows the very capable students to move ahead at their own rate. They are not held back by the confines of working within a group that may not be able to move ahead at the same rate that they are able to progress.

There was another aspect of what was happening in our classroom, something that does not appear on any of the charts or graphs but that visitors to our classroom commented on and said was contagious. It was the energy that they could feel in our room or, more specifically, the enthusiasm the students had for reading. Some of the visitors were amazed to see that when students were given the choice of what to read, they did read...and they loved it. I wrote about this in my teaching log toward the end of January:

> I must now give the next end-of-the-book test that I have agreed to give. But the tests will not show the way that Joshua devours books. The tests will not show the intense looks on the faces of Joey and Stephen as they attempt to read yet another new book together. The test results will not reflect the feeling of satisfaction that causes Shanna to glow as she comes to show me her response to the story of Pinocchio...that it teaches you not to talk to strangers and not to lie. The test results will not show the feeling of importance that Leslie has when she is able to help a classmate read a book.

I was beginning to see that giving my students the freedom to choose their reading materials was, in effect, giving them ownership of the reading process.

I was also noticing other changes in my students' reactions to reading. Before our next trip to the town library, we talked about how to find a book by the author's last name. The students were now aware of more authors. This gave them a place to start once we arrived at the library, so our trips there became more enjoyable. From amid the stacks of the children's section, I would now hear cries of "Oh look, here's a Rosemary Wells book" or "Mrs. Timion, I've found a whole section of Beatrix Potter books!" The students were delighting in choosing their own books. We even began having our quiet reading or reading in pairs time at the library because the students were so anxious to begin reading the new books they'd found.

During my school vacations, I had time to reflect on my students' work in the readers workshop and also on my own research. In April, I compiled my results on their reasons for reading certain books (see Figure 3). I was interested to see that 15 students preferred books that they or other students had written themselves, and I was not surprised to see that "can read" was the most common response.

During this time for reflection, I also realized that my students needed to learn some new ways to think critically about the books they were selecting. I searched for strategies in books and articles by other teachers who had

Figure 3
Students' Strategies for Choosing Books

Reasons given at conference for selecting a book...

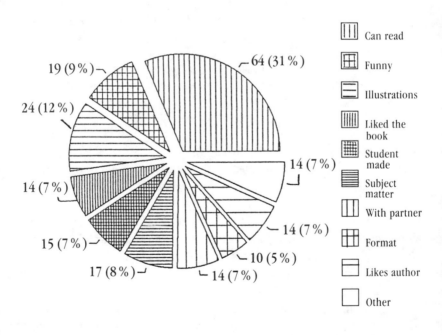

Note: Percentages reflect multiple answers from 22 children (over seven months).

used the readers workshop approach (e.g., Graves, 1989; Hansen, 1987; Hornsby, Sukarna, & Parry, 1986). I borrowed from Hansen the idea of having the students categorize the three books they brought to reading conferences by level of difficulty: "easy," "working on," or "challenge." After vacation, I found that, almost without exception, the students categorized the books the same way that I would have.

I also began to wonder how children determine that they can read the books they choose. After vacation, I began asking this question at individual reading conferences. One student after another told me, "I look at the words."

Change and Progress

Although many of the students were experiencing success, taking risks, and reaching new levels of achievement, Robert appeared to be at a standstill. A note from his mother expressed her concern as well. She said that Robert just wanted to read the same books over and over again, that he was simply memorizing the words and looking at the pictures so that he would know what to say for each page. She asked what she should do to help him.

When I wrote back to Robert's mother, I tried to reassure her. I encouraged her to keep spending time each evening with Robert and books. I told her that educators are discovering that memorizing texts and repeating stories—that is, imitating reading-like behavior—may be a step toward acquiring written language, like crawling before walking. Although I, too, was somewhat concerned about Robert's slow reading progress, I was confident that when he was developmentally ready, Robert's reading skills would increase. He truly appeared to enjoy books, and often when I made my rounds during quiet reading or reading-in-pairs time, he would stop me to share something from the book that he was working on.

For his next reading conference, Robert chose one of the books he had written himself. For his conference the following week he brought two books that he had used in previous conferences. Robert was on a plateau as far as reading development was concerned.

Patrick's progress appeared to be in some sort of holding pattern as well. I noticed that he was taking risks by selecting books that I had not read to the class for his quiet reading material and for reading with his partner. But when it was time for his individual reading conference, he chose "safe" books, books that were very easy for him to read. For two of his conferences in January and February, he chose books that his classmates had written and published. These were books with very few words.

After the February vacation, however, Patrick began to move forward again. From that point on, he became a book scavenger. He discovered books stored behind a chair in the library and books tucked in the bottom shelf in our classroom; there was no book anywhere that was safe from Patrick's scrutiny. When he came to conference and began to tell me about each book he had brought, it was as though he was telling me about a good friend. Through our book talks I discovered that he had internalized the meaning of the books he had chosen. For example, in response to a book about a sister and brother at Christmastime, Patrick wrote: "I think whoever has a sister or a brother, it might be complicated." After reading a book about a dog who flunks miserably at obedience school, he wrote, "I think when Pinkerton went to obedience school he was confused."

As I read over my notes and tabulated the ways my students decided which books to read, I realized that in the last couple of years my teaching style had changed dramatically as I moved to the readers workshop format in my reading program. I decided that it was time to rearrange our classroom to reflect this change.

For one thing, I needed a classroom arrangement that would allow more space to display books. In our current arrangement, about half of the bookshelves were blocked by our piano and a portable bulletin board. I also wanted to expose more of the bulletin board so that we could display more student work. I devoted one Saturday to this project and was able to accomplish the desired result. We could now display books the entire length of our classroom, and the students could now get to the books more easily.

This new arrangement did open up our classroom space. We liked the effect. There was one minor drawback to all of this, however. For years I had held back a few books in a small bookshelf on the counter by my desk. These were books that I planned to save for special occasions—holidays, science units, and so on. In previous years these books had been left undisturbed. But this year, when the students were making decisions about their own reading materials, they considered all books in the room to be fair game. After the change in room arrangement, they found this bookshelf and began to dip into that "private" collection. Although those books had been in that part of the room for years, no other class had been curious about them. I attributed the change with this class to the fact that these students were taking very seriously the choice of books they would spend the time and effort to read. Also, their curiosity about books had been nurtured and encouraged.

Around the beginning of March I changed the guidelines for Book Share a bit. I told the students that rather than just telling about any book that they had read, they should tell about good books they had found that most of the class had not read. It was rather like the author's circle in our writers workshop (another reading/writing connection). After the student told a little about the story, she or he would read a page or two from the book—just enough to entice classmates to read the book themselves. At the end of Book Share, the students could ask questions of the child who shared the book.

Perhaps giving students a vehicle for sharing new books sent them searching for new and different reading materials. I only know that when I spoon-fed them one story at a time from the commercial reading programs, they appeared to enjoy reading but they were not curious about books. I believe that my previous students actually saw reading instruction and the reading of books as two distinct activities. Books most often remained on shelves where I had arranged them. On the other hand, this new readers workshop routine was a messy process. I had to talk often to the class about handling books carefully and putting them back on the shelves gently. Finally, I resorted to appointing bookshelf helpers each week to help keep our classroom collection in order. But the important thing was that the kids were reading the books.

In March, as I surveyed the class during quiet reading time, I noticed that some of the students were flitting from book to book, simply looking at one for a few minutes and then moving on to another. They were using books, but I wanted them actually to be reading them by this point in the school year. So once again, I took my cue from our writers workshop format. At the beginning of the quiet reading time, I would circulate around the classroom with a clipboard and a bunch of books from different reading levels. If I noticed that a particular student was struggling with her or his book, I would let that student choose a new one from the batch that I was carrying. I'd try to match the reading level or interest of the student to the book. Thus, I added yet another strategy to enhance my students' book-selection process.

By the seventh month of first grade, most of my students had developed a system for selecting books. Patrick, still a scavenger, had found another favorite author. An entry in his reading log in April stated, "This is a very,

very good book. Eric Carle is my favorite author. It was a story about a tiny seed that grows and grows to a big flower."

Patrick progressed steadily and at an accelerated rate throughout first grade. His parents were amazed at his development as a reader. His attitude toward reading at home, they reported, was quite different from that of his older brother, who saw reading as a chore. They said that Patrick exhibited a love for books, and that he read at home when time was provided in their busy family routine. They also said that when Patrick was first beginning to read on his own, he would often choose to read the same book over and over again and that as he developed he would try to read most any printed material he encountered, including signs, cereal boxes, baseball cards, and newspapers.

Robert's story is quite different. While the majority of the students were still telling me that they were selecting books because they could read them, Robert continued to select books because of appearance or illustrations. I watched him on our trip to the town library in April as he chose a book by its cover. He did not even look inside the book before he checked it out. Not until the next day, during quiet reading time, did he actually open the book and look at the words. Once he opened it, his interest was immediately taken up with the pictures and diagrams of earth-moving equipment. His major concern in selecting reading material clearly was not whether he could read the book.

At first this behavior rather irked me—after all we'd been through with books and words and more books! But as I looked back in my record of the individual reading conferences, I noticed that Robert almost always said that he picked a book because he liked the illustrations. This was his "system" for selecting reading materials.

It wasn't until late in April that Robert had a conference in which he varied from his usual reason for picking a book. He said that he had chosen this book by Bill Martin Jr because he liked the sound of the words. The book, which incorporates the letters of the alphabet in a rhyme with a definite beat, had had a wide appeal in our classroom. Often I would overhear Robert reciting this rhyme to himself as I passed his desk, or as he was on his way out for recess.

Finally in May, Robert's responses to the questions about why he chose books became quite varied. At one conference, he stated that Mercer Mayer was his favorite author; at another he said he picked the book because he thought it was "cool." Robert was beginning to interact with text. In mid-May he brought an Eric Carle book that he had brought to an earlier conference in January. In my anecdotal record of the conference at that time I had written, "Robert could tell the story of this book, but he could not read it. We sounded out the word h-a-d but that was not an easy task for him." But when Robert chose this same book for his individual conference in May, there was quite a different entry in my notebook:

> Robert could talk about the storyline of this book. He categorized it as a "challenge" book for him, but when he began to read from the book, he attacked all the hard words and was able to pronounce them after looking at the illustrations, using context clues and sounding them out. Robert even went back and corrected his miscues. This is the first time I have seen him do this. I am amazed at his progress and attitude toward reading.

The book that had once been a challenge for him was now a "working-on" book.

Robert's seventh birthday was May 28th. His father gave him a fishing pole, but when his mother came in with cupcakes for the class, she whispered, "I can't wait for Robbie to open his big present tonight. It's a 19-volume set of books." I couldn't help thinking that his mother's enthusiasm for books would be contagious. Later, when I was able to sit down with Robert's parents for an interview, they expressed their delight at the progress they had noticed in Robert's reading at home. They talked about the fact that his interactions with books at first had been a cause for concern for them because he constantly chose the same books and read and reread them many times until he had memorized them. They had not considered this to be reading. They said that they had encouraged Robert to read at home, had visited the library with him, and had bought him the books for his birthday so he would have books that were within his reading range at home.

My notes concerning Robert reflected the fact that he had enjoyed looking at books all year. The illustrations remained an important part of any book for him, however. He relied on the illustrations and photographs for context clues and information in the text. His parents also had noticed his fascination with the illustrations. When Robert wrote his own pieces in writers workshop, his elaborate illustrations were always the first thing on his paper.

It was almost the very end of the school year when Robert experienced the turning point in his reading development that many of his classmates had experienced in January. I was sorry that summer vacation followed so closely this point in Robert's reading development.

Reflections on the Year

As this school year progressed, I began to see individual patterns in the way my students selected their books. Most students would go directly to a specific section of our classroom, school, or town library. Some, on the other hand, would peruse the bookshelves until they found the particular book they were looking for. One or two appeared to wander aimlessly among the books until one—usually one that I had read to the class—caught their eye.

The value of making reading/writing connections also became apparent in my classroom. During the first months of the year, students often chose to read books that they or their peers had written. These books seemed to provide them with familiar language and topics as well as a personal relationship to the text that helped them get involved with reading. I speculate that it also helped them see that the authors we studied were real people, just like them.

By reviewing my data and notes, I have also come to realize how important it is for me to "set the stage" for the reading process by making the books in our classroom readily accessible to the students, reading to them at least twice a day, and sharing my genuine love for books. I saw the value of offering reading to my students in this way when one rather immature student, for whom retention was being considered, came to me in early June and said, "Mrs. Timion, I just love reading." Paper-and-pencil activities were still difficult for this child. If he had been forced to sit quietly all day completing worksheets and workbook pages, if he had been expected to read unpredictable language at a level that was too difficult for him, I feel certain that he would not have developed a love for reading.

I have come to realize that selecting the right book is a very important part of the reading process for the beginning reader, just as it is for adult readers. Like the prewriting activities in our writers workshop, book selection is a prereading activity and needs to be nurtured and developed. It appears that once a student discovers a method of choosing books that works for him or her, he or she often uses that method again and again. Some students used the favorite-author method; others preferred to select books by topic or on a recommendation from a friend. Whatever their method, my students had definite patterns for choosing their books. Ashley, for example, read almost exclusively about animals, both fiction and nonfiction. She even wrote about animals. Joshua loved mystery books, and our whole class was on the lookout for books for him. When we saw a mystery book, we automatically thought of Joshua. Katie, on the other hand, read almost anything she could get her hands on. She did not appear to be too discerning in her choices; she simply loved to read. She was our first student to risk reading a "chapter book" with very few pictures. But after that great accomplishment, she was content to read very easy books for quite a while. It took a lot of self-control for me to let her read these books for a few weeks; to my relief, she eventually did get back into chapter books. She even began bringing them from home and secretly distributing them, as if they were contraband, to some of her friends.

Clearly I cannot say that reading development is constant and smooth, that each book a student picks will be more difficult than the last one, or that a graph of the difficulty level of the books that a particular child has chosen to read throughout the year would resemble a diagonal line. Instead, the developmental graph seems to resemble a profile of the Rocky Mountains, with numerous peaks and valleys.

As I watched my students develop into diverse, independent readers, I began to realize the power that I had given them when I allowed them to choose the books from which they learned to read. I glimpsed the bigger picture—the way that the commercial, prepackaged reading programs have worked against individuality and promoted conformity. They had assumed that all students have the same learning style and learn at the same pace. Commercial programs essentially ignore the fact that different life experiences elicit different responses and different ways of making meaning from text. Individual preference for reading materials is never a consideration.

I began to wonder if by preselecting and packaging the doses of reading material we were telling the students that choosing their own books was too difficult. Thinking back, I realized that in the past I had taken the freedom to select reading materials away from my students and then wondered why they were not choosing to read. But when the students were allowed to choose the books that they wanted to read, they *did* read.

I have learned that it is important for students to spend their school days in a joyfully literate environment where books are displayed and celebrated. I have learned that reading books should be the primary activity in a reading program rather than being considered a quiet activity that students may do when they have finished their "real" work. It is important to make *reading*, rather than learning *how* to read, the top priority.

When I used the commercial programs to teach reading, the trade books in our room were basically decoration; the students did not show much interest in them. In some ways the books were intimidating to them: they hadn't seen flashcards of the words in these books, and the rich language differed from the control vocabulary they had been taught. There was not much transfer between the reading work that we did in school and the actual reading of books. But in the readers workshop format, students at all stages of development read books and found reading to be both a pleasurable activity and a way to gain information. I hope that these attitudes will last a lifetime.

It is my job to expose my students to the world of books and to give them ownership of their reading process by allowing them to choose which books they will read. Sometimes if a student is overwhelmed by the multitude of books available, I narrow their field of choice to two or three in order to make their decision easier. But right from the start, when you're going to read, the first step is to select a book.

References
Atwell, N. (1987). *In the middle*. Portsmouth, NH: Heinemann.

Graves, D. (1989, November). Research currents: When children respond to fiction. *Language Arts, 66*, 776-783.

Hansen, J. (1987). *When writers read*. Portsmouth, NH: Heinemann.

Hornsby, D., Sukarna, D., & Parry, J. (1986). *Read on: A conference approach to reading*. Portsmouth, NH: Heinemann.

M. Joan Throne

— E L E V E N —

A Special Needs Student in a Reading/Writing Workshop

*T*hough all my sixth grade students, including those with special needs, seem to benefit from participating in our process-oriented reading/writing classroom, I felt I needed to study their responses carefully to verify that my approach was an appropriate one. I decided to observe one student closely. Anne had serious learning disabilities and problems involving self-esteem. What would happen to her in my classroom? Most of the study described here focuses on Anne's growth as a writer and as an active participant in the community of learners in my classroom.

My study looks at Anne in both the reading and writing workshops (Atwell, 1987). With respect to the writing workshop, I take a special look at a story Anne wrote and revised, and at how important being able to use the word processor was to her. Then, because spelling was such a problem for Anne, I include a section on spelling strategies we hoped would help. I also look at timed writing, its effect on Anne's fluency in writing, and its contribution to her belief that her responses were valued.

Informational reading and writing is discussed in a separate section. I wondered what would happen to Anne, whose reading and writing ability were supposedly below grade level, in a situation where she would be expected to gather information, write papers, and present what she learned to the other students.

Something I couldn't seem to put into a special section was Anne's growth as an active participant in a community of learners. I hope, though, that it permeates this chapter. Perhaps there is nothing as important that we can do for our special needs students than to help them become a part of that community.

The First Day

I couldn't find my way through the school at first because I didn't look around at the end of the year to see where our class was going to be. I found my way somehow, don't really remember. Well, ummm, I was in front of the room, and I was staring at it for awhile. I looked at who was going to be in our class [the names were on a chart outside the door], and I felt really terrible because a bunch of kids from my old class was going to be in this year's class, like Sandy and Laura and Cathy and a bunch of kids I knew.

Well, I walked into the room and everybody was sitting down. None of the boys were there, but well, I sat down in a group [of desks] and all the boys came in. See the girls were first, and then the boys come. I sat down and everybody and there was and all the boys sat down next to me. I thought it was terrible that I had to be in an all-boy group the beginning of the year, but I lived. Well, a few days later we changed groups. That was better.

(from a taped interview with Anne)

Only a few students were in the room when a girl with hazel eyes and medium-length dark blonde hair walked in. "Take a seat, anywhere," I invited.

"I'll sit here," she said, and, ignoring the students who were already in the room, she sat at one of the few places where her back would face most of her classmates.

Gradually desks were chosen, and my 26 sixth graders and I were ready to begin our first day of school. "I'm Mrs. Throne," I said. "I like beginnings and sixth graders. I think we'll have a great year. Now, please tell me your names and a little about yourselves if you don't mind. I'm getting older, and I'm going to need some help remembering everyone."

I knew a lot about Anne before she told me her name. She was the girl who sat with her back toward most of the class. She was the only girl in a group of four boys. She stared straight ahead. Her hands were folded on her desk. She hadn't joined in the earlier joyful reunions during which students screamed with delight as they greeted friends. She sat isolated and alone in a class filled with students.

(from my notes and recollections)

The Plan

Last year the learning specialist and I were members of our school's teacher-researcher group. I was closely observing English as a Second Language (ESL) students that year and trying to learn more about how a process-oriented reading/writing classroom could help them learn English. The learning specialist knew that I agreed with the view that, unless a problem is extreme, special needs students benefit from participating in that type of classroom. She began coming to my room for half an hour a day, four days a week, to work with students who had learning disabilities instead of having those students leave the room to see her. We decided to continue these visits in the upcoming school year.

Near the end of last year the learning specialist talked to me about Anne, a fifth grader. According to tests, Anne was weak in short-term auditory memory, auditory discrimination, visual memory, spatial relationships, and visual motor integration. Her visual motor integration problem seemed to be the most serious. She was reading below grade level and had much trouble putting thoughts on paper. She also had poor self-esteem.

Due to the nature of her problems, the recommendation that she be placed in a self-contained learning disabilities class seemed warranted. However, our specialist thought Anne would benefit from being a member of a class in which the teacher used a process approach to teach reading and writing. She agreed with the school psychologist, who had said that Anne might achieve more success in an environment where she could be made to feel secure and supported academically as well as socially.

Graves (1991) suggests four essentials for a successful writing-process program: time to write, choice of topics, response to writing, and the establishment of a community of learners. Those same four ingredients may also be essential to a successful reading-process program. In both reading and writing, establishing that community of learners is important for promoting trust and risk-taking.

I focused my research on Anne. What would happen to her in such a classroom? Would the process approach be beneficial to her as a reader? Would she grow as a writer? What would happen to her in the informational reading and writing program? Would she become a part of that community of learners I hoped to establish? Would being a part of this type of classroom improve her self-image? Though I planned to focus on writing, I hoped my study would increase my knowledge about how to meet the needs of students with other special problems in my classroom as well.

I decided to enter my observations in a journal several times a week and to reread those observations every two or three weeks to reflect on what I had observed. Interviewing Anne, her mother, her former teachers, and the learning specialist was also part of my plan. I would use the tape-recorder for some of the interviewing sessions and would videotape at least one sharing session. I would copy samples of the writing Anne did throughout the year and ask her and my other students to fill out writing surveys periodically.

Early in the year, I learned that I had underestimated the seriousness of Anne's problems. At one point in my journal I wrote, "I may be in over my head." The school psychologist compared Anne's problems with that of a stroke victim's. She said that sometimes stroke victims cover their faces and shake their heads when they realize that what comes out of their mouths isn't what was in their heads. Sometimes that happened to Anne. She seemed to find herself saying something different from what she intended. When that happened, she held and shook her head in dismay.

Strengths Revealed in the Reading Workshop

For a community of learners to develop, each student needs to believe that he or she has something of value to contribute. I knew that Anne, like every other student in my class, would have areas of strength—areas in which she could make valuable contributions. In September, I learned that Anne had strong math ability; later I made several surprising discoveries about other areas of strength.

In the first month of school, I gave the students the word "archaeologist" and asked them to use the letters in that word to make as many other words as they could. Anne was the only student to write "gist." Most of the students didn't know the meaning of that word, so she was asked to explain it (this was one of the rules of the game). She said it meant "to get the idea of something—to get the gist of it." Then she used the word "pronounced" in describing one student's problems and wrote that Dracula is "desolote and alon." In January she explained the meaning of the word "intermittently," used in Jack London's *White Fang*, with an example: "You know how you sleep and wake up and sleep." One of the valuable things Anne shared with her classmates was her rich vocabulary.

Something else she shared was her wonderful acting ability. Once or twice a week the learning specialist brought a short play to the room and some of the other students joined Anne in reading the play together. After practicing it once or twice, they would present it to the rest of the class. One play they presented was based on Barbara Parks's *Skinnybones*. I noticed a slight hesitancy in Anne's voice, but she read with very good expression. Working with Anne on these skits and plays became so popular with the other students that the specialist had to keep a record to make sure everyone got a turn.

Anne also demonstrated good comprehension when we discussed books read to the class. Reading and discussing these books usually began the reading workshop component of our class. "What is the mood here?" I asked about Mary Hahn's *Wait Till Helen Comes*.

"It's a combination of fears," Anne explained. "It's fear of Helen, fear of the pond, fear...."

Later in the year, when I was reading *White Fang* aloud, we discussed why Henry tied a burning pine-knot to his hand. Anne seemed to understand exactly what was going on when she responded, "To wake him up. He didn't want to sleep too soundly!"

In reading workshops, students usually choose their own books to read. Early in the year, the learning specialist and I read aloud some of our favorite easy-to-read books. Through our sharing, students learn that reading easier books is acceptable. Anne and many of her classmates enjoyed reading these books but they also enjoyed reading harder books.

Late in the school year, Anne chose Mark Twain's *A Connecticut Yankee in King Arthur's Court* and read it while sprawled on the couch in the reading corner. She used a bookmark to read each line, and she read very slowly. Although the book was much more difficult than most of the books she'd read, I didn't discourage her. I remembered Laura, a student in my class the previous year, who had had a problem with reading. She decided to read Paul Zindel's *The Pigman*. I'd had my doubts. She read it very slowly and, at times, seemed to lose interest. But after a few days, I noticed Laura's head bent over that book when she was supposed to be working on math or social studies. It was obvious from her sharing and responses to questions that the book had made a real impression on her. She said it was the first novel she'd finished. No, I thought, I won't discourage Anne.

When I listened to Anne read aloud, I would notice a slight hesitancy in her speech as she hummed over some of the words she wasn't sure of. She did, however, seem to understand what she read. In October, she read to me from C.S. Lewis's *The Last Battle*, a book she had chosen herself. Without a bookmark, she seemed unable at times to stay on the line. When she came to the words "skimpy beard," she hummed over the word "skimpy." But when I asked her what kind of beard he had, she said, "puny."

She insisted on understanding. When she was reading Betty Mac-Donald's *Miss Piggle Wiggle* to me, both she and I found one part confusing; on her own, Anne said she needed to read that page again. In a class discussion about what to do if we come to something hard to understand, Anne said that when she reads "hard stuff," she reads it over and over again.

How is it that Anne, who scored low on standardized tests in reading, could solve—accurately and without help—word problems on tests from a difficult sixth grade math book? Anne had good comprehension that didn't show up in the results of standardized tests. When she found that her class would take the Iowa Tests of Basic Skills, Anne said, "Oh, no. I have such a hard time filling in those ovals." When I talked to her mother about my belief that the reading tests were not measuring her reading ability, she compared the tests with measuring Anne for shoes. She said her shoe size couldn't be checked using the regular methods because she has a high arch and needs large shoes.

Our reading workshops generally ended with students discussing books they were reading. Although they discussed books with each other in informal ways throughout the day, the discussion at the end of the workshop had more structure, with one student sharing and the others asking questions. Anne, who treasured the solitary quiet reading time, would share her books in small groups and with the entire class enthusiastically when given this opportunity.

The literature log (Atwell, 1987), or reading journal, is another vehicle for students to share information about books. In these logs, students write letters to their friends or to me about books they are reading, and we write back. For the most part, this year's students addressed letters in their logs to me. A typical letter from Anne early in the year said, "Dear, T I have ben reading those James Stevenson Books. Do you lick that riter. Anne N." By the end of November, I was finding her letters more interesting: "Dear, T I have bene reading the EDgarallen Poe Year Book. The first story was vay skary it freakd me out! *Anne N.*" The letters were also becoming longer: "Dear teach, I hav not read alot sens I rot you last but I've had lots to dow. I'm still reading Taming the Star Runner by S.E. Hinton it has goten boring sens I read it last. Anne N Ps. Can I go to the lidary to get informashon for I Searh on Greasee and rome."

It was interesting to note her correct use of the apostrophe in two places in this letter. It was a skill we'd discussed in an individual conference based on a paper she had put in my basket during writing workshop.

Progress in the Writing Workshop

Our writing workshops usually began with a minilesson on a special need I'd observed. All types of subjects came up: possessives, choosing topics, good beginnings, quotations, and so on. Anne would pay close attention to these short lessons and, in discussions, would show good understanding. After the lesson, I would ask students to tell me what they planned to do that day. Then, while I met with individual students for short conferences, the others began writing.

In an interview, Anne's fifth grade teacher told me that Anne had lots of good thoughts but that expressing them on paper was a problem. She said Anne's actual writing was minimal, difficult to read, and contained many spelling errors. In early September, I observed the same problems in Anne's writing. I also observed that Anne often wasted time during writing workshop, tracing pictures and reorganizing her desk more than she wrote. I couldn't help but think, however, that in her shoes I would do much the same thing. I'm not sure how much criticism about my writing I could take before I decided I'd be better off tracing pictures. In looking through her records, I read again and again about her poor spelling, problems with capitalization and punctuation, and illegible handwriting. Though she'd received remedial help since second grade, these were still problem areas for her, and more practice was recommended. If I were Anne, I would have little motivation left.

It was important for Anne to know that there was much more to writing then those superficial aspects. Rhodes and Dudley-Marling (1988) make the point that "If the audience, including teachers, is most concerned about students' ideas, students will learn to focus on the expression of ideas when writing" (p. 113). I wanted Anne to know that her ideas were important. When she wrote, "I lick working with ofer pepepl its more fun than doing work olon," we discussed my plans for working in groups. When she wrote, "I think that If a kid is pronst with having prodlems with puting ideas on papers, the teacher shod let the pearson use the computer more," I tried to provide her with more computer time.

Our school is lucky enough to have some classroom computers; I have two terminals and a printer in my class. Anne discovered the word processor in September. That discovery led to two important events. First, it opened up a whole new world of writing for her. She stayed after school to write almost every afternoon I would permit it. And that opened the way for the second event, the beginning of friendships. Before long, Heather, Susan, Monica, and others also wanted to stay after school. Since Anne learned to use the word processor first, she became their teacher. They stayed after school to write, talk, eat cookies, and become friends.

It was very important to Anne to make friends. "Back then," she told me about last year, "they were all in one group, but now I think they are getting a little better. The group is getting much better. They're talking to other kids, doing stuff with other kids. Last year I just didn't feel like I was included in any of it, but this year I'm being included in more things and doing more things."

Before the end of September, Anne began using her writing time to better advantage. She'd learned that I meant it when I said she should get her ideas on paper and not worry about spelling and punctuation. We'd work on those things when she decided to "publish" something. She was happiest when she could use the computer, but would also write with pen and paper.

She became very interested in working on a newspaper about herself. A poem she wrote for her newspaper exemplifies how she, and many of us, feel at times when we try to think. It was selected for inclusion in our class newspaper. An edited version follows:

A Truly Horrible Experience

I CAN'T THINK!!

I can't think!!

My brain is gone!!!

SLISH slish slish slish

OH!

Here it is.

Anne enjoyed putting her first newspaper together so much that she decided to work on another. Later in the year working on our class newspaper was one of her favorite writing ventures. With her friend Heather, she worked on a section they titled "Coming Attractions." Together they turned in a nicely edited paper.

The process involved in putting together our class paper went this way: After students have edited their own pieces, they place them in my "edit" basket. As their final editor, I go over their papers, note a couple things they do well and a couple things with which they need help. We discuss these areas in short individual conferences. Students get much of the help they need from other students before they turn a paper in to me. They may discuss it with another student during the workshop, or with a small or large group at the end of the workshop.

For this sort of sharing to take place, a trusting community needs to be established. Students need to be able to count on responses being made in a kind and helpful way. My efforts to help them learn about responding took two forms: I shared my writing and discussed the kinds of responses that are most helpful, and I modeled constructive criticism by responding to their writing out loud.

I didn't notice at first that Anne didn't often read to the large group. Then one day, I mentioned to her that a story she'd written would be interesting for the entire class. She said she wanted to practice reading it before sharing it with everyone. She explained that sometimes she can't read her spelling, but I didn't think that was the whole problem. Reading the skits and plays went well because she practiced first. I learned to plan ahead with Anne so she knew when she would be sharing her writing and would have time to practice.

A Closer Look at One of Anne's Stories

Anne is a hard worker, more than willing to do her share to improve in her writing. She spent long periods between November and early spring working on a story about her brother's accident and made great progress with each new draft. She chose this as the best story she'd written, "bekos its worded great."

"Is this story true?" I wanted to know.

"Well, part of it is," she said, "but I added stuff."

She wrote her draft by hand in November. She told me that she marked all words she thought she had misspelled with a pink marker. In Figure 1, I've circled those words and penciled in the other changes she made (I also crossed some of her t's).

In editing her first draft, Anne was most concerned with spelling. When I told her not to worry so much about spelling, she replied, "But I

Figure 1
Anne's First Draft

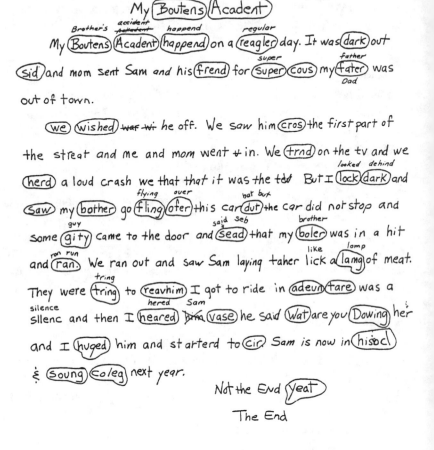

want to spell it right." In both her first and second drafts, she tried out
different spellings to see which words looked right. She used my battery-
operated spell-checker and the spell-checker on the computer, but that only
helped if she was close to the correct spelling.

When she wrote her second draft in December (see Figure 2), spelling was less of a problem and she made some interesting revisions. She tried a different title and decided that "going out for groceries" fit the meaning of what happened better than "going out for supper." In draft one, she wrote that somebody came to the door to tell them her brother was hurt. In draft two, she decided that it made more sense for them to run outside after hearing a crash. She knew that she sometimes confuses "b" and "d," and in this draft she occasionally corrected that.

She wrote several more drafts, using the computer for a couple of them. In one draft she ended the story, "I got to go in the ambulans and I felt a cold like the angol of deith was thar but he wasent Sam lived and is going to colleg this Agustest." Anne decided to read her story to the entire class so that they could help her decide on an ending. She told me she wanted to practice reading it to herself first.

She began her sharing by explaining that she couldn't decide which of the endings to use, the long one or the short one. As soon as she finished reading the story with one ending, hands went up. Her classmates were anxious to respond. "Do you want to read your second ending first?" I asked.

"No," Anne said. "I'll answer their questions first."

Her story captured the interest of the class. James complimented her on the descriptive words she used and wanted to know which parts were not true. Anne explained that the angel of death wasn't true. Monica and Carol also said they liked the words Anne used, and Monica wanted to know if the car really left. Anne assured her that it had. Linda liked the way Anne told how she felt in the ambulance but wondered if she should work on the part where she said it was a nice day but then said it was a nice night. Anne said she did need to work on that part. Finally, Monica asked, "What was your other ending? You said you had two."

Anne read her second ending to the class. This ending cast the entire story as a performance of a play. Anne read the part of herself with great expression and even included in the dialogue an argument with a member of her fictional audience.

Pattie responded immediately. "Your second ending was more active," she said. "I liked that better." Laura said she liked the way Anne had people talking back and forth and wondered where the second ending began. Anne explained that it picked up right after "He's alive." Linda was concerned about confusing the reader. She suggested that Anne could say something like

Figure 2
Anne's Second Draft

My Brather's Hit and run

My Brother's Hit and run happend on a day just (lick) this one. It was warm outsid [b] dut I [d] bon't no way. It was [d] bark and mom sent Sam and his [friend] frend out side for [groceries] grosares [be] cos my Dad [went] ~~was~~ out of [town] ~~towen~~ [towne] and had the car.

Me and my mom [washed] (wtoshed) Sam and his ~~broter~~ [friend] frend cross the [first] ~~ferst~~ part of the [street] streate [streate] and we went in side and [turned] tearnd on the T.V. And we herd a lowd crass I [trend] ~~terd~~ aro[a]nd and saw Sam go flying over a car but the car did not stop it [Why bibn't stop.] [K] cept on going. ~~We~~ I ran out and sam was laying on the cart like he was beid. Pepole were [trying] (tring) to [revive] ~~reavive~~ [him] hie. Thay put him in the [ambulance] ~~amdulins~~ and I got to [with him] ~~rid in~~ [to the hospital] ~~the amdulins too.~~ [It was quite to quite] ~~Thar was a deid silinsin~~ [in the ambulance] like someting big is going to hapon. I herd somting [was it] it ~~-~~ was Sam!! [He] is al[your was]l alive.

The End

No No No

~~cut~~

it's Not the End Yeat!!!

he's still alive, I wont, to Know wait he's doing now
ok he is 17 and going to college next year, is that [enough] ~~enof~~
It's not the end yet is it
yes!!! the end

"'Oh, no,' said a man in the audience." Laura picked up on that and said, "Yes, like 'a voice from the audience said.'" Anne indicated that she appreciated their help.

Everyone seemed to agree that the second ending was best, but I wanted to give my opinion. When Anne called on me, I said, "In the first ending, you told about something cold passing. I liked that because you're telling about something that almost happened but didn't." Anne assured me that she was keeping the part about the coldness. I added that I thought it added a touch of mystery. Anne is at her best in discussions and obviously enjoyed the interest in her story.

She used the word processor to write the final copy of her story before putting it in my edit basket. The final version appears in Figure 3.

Figure 3
My Brother's Hit and Run

My Brother's Hit and Run

My brother's Hit and Run happened on a night just like this one. It was a warm night but I didn't know why because it was in the middle of february. My brother Sam was just about to leave to go get soom grosary stoor to get soom food. Because my dad was out of town and had the car.
Me and my Mom watched Sam cross the first part of the street. We went in side and turned on the T.V.
Then we herd a lowd crash so I ternd arond and sow Sam with his bike go flying over a car but the car didn't stop it kcpt on going why didn't stop? Me and My Mom ran out the door to see if Sam was was deid he wasent "Thank God" I got to go in the ambulans and I felt a like cold the angol of deith was thair and ten the cold was gon and Sam seid Anne wait are you doing hear..
THE END
NO, NO NO seid a voise from the audince It's not the end yet he is still alive I wont to know wait he doing now.
Ok he is going to college in AUGUST That enough.
IT'S NOT THE END is it
YES!!!!!!!
THE END
Some of this story not true.

In a short conference about this story, we discussed the skills she knew and used and those she needed to learn. But more important than discussing those skills, I wanted her to know how much I liked her story and how much I hoped she'd let me help her publish it in a more formal way.

Anne had used some of her classmate's suggestions. She tried to make clear just who was talking after the end of her main story. She addressed the confusion about the time of day. I think she tried to make everyone happy with the ending of her story. As an actress and a writer, Anne always considers her audience. That it is very important to her to draw others into her story is obvious in the revisions she made.

Revisions aren't always an improvement. I liked the way she described her brother "lying there like a lump of meat" in her first draft, but she never used that again. I thought her description of the ride in the ambulance, "dead silence like something big is going to happen," was terrific, but she chose not to use it after the second draft. Anne saw all kinds of possibilities and had difficulty choosing the best one—but "best" is, after all, a matter of opinion.

I asked Anne how the computer helped her. Much of her editorial process is evident in her answer: "Well, the computer helps me a lot because I don't have to write down what I say and what I think 'cause it's really hard for me to write down what I really think because when I'm thinking it's just blob, blob, blob. I don't have the time to write out the words, and try and correct myself too much. I'm just terrible at that. When people say for me to not to correct myself and just do it after, I always when I see—oh, that's wrong! I have to go back and correct it or I'll be terrible. But in the computer...you can write it down and you can go back and correct it and it won't be as messy and stuff like that. In my writing I'm really a neat person...."

Working on Spelling

Although the computer helped Anne tremendously in her writing, the program we tried for spelling didn't seem as helpful. It did make it easier for her to learn to spell lists of words, but what she learned didn't seem to transfer to real writing. Learning lists of words from a spelling book wasn't the answer for her either.

When I asked her about spelling, she said, "I don't think [the computer program] helped me much because I really can't remember the words.... I think it's terrible. I really want to learn how to spell words. It's just that I really can't. I can't remember the words. It's terrible. And I don't think people with the same problem will be able to either." Still, Anne was the student who noted that I had misspelled "chemistry" on a chart I made. Another mystery.

Although I didn't want her to be so concerned about spelling that her writing fluency would be inhibited, at one point in early spring, I decided that we weren't working hard enough on spelling. I gave her five words to learn to spell, words that she had misspelled in her own writing (*discussion, because, like, easy,* and *what*). She said she would learn them, but I didn't see much evidence that she was really committed. When I asked her a few days later how she was doing on learning to spell those words, she became upset with me. "Now you are just like all my other teachers," she accused.

"You can use the computer to practice spelling them," I suggested, but I could tell she was angry.

We were involved in a science fair on the day Anne was to take her test on her five words. To be honest, I had much more on my mind than that test, but it seemed to be the only thing on Anne's mind. "When do I take my test?" she asked.

"Are you ready for it right now?" I responded.

She assured me she was, and while the rest of the class moved desks around and took out science experiments, Anne took her test. She did very well. She spelled *because* "becuase," but when I asked her to take another look at it, she corrected it. She began the word *discussion* with a "b," and we talked about the problem of confusing those letters. I had no doubt that she deserved high marks on that test.

"Anne, I have a feeling we should do more spelling this way. What do you think?" By now Anne knew I wanted her to tell me the truth. When she nodded her head in agreement, she was sincere. As time went on, she became the one to remind me that she needed words to learn. She was very proud of herself for remembering how to spell *because* in her final version of "My Brother's Hit and Run."

Jennie, a student for whom spelling posed no problem, decided one day to help Anne with her spelling. I don't know how that happened. It was a joy for me to see the two of them working together. Anne, with Jennie's help, started to do very well on her tests, but just as important, she had made another good friend.

Response Journals

Early in the year the students began writing in what I call their RJs (response journals). Because I like journals in all subject areas but find keeping separate ones cumbersome, my students keep only two: one is their literature log, and the other, the RJ, is for all subject areas. Sometimes I choose a topic for them to respond to in their RJ; other times students choose their own topics. My usual procedure for writing in the RJ is to decide on a topic, set the timer for five minutes, have everyone write without stopping, and then all share (without class response). The only concern should be to get ideas on paper. I write and share my draft too, which helps the students believe me when I say that every writer writes drafts.

Anne enjoyed sharing her work almost from the beginning, but I noticed that when she spoke she didn't always read what she had written. One time this was particularly apparent was during an assignment in October. I'd said we shouldn't have computers in the room because they really caused a lot of problems—not meaning what I was saying, of course. Then I asked the students to write a five-minute response to what I had said.

Since five students from the University of Maryland were visiting that day, I asked for volunteers to share their responses. I was a little surprised at her bravery, but Anne raised her hand. She looked at her audience so much when she shared that I knew she hadn't really written all that she said, although she made it sound as though she were reading it. She made the point that it wasn't fair that people who had problems with writing might be denied the use of a computer because other people had misused the equipment.

After she shared, she sat down, covered her face with her hands, and shook her head. Later, I asked her why she felt unhappy after sharing. She said she hadn't said all she wanted to say and that she'd said "uh" too often. What Anne often misses is the fine impression she makes because of her thoughtfulness and her sincerity.

Another occasion when these qualities came through was in March when we were sharing responses to Louis Sachar's *There's a Boy in the Girls' Bathroom*, a book I had read to the class. Anne began reading her response, then asked if she could just tell it. I agreed. She said the boy's problem reminded her of her own problem. She said she talked with our learning specialist, like Bradley talked with the counselor. She said that now she is better, just like Bradley was.

This timed writing in response journals seemed to help Anne with fluency. Her longest responses came when the topics were her choice. On one of those occasions she wrote at some length about why sixth graders should be allowed to chew bubble gum and how unfair the teacher was for not permitting it. Her classmates were nodding their heads in agreement as she shared. (In my own defense, let me say that I was very tired of seeing bubbles and hearing those pops!)

When asked what she thought of timed writing, Anne said, "It helps me in writing faster and just not thinking about every single word." She verifies what Rhodes and Dudley-Marling (1988) have to say about this type of writing: "Most students would have plenty to say if they would only leave behind their nearly paralyzing concern about conventions, spelling in particular" (p. 114).

Informational Reading and Writing

My approach with reading for information and writing to express that information is to integrate them into the reading and writing workshops. First, I have the class brainstorm, listing on a chart everything they can think of that has anything to do with the subject to be studied. Then I give each student several index cards and we go to the library with our chart. Students search the shelves and card catalogs, looking for books that might fit any of the topics listed on the chart or any additional topics that might be of interest. When they find appropriate books, they note titles, authors, and page numbers on their index card. When we get back to the room, I help the students put the information they gathered on large charts. Then we categorize the information.

As students are reading about the general subject and are finding information, they begin choosing specific subtopics that interest them for an I-Search paper (Macrorie, 1988). Students may work alone or with a partner. A chart listing each student and his or her chosen topic makes it easier for classmates to help each other gather information. A culminating activity is the sharing of the finished paper and, perhaps, a special project. The audience responds by making observations and asking questions.

Early in the year we were studying "Bulbs and Batteries." My students expanded on that unit to include everything they could think of that had something to do with electricity. Anne decided to find more information about Faraday and Franklin and their experiments. On the day she informed the class of what she'd found in her search, she shared from her writing the story of her hunt for information: "The first day I was stuned how little thar was on expramets exepet for do your own expramets but a friend fond a book...which was a hug help in my search for informashon." At the end of her report, she answered her classmates' questions with authority. Anne was becoming known as a fine student who did thorough work.

From time to time students wrote proposals to do an I-Search on their own. A proposal Anne made was to learn more about Dracula. She found that "Dracula flies all over the world for prey. Life for Dracula is a hunt for prey." She almost had me sympathizing with her character when she shared, "I think that his desolote and alon. With no life out of finding blood at eney coust." Again, as with previous reports, Anne had knowledge to share that her classmates were eager to hear.

In January, Anne presented another I-Search project, this time about Alexander the Great and Aristotle. She put on a skit in which she played several parts. She began in the role of a rather belligerent contemporary student who had a report due the next day. This girl had no luck at the library, so she went back home and fell asleep. When she woke up, she found herself in a strange setting. It seemed to be a classroom where students were listening intently to a man who seemed to be a teacher. She discovered that the man was Aristotle, and one student who seemed to be hanging on his every word was Alexander the Great.

When a student gave an I-Search presentation, we all wrote our responses to the presentation in our RJs and then shared them with the presenter. Everyone seemed to enjoy receiving written responses from their classmates. Anne wrote that she liked hearing the responses because it brought up her spirits when she thought she'd done badly.

In an interview in March, Anne said about informational writing, "I go down to the library and get billions of books on one subject and I read them and then I just go back and stick the information in the back of my mind. During writing time, I take that information in the back of my mind, I use a computer, and I just zip it out." After Anne did her search for information about Aristotle and Alexander the Great, I watched as she did just "zip out" a report of about 250 words from the back of her mind. There seemed to be no struggle for words.

A Special Group Activity

John, a young man who often comes to our school as a substitute teacher, became interested in my class and offered in March to make up a game for the students to play as the culmination of our study of Ancient Greece and Rome. Although I was reluctant about the idea because of the competitive nature of the game he suggested, the students voted overwhelmingly to participate. I decided that the game might give me an opportunity to see how Anne retained information from her reading, so I threw in my support as well.

John gave each student a list of names and terms to study in preparation for the game. The students chose three leaders. These leaders, in private, chose members for their teams. The students on each team worked together to plan strategies and to help each other learn as much as they could about the subject. From my observations, it seemed the whole class was working hard to prepare for the contest.

I overheard Anne begin to explain to her group how she used a tape-recorder to learn things. When some students in the group interrupted to talk about writing questions and answers on paper, Maureen suggested they listen to Anne. Anne explained that she tapes things she wants to remember. Then she listens to the tape.

The big event was a simple contest in which teams were awarded points for correct answers given in response to John's questions. First one team then another team was in the lead. The team I thought would win came in last. Anne's team won.

When I walked into the faculty room for lunch, John was talking about the game. "There was one little girl," he was telling the other teachers, "who was shaking, but who kept getting the right answers." That girl was Anne.

In our discussions and in their response journals, the students expressed enthusiasm for that game. Linda said that it was fun to see kids who started out not knowing anything learn so much—even kids who weren't on her team. Sandy said she didn't feel one bit bad that her team lost even though they had worked so hard. She said they'd learned a lot. Anne wrote in her RJ, "It was fun and I think pepol learned alot. I think that copatighin [competition] is good cos it mack us study more. I think we shod have more tearnants [tournaments] so we can lern more." However unsure I am about such competitions, I am very sure of the value of the kind of teamwork that went into preparing for the big day.

Anne's Growth

At the beginning of the year and again at the end, Anne and her classmates were asked to fill out a writing survey (Atwell, 1987). It is interesting to compare some of Anne's early responses (which appear in italics) with her later ones. (I've corrected Anne's spelling.)

1. How do people learn to write?
I think that you have to be able to put words down on paper.
Reading a lot.

Anne's second answer seemed to be a natural outcome of our book discussions. How did Mary Hahn, the author of *Wait Till Helen Comes*, set the mood in some of those scary parts? How did Jack London get us to care about his characters? How do authors use foreshadowing to keep us reading? These sorts of questions helped students to learn useful techniques for their own writing. When I asked Anne to explain her answer for me, she said, "Well, I think first you should be able to put down words on paper, but then you should read a lot to pick up a style of writing."

2. Why do people write?
Because it lets go of some of the tension.
To teach people and to let out emotions.

Anne's concern about audience grew throughout the year. She learned that through writing she could teach others whatever it was she wanted them to learn. She was interested in Dracula and wanted others to share her interest; her writing served that purpose. It was also a good way for her to express her emotions. In her response journal, she shared and expressed much of what she felt. We all want an audience, but for Anne, with her interest in acting, perhaps an audience was even more of a necessity.

3. How does your teacher decide which pieces of writing are the good ones?
She reads it and goes over it and checks the mistakes.
She doesn't. You do.

At the end of the previous quarter, I had asked the students to select their best piece of writing and explain to me why it was the best. That probably helps explain Anne's answer. As I mentioned earlier, Anne selected "My Brother's Hit and Run" as her best story. Her reason was that it was "worded great." What was especially interesting was that she selected it before she'd received her classmates' responses to her story, before they'd all complimented her for the words she used.

4. In general, how do you feel about what you write?
I hate it. It stinks.
Pretty good.

I was delighted to read Anne's second response. Sharing her writing with friends and receiving their supportive responses did much to convince her that her writing has value.

For Anne I had one more question. I asked it near the end of the year and taped her answer. I told her that early in the year I'd noticed she wasted time during writing, but that this had changed. I asked her to explain the reason for the change. She said, "Well, I think it's when I got used to the sixth grade and stuff like that and that I got to use the computer more...and I felt better about myself with the other kids."

I could have guessed she'd mention the computer in her answer, but I wouldn't have guessed she'd mention the connection between writing and feeling better about herself in relation to the other students. Making that connection showed great insight on Anne's part.

Some days Anne writes when she could just relax with a good book. On one spring day we went outside to read under a tree. I watched as Anne took out paper and pencil and began writing.

"Tell me what you're writing about," I asked.

She said, "It's another almost accident. It's based on something true. I'm just adding things. Is it time for our kickball game?" It was Friday and Anne's last day to be a kickball team captain.

"Do you really want to leave this shade to play kickball?" I asked. Yes, of course she did—they all did. As I watched them play their game, I had to think back to the beginning of the year when Anne had walked into the room and sat with her back to most of the other people in her class. It seemed so very long ago.

References

Atwell, N. (1987). *In the middle*. Portsmouth, NH: Boynton/Cook.

Graves, D. (1991). All children can wright. In S. Stires (Ed.), *With promise*. Portsmouth, NH: Heinemann.

Macrorie, K. (1988). *The I-Search paper: Revised edition of searching writing*. Portsmouth, NH: Boynton/Cook.

Rhodes, L., & Dudley-Marling, C. (1988). *Readers and writers with a difference*. Portsmouth, NH: Heinemann.

Future Directions

Robert J. Tierney

— T W E L V E —

Ongoing Research and New Directions

*S*everal years ago, in an article written with David Pearson, I offered the following vignette of a classroom (Tierney & Pearson, 1985):

> "All right," says fourth grade teacher Amy Franklin, "it's time to work on reading. Turn to page 53; read the story; answer the questions; and then move to your skill worksheet. When you finish the worksheet, pull out your skill folder and mark your progress. Then check your daily assignment. If you're working in skills, check your chart and select a skill sheet that matches your progress. If your assignment today is free reading, find a blue dot book. Remember, blue dot books are intended for you."
>
> After a while, the reading coordinator, Tom Benson, drops by and chats briefly with Amy. As he's leaving, he says, "If there's anything I can do to help, Amy, let me know. And remember, I need a summary of skills for each child" (p. 14).

As we stated in the same article,

> Despite their hard work and humanistic goals, many teachers were locked into a production-line mentality. They accepted the responsibility of positioning students within the system, assessing progress according to prescribed sets of skills and subskills, providing appropriate practice materials, and keeping voluminous records of it all (p. 14).

At that time, it seemed as if students were expected to fit the system rather than the other way around. While reading and writing assignments were included in the literacy curriculum, they were not interrelated. Nowadays, I would suggest a vignette with somewhat different features:

The students are working in different areas in the classroom. There is a hum of conversation. Eleanor can be overheard saying to Paul, "I'm going to use your name in my story." Paul says to Timothy, "Let's work together on our report. Do you have the plans we wrote down?" Ivan says to Roberta and Rachel, "Can I share my story so far?" The teacher is chatting with Peter and Jessica about their progress.

The teacher asks the students to gather for group sharing time. At this meeting, Juan shares his story and responds to his classmates' questions: Why did you write the story? Where did you get the idea? What will you write next? Then Paul and Timothy discuss their plans for a report, including where they will go to explore ideas and some of the discoveries they've already made. The teacher then introduces a text presented in an oversized book. As the teacher and students discuss its topic, they make predictions, offer comments on the text, and sometimes read along with the teacher. The students then move to reading their own trade books.

The principal comes into the room. After chatting briefly with the teacher, she sits down with a couple of children and asks them to share their portfolios with her. She tells them, "You have a wonderful range of selections you have written and read, as well as projects you have done. Some of your comments suggest that you chose some of them because they were things you discovered for yourself. Can you tell me about some of the reasons you chose these to go in your portfolios?"

These two vignettes afford a glimpse of some dramatic shifts in how reading and writing instruction is approached. Figure 1 lists some of the shifts in views of reading and writing that have occurred over the past 20 years or so; Figure 2 describes some of the shifts in practice.

The shifts highlighted in the two figures, along with others, were fueled by developments on a variety of fronts. Researchers' thoughts about reading and writing began to be influenced by work in a variety of areas: the process-oriented research in writing, theoretical discussions on the pragmatics of reading and writing, studies of developing readers and writers, research on

Figure 1
Shifts in Viewpoints

1970s	1990s
Reading is receiving; writing is producing.	Reading and writing are composing, constructing, problem-solving activities.
Reading and writing are means of translating or transmitting ideas.	Reading and writing are vehicles for thinking.
Reading involves understanding the author's message; writing involves making your message clear for others.	Reading and writing involve interaction among participants as communicators, as well as the pursuit of self-discovery.
Reading and writing occur in a social context.	Reading and writing involve social processes.
Reading is a precursor to writing development.	Reading and writing development go hand in hand. Early writing is an avenue for reading development.
Writing development requires mastery of spelling conventions; reading development begins with mastery of skills and subskills.	Writing development involves invention as students pursue temporary spellings, negotiate conventions, etc. Reading development occurs naturally as students explore meaningful literacy experiences.

reading and writing processes, and studies examining the impact of learning from text. Consider a brief review of some of these developments:

- In conjunction with the process-based descriptions of writing as a problem-solving experience and composing activity, reading researchers developed models of the reader as writer, which complemented and extended the schema-theoretic traditions of constructivist views of meaning making.

- Developments in linguistics, especially pragmatics, prompted reading and writing researchers to describe meaning making in terms of author-reader interactions and the social dynamics of interpretative communities (i.e., reading and writing are similar to conversations).

- Studies of preschool literacy development challenged age-old notions of how literacy was acquired and brought to the fore the extent to

Figure 2
Shifts in Practice

1970s	1990s
Reading and writing are taught separately.	Reading and writing are taught together.
Reading and writing skills are listed separately.	Reading and writing programs are developed from a list of skills and behaviors that apply to both processes.
Writing is excluded from reading; reading is excluded from writing.	Writing and reading occur together in collaboration.
Single texts are used to read or write.	Multiple texts are used to write, synthesize, pursue projects, develop reports, or analyze.
Beginning reading involves reading readiness activities.	Beginning reading involves shared reading and opportunities to write.
Early writing involves dictated stories and activities focused on mastering conventions.	Early writing involves allowing students to approximate and pursue conventions based on emerging hypotheses about language and how it works.

which reading and writing are intertwined and work together from a very early age.

- Studies of the relationship of reading and writing to thinking and learning indicated that when writing and reading were tied to one another, both thinking and learning were enhanced.

These developments did not occur in isolation. In many ways, research on these topics added to the findings of schema-theory, which emerged in the early 1970s, and to the growing interest in instruction. At the same time, this new approach in research was shaped and spurred on by what was happening in schools. Indeed, a great many of the major shifts in literacy education related to reading/writing relationships were sponsored by teachers and other education personnel, who embraced process writing, literature-based programs supported by classroom libraries, whole language views and methodologies, writing across the curriculum, the importance of such things as invented spelling and shared reading to early literacy development, and a shift toward integrated curricula with simplified and reduced skill listings.

In the 1980s classroom teachers encountered the work of Graves (1978), who validated their grassroots explorations of reading/writing connections in his published research. It became obvious that (1) writing has ties to reading, (2) reading and writing work in synergy, and (3) adopting a writer's approach to reading (or integrating reading and writing) involves being more process oriented and offering more in the way of collaborative activities.

Will the reading/writing research continue to shift directions? Perhaps. I believe, though, that the shifts are over. Instead, I anticipate that further developments will build on or extend the shifts that have already occurred. In this regard, let me describe what new ideas are influencing my own thinking and research.

Intertextuality and Integration

During the 1960s, reading and writing instruction were kept separate for the most part. During classroom reading time, writing was rare; during writing time, reading was rare. In the 1970s and 1980s, researchers and educators became interested in the impact that reading and writing had on one another. As a result, teachers and researchers often used writing assignments as precursors or follow-ups to reading. At this time views of reading and writing relationships seemed to be tied to the transfer value between the two.

In the later part of the 1980s, a number of researchers shifted away from viewing writing as a learning tool or adjunct for reading, and interest grew in the synergism that occurred when reading and writing worked together. The relationship was seen as straightforward, however, and most teachers and researchers focused on reading and writing single texts. At the end of the decade, a shift toward a more dynamic view of reading/writing interrelationships became the focus. An image offered by a group of educators seems relevant:

> A learner is only a partial biologist, for instance, if he [or she] cannot read or write to discover information and meaning in biology. When a student takes the results of his or her observations about lobsters, reads, writes a draft, talks, reads, then writes again, he or she learns what it is to think critically (Guthrie, 1985, p. 15).

In accordance with this shift, attention turned to reading and writing multiple texts. In the course of working on assignments or developing projects, for example, students were encouraged to use several sources (reference books, literary selections, films, input from peers, and so on).

The relationship between intertextuality and learning outcomes (including thinking critically) seems central to this new interest of researchers. William McGinley and I (1989) posited that the nature of the relationship between texts contributed to the tensions, overlap, and transactions at the heart of learning. As learners crisscross between published texts, their own writing, and the writing of peers, a kind of dialectic between ideas emerges; this exchange facilitates shifts in thinking and builds momentum for further learning.

Studies that offer detailed descriptions of learning contexts for early literacy development consider intertextuality in a similar way. For example, on the basis of her observations of first graders, Short (1986) argued that the potential of learning and thinking changes when the classroom environment encourages students' use of multiple texts. Rowe (1987) studied literacy learning for three- and four-year-olds in a daycare setting and concluded that two general types of intertextual connections are important: the formation of shared meanings with others and links with literacy experience. In conjunction with exploring the literacy learning of preschoolers, Dyson (1988) highlighted the role of the interrelationships between forms of expression (children's writing, drawings, talk, and so on) and posited this thesis:

> Children's major developmental challenge is not simply to create a unified text world but to move among multiple worlds, carrying out multiple roles and coordinating multiple space/time structures. That is, to grow as writers of imaginary worlds, and, by inference, other sorts of text worlds as well, children must differentiate and work to resolve the tensions among the varied symbolic and social worlds within which they write—worlds with different dimensions of time and space. And it is our own differentiation of these competing worlds that will allow us as adults to understand the seemingly unstable worlds, the shifts of time frames and points of view, that children create (p. 356).

It is noteworthy that these studies all emphasize the power of a learning environment that facilitates transactions and tensions among texts. Still, research in this area is in its infancy—especially instructional research that explores when and how learners might negotiate such interrelationships and what they might gain from them. To date just a few studies have focused on the instructional implications of intertextuality; these studies have looked at students' perspectives, expertise, stance, sense of authorship and authoring, and overall abilities and the ways these factors influence the strategies and reasoning students use (see, for example, Ackerman, 1989; Greene, 1989; Kennedy, 1985; McGinley, 1988; Nelson & Hayes, 1988; Spivey, 1984; Spivey & King, 1989).

On first glance the ramifications of the shift away from dealing with the transfer between a single written text and a read text and toward how learners crisscross multiple texts may seem minor, but I believe they are serious. In particular, the ramifications for practice seem immense. Whereas most uses of reading and writing involve connections with other texts and other learners across time, most of our pedagogy has been tied to research and practice with a single text and has assumed that students approach that text in a linear, content-driven fashion.

Dynamic, Complex, and Situation-Based Thinking

Simultaneous to the shift away from viewing reading and writing in terms of transfer value, other major shifts have occurred in our thinking about the nature and role of reading and writing in learning situations.

First, studies suggest that the thinking involved when one is reading and writing varies even in a single instance of writing (e.g., notetaking in a lecture) or a particular reading mode (e.g., reading a chapter in a content area text). In other words, the thinking associated with reading and writing is both dynamic and complex. The nature of thinking is apt to vary depending on changes in the learner's purposes, emerging understanding, and the context for learning, as well as the content being addressed. For example, reading lecture notes might initially simply highlight ideas, but as a reader proceeds, the notes may become a basis for hypothesizing. Learners are apt to enlist a variety of reading-thinking and writing-thinking procedures as they shift gears and directions within different learning situations.

Second, a growing number of theorists have argued that learning cannot be approached as generalizable across contexts. This view holds that learning is fundamentally tied to contexts—that is, it is "situation based"— and to cope with variations across situations learning requires flexibility rather than the rigid use of strategies taught in a prescriptive fashion. The ability to approach learning in different ways across contexts (and even within the same context) develops as learners are exposed to different situations.

So what do these notions suggest about how reading and writing work together? I think that they should lead us to view literacy as dynamic and varied. In contrast, past research has tended to approach reading and writing activities as static. We need to move to think about reading and writing working together in terms of multiplicity and heterogeneity.

Multimedia and Multilayered Learning

Coming on the heels of these developments are new technologies that integrate material from multiple sources into multilayered, multidimensional, and multimedia texts. These developments extend our view of literacy beyond reading and writing to the integration of sounds and images with words. How does the combination of these media contribute to learning? How does it affect the way students approach learning?

Engaging in reading and writing with multiple texts appears to offer possibilities that writing without such sources does not, and it seems that the interrelationships among print and other media may afford similar potentials. Pierce (1966), for example, suggested that translation of ideas from one symbol system to another affords new ways of knowing that enhance ongoing learning. Working from these notions, Siegel (1984) offered powerful demonstrations of the increased learning and more open attitudes toward meaning that emerge when illustrations are used as vehicles to promote understanding.

This new line of inquiry has prompted a resurgence of interest in drama and the visual arts as ways of knowing and considerable attention to technologies with graphic interface capabilities. Dramatic presentations of issues raised in books, student writing, and discussion are being explored as a means of furthering understanding of those issues. Technology has made it easy to integrate material from multiple sources—text, graphics, sound, and visual images—into multimedia texts and has spurred inquiry into how learning changes when the nature of reading and writing change.

My colleagues and I have been examining the impact of multimedia presentations on education, including how students' learning, strategies, and views of text are affected by this sort of presentation. For example, we have recently begun examining video technology as a tool for learning. In particular, we are studying shifts in students' use and understanding of how video can help them learn, as well as the types of learning students pursue with video. Our goal is to understand the evolution of video as a mode of learning in the same spirit with which literacy educators have been learning about literacy development among young children.

Assessment: New Visions and Better Alternatives

As a person intrigued with the effects of reading and writing (in all their incarnations) on learning, I find myself in constant search of ways to tap into what learners are thinking and doing. Shifts in my understanding of the impact of reading and writing on learning would be limited, if not stalled, if I were not willing to pursue new ways of observing and evaluating learners. Unfortunately, studies exploring viable assessment alternatives that reflect shifts in literacy theory and instruction are still lacking. How might teachers acquire the assessment data they need to make well-reasoned decisions on learning? How do we give students feedback to encourage their learning?

I believe there are two issues to be resolved with regard to a needed shift in assessment approaches: (1) researchers must rethink literacy and how literacy achievement is depicted; and (2) educators must design assessment procedures that reflect what we know about reading and writing and that work in classrooms in a positive and enriching manner.

Reconceptualizing Literacy

Recently my colleagues and I have been pursuing an approach to literacy assessment that takes into account three self-evident yet often overlooked ideas: (1) evidence of literacy development may vary from individual to individual; (2) literacy may develop in a multidimensional rather than a one-dimensional way; and (3) the elements of each dimension of literacy development may differ for different people. Given these notions it seems clear that assessment instruments must be flexible.

My colleagues and I hope to be able to develop assessment tools that take into account these and other current ideas about literacy—that it is made up of a repertoire of abilities and is flexible, dynamic, varied, idiosyncratic, situation based, open ended, multidimensional, and multicultural.

To this end we have begun to elaborate on literacy's various dimensions and how they might be depicted. Consider, for example, literacy events in your own life. One might involve your engaging in a host of reading and writing activities when sending out a memo to colleagues. Some of the salient features of this event might include the social negotiations you pursued en route to developing the memo, the quality of the reasoning reflected in the memo, and the intended impact of the memo on others. Another event might involve looking through a student's portfolio and your class notes or records as you formulate a written report for the child's parents. The salient features of this event might be the strategies you use to study these sources and formulate the report. Other literacy events might involve the reading and discussing of newspaper or magazine articles.

Literacy abilities have traditionally been represented by a form of summary grade (A, B, C, etc.) or score (grade equivalency) which rather grossly judges an individual's performance, usually by a form of comparison with others. While such an approach may be easy to apply, its relationship to any kind of useful reality is questionable. Such scores have the potential to simplify the differences between students, distort the complexities of students' engagement in literacy, and disregard literacy's multifaceted nature. Furthermore, such scores do not allow one to achieve any kind of image of the nature of different students' literacy experiences.

An alternative to this form of summary might be to generate profiles based on an analysis of literacy events. City skylines are a useful metaphor for visualizing such profiles. Imagine different cityscapes. Each has a variety of structures that vary in size, design, function, and other features as well as in their relationships to one another and to the whole. While each city might have buildings dedicated to banking, government, and so on, the buildings themselves are usually unique to each city; each cityscape, therefore, is different, as one would expect. As one discusses improvements and city planning, some consideration might be given to what has worked in other cities, but most of the planning is done in terms of the individuals' city's geography and its emerging character. The parallels to literacy and literacy development are apparent. Each individual's literacy development might be depicted by structures not unlike city buildings. These structures emerge based on a consideration of different literacy events; they are designed to represent the features that are salient to these events. One of the structures might relate to projects that the students pursued, another to journals, and so on. Just as differences in the profiles of cities are to be expected, differences in the profiles of students could be expected.

As we have considered the various dimensions that constitute literacy, we have explored such superordinate features as genre, the social dimensions of literacy and the nature of the collaborations in which students engage, the nature and quality of processes and reasoning involved in literacy tasks, as well as the outcomes and ramifications that emerge. For a single literacy event—or slice out of the student's ongoing literacy experiences—we can depict the way a student negotiates a particular text type. As we move to another literacy event, different facets emerge or are highlighted in different ways or to varying degrees.

We have found this multidimensional view valuable in profiling learners' literacy development. Rather than being collapsed or simplified into one model, the profile can be examined in various ways. We can, for example, examine reading development and attitudes with particular types of text (say romance versus biography), both separately and together. Variations in development can be seen immediately and serve as a basis for appreciating an individual's strengths and weaknesses. We believe that performance on standardized tests could be *added* to the profile rather than subsuming the whole profile. Indeed, we suspect that a comparison of test results with other elements in the profile will highlight some of the sampling problems inherent in testing.

Obviously there are a host of other methodological possibilities these profiles might yield. Important to consider, however, are the dimensions themselves and the elements within the dimensions. We suspect that the way students' literacy experiences will be configured across the dimensions may require the use of multidimensional sampling procedures instead of uniform or standardized sampling procedures. Rather than require different students to manifest literacy in exactly the same ways, we see a list of overlapping possibilities and variations. The flexibility of the dimensions allows for differences in the overall configuration of literacy development. Furthermore, depending on the needs of the viewer, the picture presented could show a broad range of skills or focus on individual students' specific strengths or weaknesses.

Alternative Assessment Possibilities

I have also been exploring the use of portfolios as a vehicle for engaging students and teachers in ongoing assessment. In particular, I have studied how portfolios provide students with trustworthy visions of their literacy learning experiences and vehicles for learning about themselves and their development. The overriding theme of my research on portfolios is the assessment of assessment: What kinds of images of literacy do portfolios afford? How do these images help students, teachers, and parents? Central to my interest in portfolios is my belief that they can be consistent with current views of literacy and learning and enrich teachers', students', and parents' views of education. Portfolios are not panaceas, but if they are thoughtfully developed and implemented, they have great potential—especially in terms of linking classroom assessment practices with instruction. If, on the other hand, they are used haphazardly or rigidly, portfolios may not fulfill their promise.

Portfolios, however, will never be the whole answer. There is an enormous need to develop procedures by which teachers can explore various aspects of reading and writing that resist measurement. These include procedures to assess knowledge shifts, meaning-making strategies, the use of skill clusters, the social dimensions of literacy, and the intertextual nature of literacy learning.

A Pedagogy for Empowerment

McLaren (1989) argues that schools should be teaching literacy that "frames reading and writing in terms of moral and political decision-making":

> Literacy in this view is not linked to learning to read advertisements and becoming better consumers, or escaping into the pages of romance novels or spy thrillers; critical literacy links language competency to acquiring analytic skills which empower individuals to challenge the status quo (p. 19).

Often I begin my course on teaching reading and writing by saying "If thinking critically is our goal, then perhaps we should exclude reading and writing from our classroom." As discussion unfolds, students in my class have little difficulty identifying the ways literacy instruction is used to subjugate and indoctrinate: the extent to which teachers control the floor and define "rightness" and "wrongness"; the prescribed reading material that is devoted to mainstream experiences; the neglect of cultural diversity; testing practices that support standardization rather than variation; promotion and retention practices that inhibit rather than encourage learning.

One recent development that has serious implications for reading and writing research is the ideological examination of our approaches to teaching, learning, and research. Some groups of researchers are asking important questions about the ideologies that underlie literacy instruction (e.g., Apple, 1988; Gee, 1990). In particular, they question whether school literacy experiences liberate or perpetuate control and subjugation, especially of minority groups. When some widely used instructional practices are examined in terms of the politics from which they developed and which they continue to mirror, conformity and indoctrination rather than empowerment and liberation emerge as the results of their use. Literacy can be used as a tool to maintain the status quo or as a means of challenging it.

Research on literacy needs to examine the sociopolitical dimensions of literacy. As Gee (1990) points out, "the study of literacy ultimately requires us to study the social groups and institutions within which one is socialized to interpret certain types of words and certain sorts of worlds in certain ways" (p. 46). Most curriculum efforts do not extend beyond the classroom walls except when it is "safe" to do so. Instead of being responsive to community needs or informed by the experiences of their clientele, literacy practices in schools may stagnate and become irrelevant. Communities are often expected to accept approaches to teaching that deny or dismiss what has occurred (and is occurring) outside of the schools' four walls. I hope we will see an increase in research and teaching initiatives that reflect a different relationship to learners and their communities.

Closing Remarks

I feel optimistic about research and practice on reading/writing relationships—but only cautiously so. There is still a great deal to address, including the issues that I have mentioned here. And I have a small word of warning to offer: I encourage researchers and practitioners to pull back from their enamorment with reading/writing connections to consider the drawbacks. Sometimes, writing and reading may stifle rather than empower. We should try to understand how and in what situations reading and writing contribute to didacticism versus dialogue, rigidity rather than flexibility, entrenchment rather than exploration, paraphrasing or plagiarism as opposed to new texts. In terms of research, I suspect that the work has just begun. Indeed, the shifts that have occurred and are occurring in our views of literacy have opened us to a research terrain that is largely uncharted.

References

Ackerman, J.M. (1989). *Reading and writing in the academy.* Unpublished doctoral dissertation, Carnegie Mellon University, Pittsburgh, PA.

Apple, M.W. (1988). *Teachers and text.* New York: Routledge, Chapman & Hall.

Dyson, A. (1988). Negotiations among multiple worlds: The space/time dimensions of young children's composing. *Research in the Teaching of English, 22*(4), 335-390.

Gee, J. (1990). *Social linguistics and literacies: Ideology in discourses.* New York: Falmer.

Graves, D. (1978). *Balance the basics: Let them write.* New York: Ford Foundation.

Greene, S. (1989, November). *Intertextuality and moves to authority in writing from sources.* Paper presented at the National Reading Conference, Austin, TX.

Guthrie, J. (1985). *Curriculum reform and strategies related to reading, writing, and content areas.* Princeton, NJ: College Entrance Examination Board.

Kennedy, M.L. (1985). The composing processes of college students writing from sources. *Written Communication, 2,* 434-456.

McGinley, W. (1988). *The role of reading and writing in the acquisition of knowledge: A study of college students' reading and writing engagements in the development of a persuasive argument.* Unpublished doctoral dissertation, University of Illinois, Urbana, IL.

McGinley, W., & Tierney, R.J. (1989). Traversing the topical landscape: Reading and writing as ways of knowing. *Written Communication, 6,* 243-269.

McLaren, P. (1989). *Life in schools: An introduction to critical pedagogy in the foundations of education.* White Plains, NY: Longman.

Nelson, J., & Hayes, J.R. (1988). *How the writing context shapes college students' strategies for writing from sources* (Technical Report No. 16). Berkeley, CA: University of California, Center for the Study of Writing.

Pierce, C.S. (1966). *Collected papers of Charles Sanders Pierce.* Cambridge, MA: Harvard University Press.

Rowe, D.W. (1987). Literacy learning as an intertextual process. In J.E. Readence & R.S. Baldwin (Eds.), *Research in literacy: Merging perspectives.* Rochester, NY: National Reading Conference.

Short, K.G. (1986). Literacy as a collaborative experience: The role of intertextuality. In J.A. Niles & R.V. Lalik (Eds.), *Solving problems in literacy: Learners, teachers, and researchers* (pp. 227-232). Rochester, NY: National Reading Conference.

Siegel, M. (1984). *Reading as signification.* Unpublished doctoral dissertation, Indiana University, Bloomington, IN.

Spivey, N.N. (1984). *Discourse synthesis: Constructing texts in reading and writing.* Newark, DE: International Reading Association.

Spivey, N.N., & King, J.R. (1989). Readers as writers composing from sources. *Reading Research Quarterly, 24*(1), 7-26.

Tierney, R.J., & Pearson, P.D. (1985). New priorities for teaching reading. *Learning, 13*(8), 14-18.

PART
— SIX —

Appendix

— A P P E N D I X —

Reading/Writing Research: 1900 to 1984

*B*etween 1982 and 1985 the International Reading Association's Reading and Its Relationship to Writing committee undertook a survey of research on reading/writing connections. The purpose of the survey was to identify all the studies available that dealt with reading/writing connections, evaluate them, and then produce a bibliography listing the best research in the field. The committee members also hoped that the survey would reveal some of the general trends researchers were following and suggest avenues for new research.

First, the committee conducted a computerized library search for all reading/writing research published between 1900 and 1982. Specifically, ERIC, *Dissertation Abstracts International, Psychological Abstracts,* and *Learning and Language Behavior Abstracts (LLBA)* were searched in order to find the intersection of "reading," "writing," "instruction," and related descriptors. A separate search for 1982 to 1984 was completed later.

Nearly 2,500 entries emerged. A graduate student assistant determined which of these entries described "research," defined very broadly as "the gathering of data for the purpose of drawing conclusions." From this subset, 273 studies that dealt with both reading and writing were retained for analysis.

The research assistant then coded the pre-1982 studies to relevant demographic characteristics. (Later, I coded the 1982-1984 studies myself.) The relevant characteristics were as follows:

1. date;

2. source (book, journal, dissertation, unpublished paper, presented paper);

3. field of journal (education, psychology, linguistics, rhetoric, literature, language, other);

4. database *(Dissertation Abstracts International,* LLBA, *Psychological Abstracts,* ERIC);

5. sex of first and second authors;

6. nationality of authors;

7. category of research question (process description, reader or author characteristics, instructional methodologies, text characteristics); and

8. primary unit of text examined (letter, word, sentence, prose, all, irrelevant).

The committee planned to prepare an annotated bibliography of "quality" research, so the next task was to determine which studies were the best. Skimming the studies' abstracts revealed an amazing variety in subject, purpose, method, apparent quality of design, and so forth. To avoid bias as much as possible, researchers identified as working in the reading/writing field were asked to rate the studies. This group included specialists from a variety of disciplines, with a range of specific interests similar to those represented in the abstracts themselves.

A rating sheet was designed to allow these researchers to respond to each abstract separately (see Part A of the Figure). They were asked to rate each study's importance (both current and historical), its contribution to specific questions, and the quality of its design, based on the impressions gained by reading the abstracts. They were also asked to assign categories to the study's design and research question (process vs. instruction; reader/author, text, or situation characteristics; letter, word, sentence, or prose units). In Part B, the researchers were asked to summarize their findings and rank the top five studies.

Figure
Research Analysis Response Form

A. Please answer the following questions for each abstract:

	Strongly agree	Agree	Undecided	Disagree	Strongly disagree
			(Circle one.)		
1. I think this study is important for others to know about.	5	4	3	2	1
2. This study is valuable now, given the present state of the art.	5	4	3	2	1
3. This study made a valuable contribution in the past but it is no longer of value.	5	4	3	2	1
4. This study was valuable in the past and continues to be so.	5	4	3	2	1
5. This study makes a valuable contribution to our knowledge of					
a. the relationship between reading and writing processes,	5	4	3	2	1
b. the measurement of reading/ writing skills, and	5	4	3	2	1
c. ways to teach more effectively.	5	4	3	2	1

6. Which of the following research methodologies was used in the study? (Circle one.)

   a. Experimental
   b. Quasi-experimental
   c. Descriptive
   d. Demographic
   e. Meta-analysis

   f. Quantitative or qualitative (circle one)
   g. Other (please specify) _____
   _____
   _____
   _____

7. Rate the overall quality of the research methodology (from what you can tell in the abstract). (Check one box.)

Very low quality	1 ☐	2 ☐	3 ☐	4 ☐	5 ☐	Very high quality

8. Which issue is the research question primarliy concerned with? (Circle one.)
   a. Process   b. Influencing learning

9. Is the research question concerned with any of the following process influences? (Circle as many as necessary.)

(continued)

Irwin

a. Reader and/or writer characteristics
b. Text characteristics
c. Situational characteristics

10. The measure of the dependent variable(s) is primarily related to what unit of information? (Circle as many as necessary.)

    a. Letter   b. Word   c. Sentence   d. Prose

B. 1. Rank the 5 best of the 20 abstracts that you received using first *quality* and then *importance to the field* as criteria. *List only 5 studies for each.* The studies may be ordered the same way or differently for each criterion. For example, one study may be a "5" in quality but only a "2" in importance.

	QUALITY	IMPORTANCE
	Abstract #	Abstract #
Highest ranked	1 _____	1 _____
	2 _____	2 _____
	3 _____	3 _____
Lowest ranked	4 _____	4 _____
	5 _____	5 _____

2. Consider the studies you chose as the five best in terms of quality. What research criteria led you to rank them as the best? Please rank and describe these criteria in one or two sentences each.

3. Consider the studies you chose as the five best in terms of importance. What research criteria led you to rank them as the best? Please rank and describe these criteria in one or two sentences each.

4. We consider you to be an expert in either process or instructional research on reading, writing, or the relationship between reading and writing. Please identify your area of expertise by circling the appropriate response below:

    1. (Circle one.)   a. Process   b. Instruction
    2. (Circle one.)   a. Reading   b. Writing   c. Reading/writing relationship

5. What criteria would you use to identify the highest quality current research in your major research area as indicated in question #4? Once again, please rank and describe these criteria in one or two sentences each.

The abstracts were then divided at random into sets of 20. Each set was assigned to two researchers from two different fields.

Because this survey was completed in 1983, it was necessary for the quality of the 1982-1984 data to be assessed separately. I completed response forms for these later studies after carefully studying the criteria identified by the experts completing the earlier survey.

Limitations of the Data

Before looking at the results of an analysis of this data, it is important to be aware of their limitations. First, the actual studies selected were limited by the nature of the bibliographies searched. Thus, the analysis here should be viewed as a description of the research listed in these bibliographies rather than as a complete description of all research available. Second, the rater for the demographic information changed for the 1982-1984 data; I, rather than the previously chosen experts, completed the quality response forms for these later studies. Third, many of the decisions, especially in the quality survey but even at the demographic level, were extremely subjective. Finally, all of these decisions were made on the basis of an abstract alone. Many of the experts complained about this (and rightly so), but the committee simply did not have the resources to copy and distribute such a large number of complete articles.

General Description

The earliest study located by the search was published in 1929. Published work on reading/writing connections was scarce until the early 1970s; another increase was noted in the early 1980s. Eighty-three percent of the studies were classified as being in the field of education, with the second most common discipline being psychology (10 percent). Rhetoric, linguistics, literature, foreign languages (for the purposes of the survey, languages other than English), and all other related disciplines each accounted for less than 4 percent of the studies. The majority of the 273 studies were found in dissertations (155); the only other common source was journal articles (81). While 34 studies could not be classified according to the sex of the first author, 97 had male and 142 had female first authors. About 17 percent of the studies were published outside the United States.

In terms of the research question being addressed, 158 of the studies were rated as primarily concerned with methods of instruction, 84 with characteristics of the reader or writer, 22 with the processes themselves, and 8 with text variables. Twenty-three focused on letter-level units of text, 6 on word units, 9 on sentence units, 48 on prose, and 186 were coded as dealing with multiple levels.

The reviewers were, on average, neutral about the quality of the studies. On a Likert scale of 1 to 5, the mean values for the first set of reviewers on the first two items on the Research Analysis Response Form were 3.185 and 3.055. According to the experts, the majority of the studies used quasi-experimental designs (115), with the next largest categories being experimental (79) and descriptive (38). Studies using quantitative data (120) were more common than those using qualitative data (53). The experts rated 133 of the studies as focusing on influencing learning and 115 as being more concerned with processes. When allowed to circle as many adjectives as they wanted, they categorized 155 studies as dealing with reader or author characteristics, 48 with text variables, and 94 with situational variables. On the issue of unit level examined, the results were as follows: letter – 42; word – 82; sentence – 112; prose – 152.

Results by Discipline

The results are more interesting when cross-tabulated by discipline. The discipline of each study was subjectively determined from a variety of clues, including the research question, the researcher's university departmental affiliation (when available), the jargon in the abstract, and so on. The purpose was to establish authors' major areas of study with the assumption that this would represent the disciplinary milieu giving rise to each study.

Chi-square tests of affiliation showed significant relationships ($p \leq .01$) between discipline category and research method as categorized by the experts ($\chi^2 = 109.8$, $df = 30$, $p = .00$), the field of the journal of publication ($\chi^2 = 126.3$, $df = 25$, $p = .00$), the source of entry ($\chi^2 = 61.9$, $df = 18$, $p = .00$), the period of publication (investigated in more detail in the next section), the first author's nationality ($\chi^2 = 45.35$, $df = 6$, $p = .00$), the research question as rated by the experts ($\chi^2 = 99.17$, $df = 18$, $p = .00$), and the unit of text examined ($\chi^2 = 64.75$, $df = 24$, $p = .00$). No significant relationships were found between discipline and the expert quality ratings or between discipline and the sex of the authors.

Since educational and psychological studies together made up well over 90 percent of all the studies identified, the bulk of the following analysis will examine these two groups of studies.

The differences across disciplines in terms of research methods are occasionally surprising (see Table 1). Of the 26 psychological studies, 7.7 percent used quasi-experimental and "other" designs, compared with 32.3 percent of the educational studies. This is as might be expected since the psychological studies are less concerned with ecological validity in real classrooms. Thirty-one percent of the educational studies were classified as using true experimental designs—higher than might have been predicted, given the second-class status often afforded to educational research by other disciplines. The only other discipline using experimental or quasi-experimental designs was rhetoric (2 out of 8 studies), loosely defined as the teaching of English at the high school or college level.

Table 1
Discipline of Research Studies, by Research Method

Quality	Experimental	Quasi-experimental	Descriptive	Demographic	Meta-analysis	Other
Education	62	51	69	2	3	14
Psychology	6	2	14	1	3	0

Most of the studies published in the form of journal articles tended, naturally, to appear in journals devoted to the same discipline addressed in the article. The one interesting finding here is the overlap in education and psychology. Of 54 education articles, 17 appeared in psychology journals, while 8 of 24 psychology articles appeared in education journals. Also of interest is the finding that education studies appear in all kinds of journals. In this instance, 5 education studies appeared in rhetoric journals, 3 in linguistics, and 1 in a nonspecific journal category.

Half of the educational studies were found in *Dissertation Abstracts International*, with the second most prominent source (77 of 227 studies) being *Psychological Abstracts*. The 26 psychological studies were split between *LLBA* (12) and *Psychological Abstracts* (13), with a single study appearing in *DAI*. One wonders if doctoral students in psychology were discouraged from conducting dissertations in the area of reading/writing connections.

Almost 90 percent of the educational studies originated in the United States, whereas the psychology studies were more evenly split between U.S. (40 percent) and non-U.S. (60 percent) authorship. This could be because more international journals on psychology are entered into the computerized bibliographies than are international education journals.

As might have been expected, the educational studies were more likely to focus on instruction than were the psychological studies, which tended to examine reader/author characteristics. Of course, because the discipline category assignments were largely subjective, it is impossible to know how much the research question determined the discipline category—that is, the fact that a study examined instruction might have led to its being labeled an educational study. Viewed in this manner, this information might be better interpreted simply as validation of the discipline categories.

Finally, although the majority of both the psychological and educational studies were classified as involving more than one text level, the remaining psychological studies were most likely to focus on letter-level questions, while the remaining educational studies were most likely to focus on prose-level questions. This probably reflects the psychological emphasis on perception versus the educational stress on comprehension and composition.

Results by Publication Period

Perhaps the most interesting results stem from analyses of chronological trends in the data. The committee hypothesized that there might be a shift in the type and number of studies investigating reading and writing some time in the early 1970s. This was when educators were feeling the full impact of psycholinguistics and cognitive psychology. In terms of reading comprehension research, "basic" research on processes came into vogue during this period, and the earlier emphasis on letter and word decoding gave way to a new interest in prose variables. We also hypothesized that there might have been another shift in research type more recently. Again, in terms of comprehension research, there has been a resurgence of interest in instructional studies, ecological validity, and alternative methodologies over the past 10 to 15 years. An informal examination of the data suggested that these shifts did, in fact, occur.

In order to investigate these hypotheses statistically, the data were divided into three "eras," with 1929-1971 deemed the "early research period," 1972-1981 the "psycholinguistic research period," and 1982-1984 the "recent research period." Of course, it must be remembered that the studies in the recent research period were coded by a different researcher than those in the earlier two periods. Thus, interpretations of differences between the recent and the earlier periods should be viewed with caution.

Chi-square tests of association revealed significant relationships ($p \leq .01$) between the research-period categories and several of the demographic variables: the database ($\chi^2 = 33.16$, $df = 6$, $p = .00$), the source of the publication ($\chi^2 = 16.03$, $df = 6$, $p = .01$), the rated discipline ($\chi^2 = 31.6$, $df = 12$, $p = .00$), the research question ($\chi^2 = 47.44$, $df = 6$, $p = .00$), and the unit examined ($\chi^2 = 89.69$, $df = 8$, $p = .00$). Tables 2 through 6 show the frequencies in each category.

An examination of Tables 2 and 3 suggests the following interpretations: During the early period, the majority of the studies were in *Dissertation Abstracts International*. LLBA became a useful source during the psycholinguistic

Table 2
Sources of Publication in Each Research Period

Period	Dissertation Abstracts International	LLBA	Psychological Abstracts	ERIC
Early	24	0	4	0
Psycholinguistic	55	34	56	12
Recent	44	5	37	2*

*Not searched in late 1982-1984; this figure from early 1982.

Table 3
Types of Publication in Each Research Period

Period	Journal	Dissertation	Paper	Unpublished
Early	3	21	0	0
Psycholinguistic	42	84	9	1
Recent	36	50	0	0

Irwin

period, but fewer studies were found there in the recent period. Finally, *Psychological Abstracts* seems to be an increasingly useful source when the results are seen as percentages of the total for the period. Table 3 similarly suggests that the percentage of studies in the form of dissertations has decreased and that the percentage published in journals has increased.

Tables 4 and 5 should be viewed with caution because of the extremely subjective nature of the categorizations by discipline and research question and the change of rater for the recent period. In terms of discipline, Table 4 indicates that during the early period most of the studies were done in education. During the psycholinguistic period, psychology, linguistics, and literature entered the reading/writing field. During the recent period, rhetoricians, foreign language specialists, and researchers from a variety of undefinable disciplines (probably interdisciplinary) entered the area. Again, this generally verifies the committee's original predictions.

Table 4
Discipline of Studies in Each Period

Period	Education	Psychology	Linguistics	Rhetoric	Literature	Foreign language	Other
Early	26	1	0	0	0	0	0
Psycholinguistic	135	17	3	0	2	0	0
Recent	66	8	0	8	0	1	3

Table 5
Research Question Categories in Each Period

Period	Process	Reader/Author	Instruction	Text
Early	1	2	25	0
Psycholinguistic	5	42	105	4
Recent	16	40	28	4

An examination of Table 5 suggests that, as predicted, the percentage of studies dealing with instructional questions decreased during the psycholinguistic period. At the same time, reader/author questions were examined more often. Process questions were not systematically examined until the recent period, and, in contrast to our prediction, the resurgence of interest in instructional questions could not be detected by the end of 1984.

The data in Table 6 are perhaps the least reliable, since the research assistant making these judgments expressed discomfort with his decisions. Nevertheless, the table suggests an increasing trend toward looking at letter, word, sentence, or prose variables separately; a preponderance of spelling and letter-recognition studies during the psycholinguistic period; and a gradual increase in the number of studies dealing specifically with prose-level questions.

Table 6
Text Level Examined in Each Period

	Letter	Word	Sentence	Prose	All
Early	0	0	0	1	27
Psycholinguistic	18	0	1	11	126
Recent	5	6	8	36	33

Although the research period was consistently associated with rated research quality on the expert survey, it is my opinion that these results are too unreliable to report. The biggest shifts occurred between the psycholinguistic and current periods, indicating that they may simply represent the change in raters. Moreover, the reliability for these items was extremely low.

There were, however, some significant relationships between other, potentially less subjective, category ratings and the research period. Though chi-square tests were not significant for research period and type of data, research question, text questions, situational questions, letter-level units, sentence units, or prose units, they were significant for reader/author questions ($\chi^2 = 9.39$, $df = 2$, $p = .01$) and word-level questions ($\chi^2 = 8.88$, $df = 2$, $p = .01$). The analysis of reader/author variables substantiates the trend found in Table 5 for an increase in interest occurring in the psycholinguistic period; this further analysis also verifies the trend, shown in Table 6, toward a decrease in word-level studies in the recent period.

Findings about Study Quality

The survey was designed to elicit the help of experts in the field to select studies for inclusion in a planned bibliography. However, there were many problems with this procedure, the most important being the lack of acceptable inter-rater reliability on the quality ratings. For the first six items on the survey—those that asked for judgments on individual studies' quality or importance (see the Figure), the inter-rater reliabilities ranged from .11 (question 4) to .37 (question 6). This was probably due in part to the fact that the experts were asked to make judgments on the basis of abstracts rather than complete research reports. Another possible source of disagreement was the fact that the two raters on any given abstract were always from different disciplines.

On the summary form completed at the end of all the ratings, the experts were asked to select the five best studies in terms of quality and the five best in terms of importance to the field. In most cases, the same studies were listed in both categories, albeit sometimes in a different order. Any study mentioned on any of these lists was included in the committee's select bibliography, a copy of which concludes this discussion.

A few interesting results related to these quality selections did emerge, although again, inter-rater reliability was extremely low (only 26 of the 125 studies mentioned were selected by more than one expert). Of the "excellent" studies, 67 percent addressed prose issues; only 48 percent of the unselected studies were concerned with this level. It should be noted that this relationship was not found for reader/author, text, or situation-question classifications.

Approximately 91 percent of the studies deemed excellent had first authors from the United States; 77 percent of the remaining studies were also American-authored. This may be more a reflection of the fact that U.S. authors follow different conventions in abstracts than that the quality of the studies differed.

Table 7 shows perhaps the most interesting difference between the excellent and the less-than-excellent studies. The one method that was most likely to be associated with a less-than-excellent study was descriptive. In contrast, demographic studies were very likely to be selected as excellent. Experimental and quasi-experimental methods were about equally likely to be selected as excellent: There seemed to be no prejudice against quasi-experimental studies. Indeed, these were labeled "excellent" slightly more than half the time, while experimental studies were selected slightly less often.

Table 7
Quality of Studies, by Research Method

Quality	Experi-mental	Quasi-experimental	Descrip-tive	Demo-graphic	Meta-analysis	Other
Excellent	32	30	26	5	3	8
Less than excellent	38	23	67	1	3	8

We also asked the experts to identify the criteria they used to select the "quality" or "important" studies. We compiled the results without separating these two closely related characteristics.

The criterion mentioned most often was some version of "clearly significant research question." This was usually defined as a research question that would lead to useful classroom applications or that was soundly based on theory. The belief that correlational questions have little use was reported again and again. The researchers felt that all too few of the studies "clearly added to the existing body of knowledge" or had "direct classroom applications." The studies were also criticized for their relative lack of rationale.

Several experts also noticed an emphasis on viewing reading and writing as processes. They were clearly looking for research that examined the relationship between those processes and for studies firmly grounded in new theories about exactly how and why these processes interact.

Several of the researchers also mentioned the relative lack of consideration given to the contexts affecting the processes: one criterion mentioned was "shows awareness of the broad range of contributing factors to the phenomena being studied."

The quality and appropriateness of the methodology was mentioned repeatedly. Again and again, the experts said that the methodologies were inadequate for answering the research questions. On a more specific level, the measurement instruments were often criticized. Several experts mentioned that they were looking for the use of both qualitative and quantitative measures, and that multiple measures as well as multiple methodologies were necessary to examine such complex processes.

Finally, the experts often mentioned that they were looking for a thoughtful analysis of results. The implication was that many of the studies did not provide such analysis.

The experts' opinions can be well summarized with the following comments:

> But, frankly, many of the studies were not quality studies: the questions they addressed were obvious or trivial or ill-formed, and though all the methodological machinery was there pro forma, impressively chugging away, its use was not carefully thought through.
>
> I was dismayed that the process-product and correlational studies...were of such uniformly low quality. Was this just an artifact of the process by which I was assigned abstracts or is this the state of the art? Among my concerns with these studies are their relative lack of rationale...the ad hoc quality of the measurement instruments chosen, the lack of rigor in design and administration of treatments, the failure to confront results that are equivocal and to ask larger and more interesting questions about what might be going on, and the tendency to render trivial the writing process in order to study it in terms of measurable effects of one variable upon another.

Summary

These data verified predictions that the number of studies in the area of reading/writing connections increased in the 1980s, and that these studies appeared in a wide variety of journals and came from several different disciplines, with education and psychology being by far the most prominent. The survey also verified the committee's predictions that psychological studies were more likely to use true experimental designs than were educational studies, and that educational studies were more likely to examine instructional questions.

The chronological trends were especially interesting in terms of the disciplines from which the studies emerged, the research questions discussed, and the unit of information (letter, word, sentence, prose) examined. We found that the studies from the early period (1929-1971) were largely conducted by educators, the psycholinguistic-period studies (1972-1981) were often done by psychologists, and the recent studies (1982-1984) were carried out in a wide variety of disciplines. Similarly, we also noted an increasing tendency to look at reader/author and process questions in addition to instructional ones. Finally, the recent period has the greatest number of studies looking specifically at prose-level variables. All of these findings verified our original predictions that the distinct research periods are characterized by the influence of psycholinguistics on educational questions in the 1970s and the emergence of a new interdisciplinary research paradigm in the 1980s.

The survey of experts was most interesting in terms of the complete lack of inter-rater reliability on the quality ratings. This was surprising given the virtual unanimity regarding the selection criteria. Studies perceived as using descriptive methodologies (usually correlational) were less likely to be rated as excellent than were studies using experimental or quasi-experimental designs. In contrast to our predictions, quasi-experimental studies were just as likely to be rated excellent as were experimental studies. Moreover, the raters were looking for studies addressing significant research questions, studies with classroom applications or concerned with specific processes, studies that considered the complexity of the reading/writing connection, and those that used an appropriately complex methodology and included a thorough analysis of results. According to the raters, these criteria were, for the most part, unmet.

The Top-Rated Studies

What follows is a list of the studies the committee's reviewers identified as being the best of those identified in the computer database search.

Abdan, Abdulrahman A. "The Effect of Sentence-Combining Practice on the Written Syntactic Maturity, Overall Writing Quality, and Reading Comprehension of EFL Saudi Students." Ph.D. dissertation, University of Kansas, 1983. (*Dissertation Abstracts International* 44:11A).

Allen, Max, & Wellman, Mary M. "Hand Position During Writing, Cerebral Laterality and Reading: Age and Sex Differences." *Neuropsychologia* 18:33-40.

Anderson, Peggy L. "A Comparative Study of Syntax in the Written Language of Reading Disabled and Non-Reading Disabled Children." Denver, CO: University of Denver, 1981.

Armbrecht, Brenda G. "The Effects of Sentence-Combining Practice on the Syntactic Maturity, Quality of Writing, and Reading Comprehension of a Select Group of College Students in Remedial English in Southeast Georgia." Atlanta, GA: Georgia State University, College of Education, 1981.

Arthur, Sharon V. "The Effects of Two Writing Treatments on the Reading and Writing of Third Graders." Athens, GA: University of Georgia, 1980.

Atwell, Margaret A. "The Evolution of Text: The Interrelationship of Reading and Writing in the Composing Process." Bloomington, IN: Indiana University, 1981.

Baghban, Marcia J.M. "Language Development and Initial Encounters with Written Language: A Case Study in Preschool Reading and Writing." Bloomington, IN: Indiana University, 1979.

Bair, Mary R. "A Self-Generated Writing Program and Its Effects on the Writing and Reading Growth in Kindergarten Children." Ph.D. dissertation, Rutgers University, 1984. (*Dissertation Abstracts International* 45/02-A:407.)

Bebensee, Elisabeth L. "The Relationship Between Inner-City Fifth Graders' Reading Comprehension and Writing Achievement." Ph.D. dissertation, Duke University, 1977.

Bippus, Anne Clark Marshall. "The Relationship of the Quality of Students' Written Language, Productivity of Writing, and Reading Comprehension in Grades Four and Six." Ph.D. dissertation, University of Virginia, 1977.

Birnbaum, June C. "The Reading and Composing Behavior of Selected Fourth- and Seventh-Grade Students." *Research in the Teaching of English* 16:241-60.

Birnbaum, June C. "A Study of Reading and Writing Behaviors of Selected Fourth and Seventh Grade Students." Ph.D. dissertation, Rutgers University, 1981.

Bossart, Marion C. "Writing in the Reading Class." Ph.D. dissertation, Union College Humanities Center, 1981.

Bowles, Dympna J. "An Integrated Approach to Reading and Writing for College Students." Ph.D. dissertation, Columbia University Teachers College, 1981.

Calhoun, James L. "The Effect of Analysis of Essays in College Composition Classes on Reading and Writing Skills." Ph.D. dissertation, Boston University, School of Education, 1971.

Calis, G.J., Teulings, Hans-Leo, & Keuss, Paul J. "In Search of Writing and Reading Habits in the Microgenetic Phase of Letter Recognition." Ph.D. dissertation, Catholic U Nijmegen [Netherlands], 1983.

Callaghan, Thomas F. "The Effects of Sentence-Combining Exercises on the Syntactic Maturity, Quality of Writing, Reading Ability, and Attitudes of Ninth Grade Students." Ph.D. dissertation, State University of New York – Buffalo, 1977.

Carbonell de Grompone, Maria A. "Children Who Spell Better Than They Read." *Academic Therapy* 9(5):281-88.

Conlin, Mary L. "The Relationship Between the Syntactical Complexity of Expository Writing and Reading Comprehension Levels of Community College Students." Ph.D. dissertation, Case Western University, 1981.

Cronnell, Bruce. "Phonics for Reading vs. Phonics for Spelling." *The Reading Teacher* 32:337-40.

D'Angelo, Karen. "Developing Concepts of Reading and Writing Through Literature." Ph.D. dissertation, State University of New York, 1981.

Day, Barbara D., & Swetenburg, Jan S. "Where Children 'Write to Read'." *Childhood Education* 54(5):229-33.

Dreman, S.B. "A Review of Directionality Trends in the Horizontal Dimension as a Function of Innate and Environmental Factors." *Journal of General Psychology* 96:125-34.

Duncan, Patricia H. "Developing Children's Composition Following Targeted Discussions of a Literature Selection." Ph.D. dissertation, University of Virginia, 1981.

Evanechko, Peter, Ollila, Lloyd, & Armstrong, Robert. "An Investigation of the Relationships Between Children's Performance in Written Language and Their Reading Ability." *Research in the Teaching of English* 8:315-26.

Ferreiro, Emilia. "Towards a Genetic Theory of Learning to Read." *Psychologie-schweizerische Zeitschrift für Psychologie und Ihre Anwendungen* 36:109-30.

Ferreiro, Emilia. "What Is Written in a Written Sentence?" *Journal of Education* 4:25-39.

Fishco, Daniel T. "A Study of the Relationship Between Creativity in Writing and Comprehension in Reading of Selected Seventh Grade Students." Ph.D. dissertation, Lehigh University, 1966.

Flood, James, & Menyuk, Paula. "The Development of Metalinguistic Awareness and Its Relation to Reading Achievement." *Journal of Applied Developmental Psychology* 4:65-80.

Flynn, Gregory Lee. "Reading, Thinking, Writing: A Practical Rhetoric with Readings." Ph.D. dissertation, University of Michigan, 1980.

Fuller, Katherine M. "An Investigation of the Relationship Between Reading Achievement and Oral and Written Language of Students Enrolled in Reading and English Classes at Gainesville Junior College." Ph.D. dissertation, University of Georgia, 1974.

Gowda, Nangar S. "An Exploration of the Role of Language Awareness in High School Students' Reading and Writing." *Dissertation Abstracts International* 45/08A:2374.

Hall, Christine K. "Writing as a Prereading Role-Playing Exercise to Increase the Reading Comprehension of Remedial College Students." Ph.D. dissertation, University of Louisville, 1984. (*Dissertation Abstracts International* 45/06-A:1737.)

Hart, Elizabeth J. "The Effect of a Knowledge of Selected Reading Skills on the Acquisition and Retention of These Skills in Written Composition." Ph.D. dissertation, University of South Carolina, 1980.

Hinton, Pierre R. "Basic Skills: Reading Performance Test Scores and the Impact of a Writing Program." Ph.D. dissertation, Temple University, 1982. (*Dissertation Abstracts International* 43/03A:750.)

Hoffmann, Richard J., & Kesek, Andrew. "Reading Comprehension as Predictor of Growth in Syntatic Maturity and Writing Quality in the First Two and One-Half Years of Undergraduate Study." *Perceptual and Motor Skills* 56:595-600.

Hull, Arthur J. "The Effects of Instruction in Organizational Patterns on Student Writing Competence, Reading Competence, and Attitude Toward Writing." Ph.D. dissertation, Boston University, 1982. (*Dissertation Abstracts International* 43/09-A:2911.)

Johnson, Norma. "A Comparison of Syntactic Writing Maturity with Reading Comprehension." Ph.D. dissertation.

Katchen, Linda C. "A Study in the Effects of Paradigmatic Language Training and Its Transfer to the Reading and Writing Performance of Adult Illiterates." Ph.D. dissertation, University of Georgia, 1980.

Kelley, Kathleen R. "The Effect of Writing Instruction on Reading Comprehension and Story Writing Ability (Elementary)." Ph.D. dissertation, University of Pittsburgh, 1984. (*Dissertation Abstracts International* 45/06A:1703.)

Kita, Mary J. "Children's Concepts of Reading and Writing." Ph.D. dissertation, University of Virginia, 1980.

Kucer, Stephen B. "Using Text Comprehension as a Metaphor for Understanding Text Production: Building Bridges Between Reading and Writing." Ph.D. dissertation, Indiana University, 1983. (*Dissertation Abstracts International* 44/10A:3016.)

Lansdown, Richard. "Partial Sight—Partial Achievement?" *Special Education: Forward Trends* 2:11-13.

Leone, Anne H. "A Study of the Interrelationships of Writing Ability, Writing Interest, Reading Readiness and Reading Performance of a Given Kindergarten Population." Ph.D. dissertation, University of Connecticut, 1979.

Levine, Shirley S. "The Effect of Transformational Sentence-Combining Exercises on the Reading Comprehension and Written Composition of Third-Grade Children." Ph.D. dissertation, Hofstra University, 1976.

Maat, David W. "An Inquiry into Empirical Relationships Between the Reading and Writing of Exposition and Argument." Ph.D. dissertation, State University of New York-Albany, 1977.

Mackie, Barbara C. "The Effects of a Sentence-Combining Program on the Reading Comprehension and Written Composition of Fourth-Grade Students." Ph.D. dissertation, Hofstra University, 1982. (*Dissertation Abstracts International* 42/11-A:4779.)

Manson, Martha. "Explorations in Language Arts for Preschoolers (Who Happen to Be Deaf)." *Language Arts* 59:33-39.

McAfee, Deurelle C. "Effect of Sentence-Combining Instruction on the Reading and Writing Achievement of Fifth-Grade Children in a Suburban School District." Ph.D. dissertation, Texas Woman's University, 1980.

McKenzie, Moira G. "The Range of Operative Structures Underlying the Behavior of Young Readers and Non-Readers Engaged in Reading and Writing Activities." *Dissertation Abstracts International* 35(11-A):7044-45.

McRoberts-Adair, David. "Attitudes, Writing Fluency, Reading Achievement—A Comparison Between I.T.A. and T.O. Trained Children." Ph.D. dissertation, University of Michigan, 1971.

Meyer, Bonnie J.F. "Reading Research and the Composition Teacher: The Importance of Plans." *College Composition and Communication* 33:37-49.

Morrison, Virginia A. "Getting Reading and Writing: A Description of Literacy Learning Patterns in Three Urban Families." Ph.D. dissertation, Columbia University Teachers College, 1982. (*Dissertation Abstracts International* 43/05A:1400.)

Newkirk, Thomas. "Young Writers as Critical Readers." *Language Arts* 49:451-57.

Nolan, Karen D. "An Analysis of Writing in a Case of Deep Dyslexia." *Brain and Language* 20:305-28.

Noyce, Ruth M., & Christie, James F. "Effects of an Integrated Approach to Grammar Instruction on Third Graders' Reading and Writing." *Elementary School Journal* 84:63-69.

O'Donnell, John F. "An Experimental Study of the Effects of the Supplemental Use of a Psycholinguistic Remedial Tutorial Program on the Reading and Writing Behaviors of Black High-Risk College Freshmen and on Their Attitudes Toward Reading, Writing, and Other College-Related Stimuli." Ph.D. dissertation, Temple University, 1974.

O'Neill, Nancy V. "A Comparison of the Strategies in Composition and Strategies in Reading Comprehension of Eighth-Ninth Grade Students." Ph.D. dissertation, University of Georgia, 1981.

Ottinger, Joan S. "The Effect of Teaching a Story Schema on Third Grade Students' Reading Comprehension and Story Writing." *Dissertation Abstracts International* 43/04A:1039.

Peaster, Minne Y. "A Descriptive Analysis of Beginning Reading Combining Language Experiences, Children's Story Writing, and Linguistic Principles Tested after the Second Year and the Third Year." Ph.D. dissertation, Indiana University, 1970.

Pellegrini, A.D. "The Relationship Between Kindergartners' Play and Achievement in Prereading, Language, and Writing." *Psychology in the Schools* 17:530-35.

Perry, Marden L. "A Study of the Effects of a Literary Models Approach to Composition on Writing and Reading Achievement." Ph.D. dissertation, Boston University, School of Education, 1980.

Potkewitz, Lee. "The Effect of Writing Instruction on the Written Language Proficiency of Fifth and Sixth Grade Pupils in Remedial Reading Programs." *Dissertation Abstracts International* 45/08A:2467.

Quinn, Anne-Marie V. "Some Effects of Experience-Related Reading Instruction on the Written Language Development of First Grade Children." Ph.D. dissertation, University of Maine, 1977.

Robeck, Carol P., & Wiseman, Donna L. "The Development of Literacy in Middle-Class Preschool Children." *Reading Psychology* 3:105-16.

Ryan, Sheila N. "An Examination of Reading and Writing Strategies of Selected Fifth Grade Children." *Dissertation Abstracts International* 44/07-A:2105.

Schneider, Virginia L. "A Study of the Effectiveness of Emphasizing the Teaching of Reading Skills to Improve Composition Skills in Remedial English Classes at Kansas City Kansas Community Junior College." Ph.D. dissertation, University of Kansas, 1970.

Schwartz, Judy I. "A Study of the Relations Among Reading Readiness Achievement, Three Programs of Instruction in Personal Writing, and Achievement in Personal Writing." Ph.D. dissertation, New York University, 1970.

Shanahan, Timothy E. "A Canonical Correlational Analysis of the Reading-Writing Relationship: An Exploratory Investigation." Ph.D. dissertation, University of Delaware, 1980.

Shanahan, Timothy E. "Nature of the Reading-Writing Relation: An Exploratory Multivariate Analysis." *Journal of Educational Psychology* 76(3):466-77.

Shanklin, Nancy K.L. "Relating Reading and Writing: Developing a Transactional Theory of the Writing Process." Ph.D. dissertation, Indiana University, 1981.

Shugarman, Sherrie L. "The Effect of Paraphrase Writing on Sixth Grade Children's Comprehension and Recall of Expository Text." Ph.D. dissertation, Claremont Graduate School, 1983. (*Dissertation Abstracts International* 44/05-A:1405.)

Simmons, Robert J. "An Analytical Study of the Relationship of Reading Abilities and Writing Abilities of Tenth Grade Students." Ph.D. dissertation, West Virginia University, 1977.

Smith, Richard J. "The Effects of Reading a Short Story for a Creative Purpose on Student Attitudes and Writing." Ph.D. dissertation, University of Wisconsin, 1967.

Smith, William R. "Selected Batteries of Reading, Writing, and Speaking Predictor Tests." Ph.D. dissertation, University of Utah, 1960.

Snow, Catherine E. "Literacy and Language: Relationships During the Preschool Years." *Harvard Educational Review* 53(2):165-89.

Spivey, Nancy N. "Discourse Synthesis: Constructing Texts in Reading and Writing." Ph.D. dissertation, University of Texas at Austin, 1983. (*Dissertation Abstracts International* 44/09-A:2699.)

Stern, Arthur A. "Semantic Analysis: A 'Reading' Approach to the Teaching of Composition." Ph.D. dissertation, Columbia University, 1972.

Stewart, Oran J. "The Relationships Between Reading Comprehension and the Factors of Syntactic Awareness in Oral Reading, Syntactic Maturity in Writing, and Oral Reading Fluency." Ph.D. dissertation, Ohio University, 1978.

Stilley, Mary J. "An Investigation of Syntactic Maturity in Reading Comprehension and Writing Ability." Ph.D. dissertation, University of Pittsburgh, 1981.

Straw, Stanley B., & Schreiner, Robert. "The Effect of Sentence Manipulation on Subsequent Measures of Reading and Listening Comprehension." *Reading Research Quarterly* 17(3):339-52.

Sullivan, Maureen A. "The Effects of Sentence-Combining Exercises on Syntactic Maturity, Quality of Writing, Reading Ability, and Attitudes of Students in Grade Eleven." Ph.D. dissertation, State University of New York-Buffalo, 1977.

Taylor, Carol A. "The Relative Effects of Readings or Writing a Prose or Diagrammatic Summary upon the Comprehension of Expository Prose." Ph.D. dissertation, University of Kentucky, 1984. (*Dissertation Abstracts International* 45/04-A:1085.)

Taylor, Denny. "Children's Social Uses of Print." *The Reading Teacher* 36(2):144-48.

Taylor, Harold W. "Listening Comprehension and Reading Comprehension as Predictors of Achievement in College Composition." Ph.D. dissertation, University of Washington, 1981.

Taylor, Maravene B., & Williams, Joanna P. "Comprehension of Learning-Disabled Readers: Task and Text Variations." *Journal of Educational Psychology* 75(5):743-51.

Taylor, Nancy E., et al. "The Development of Written Language Awareness—Environmental Aspects." Ph.D. dissertation, 1981.

Trivelli, Elaine A. "A Study of the Effects of Sentence Combining of Eighth-Grade Students' Written Syntactic Ability and Reading Comprehension." Ph.D. dissertation, University of Akron, 1983. (*Dissertation Abstracts International* 44/02-A:383.)

Vande Koppola, William J. "Functional Sentence Perspective, Composition, and Reading." *College Composition and Communication* 33:50-63.

Wellman, Mary M. "Relationships among Cerebral Laterality, Hand Position while Writing, Reading Ability and WISC Subtest Performance." Ph.D. dissertation, University of Connecticut, 1980.

Wiseman, Donna L. "A Psycholinguistic Description of the Reading and Writing Behavior of a Selected Group of Five Year Old Children." Ph.D. dissertation, University of Missouri-Columbia, 1979. (*Dissertation Abstracts International* 40(9-A):4982.)

Wisniewska, Hanna. "Structure of Spoken and Written Utterances in Lower Elementary School Children." *Psychologia Wychowawcza* 18(2):177-86.

Wolfe, Rosemary F. "An Examination of the Effects of Teaching a Reading Vocabulary upon Writing Vocabulary in Student Compositions." Ph.D. dissertation, University of Maryland, 1975.

Wyatt, Nita M. "A Study of the Relationship of Extensive Reading to Certain Writing Skills of a Selected Group of Sixth Grade Children." Ph.D. dissertation, University of Kansas, 1960.

Yamadori, Atsushi, & McGlannan, Frances. "Reading—Integration Ideogram Reading in Alexia." *Journal of Learning Disabilities* 9:287-88.

Yusuf, Dale R. "Reading Performance Test Scores and the Impact of a Writing Program." Ph.D. dissertation, Temple University, 1982. (*Dissertation Abstracts International* 43/03-A:745.

Zasloff, Tela C. "Diagnosing Student Writing: Problems Encountered by College Freshmen (Reading)." Ph.D. dissertation, Carnegie-Mellon University, 1984. (*Dissertation Abstracts International* 45/04-A:1108.)

Note: The reviewers involved in rating the abstracts for the historical survey were James Baumann, Diane Lapp, Donna Alvermann, Thomas Bean, Robert Tierney, Ande Rubin, Susan Florio-Ruane, Gabriel Della-Piana, Patricia Anders, John McNeil, Carmen Collins, Michael Rose, Jerome Harste, Roselmina Indrisano, Alan Purves, Victor Froese, George Green, Jane Hansen, Paul Wilson, James Squire, Katherine Au, Stephen Kucer, Linda Gambrell, Margaret Atwell, Rita Bean, Peter Mosenthal, and Peter Winograd.

Author Index

Hayes, J.R., 3, 4, 8, 28, 252, 259
Head, M., 94, 105, 109, 117
Heath, S.B., x, xi, 18, 19, 28, 121, 128, 142
Henderson, I., 66, 77
Hidi, S., 60, 62, 63, 68, 69, 75, 97, 101, 103, 104, 105, 106, 107, 108, 109, 115, 117
Hiebert, E., 124, 143
Hieshima, J., 126, 144
Hildyard, A., 60, 62, 63, 68, 69, 75, 92
Hillocks, G., Jr., 21, 22, 28, 161, 165, 166, 174, 175, 188, 190, 192, 198
Hirschman, P., 177, 198
Hoddel, M., 180, 190, 199
Holdaway, D., 136, 143
Holker, K., 118
Holloway, D.W., 56, 77
Hornsby, D., 215, 222
Hottel-Burkhart, N., 60, 69, 77
Hudson, S.A., 186, 198
Huerta, M.C., 156, 159
Husserl, E., 10, 28
Hynds, S., 177, 189, 198, 199

Irwin, J.W., 56, 57, 59, 60, 64, 65, 66, 75, 76, 77, 79

Jacobs, V.A., 68, 76, 86, 87, 92
Jeffery, R.W., 184, 196
Jensen, J.M., 80, 92
Jochum, J., 186, 198
Johannessen, L.R., 161, 175, 177, 190, 198
Johnson, C.S., 99, 118
Johnson, N.S., 84, 85, 93, 97, 98, 99, 100, 102, 117
Johnson, T.D., 185, 198
Johnston, P., 104, 105, 117
Jones, R.S., 100, 110
Judy, S., 165, 175

Kahn, E.A., 161, 175, 190, 198
Kamberelis, G., 122, 133, 143, 144

Kameenui, E.J., 62, 63, 64, 78
Kamil, M.L., 94
Katz, L., 143
Kavanagh, J.F., 27
Keenan, J.M., 57, 60, 78
Kennedy, M.L., 252, 259
Kern, S., 161, 176
Kessen, W., 28
King, J.R., 7, 29, 252, 259
King, M.L., 60, 67, 68, 78, 79
Kintsch, E., 107, 108, 110, 117
Kintsch, W., 3, 28, 56, 57, 60, 62, 78, 80, 97, 98, 100, 102, 105, 106, 108, 111, 117, 118
Kirby, D., 186, 198
Kirsch, G., 187, 198
Kirschner, B.M., 8, 29
Klecan-Acker, J.S., 68, 69, 78
Kohl, H.R., 182, 198
Kozminsky, E., 106, 117
Kucer, S., 9, 28
Kuhn, T.S., 15, 16, 28

LaBerge, D., 3, 4, 6, 28, 76, 94
Laboratory for Comparative Human Cognition, 14, 28,
LaCroix, K., 94
Lalik, R.V., 116, 259
Lancy, D.F., 177, 198
Landers, D.M., 191, 197
Langer, J.A., 16, 18, 26, 28, 33, 34, 54, 87, 88, 93, 148, 149, 159, 191, 196, 198
Lankshear, C., x, xi
Lapp, D., 189, 197
LaPorte, R.E., 92
Lehnert, W.G., 82, 93
Lensmire, T., 15, 27
Lepper, M.R., 178, 179, 180, 181, 186, 190, 199
Lesgold, A.M., 60, 61, 78
Levy, B.A., 26
Lichtenstein, E.H., 86, 92
Lightfoot, M., 196
Lipson, M.Y., 29, 183, 199
Lomax, R., 7, 29
Lomax, R.G., 185, 199
Long, J., 92
Lopez, B., 68, 69, 78

Lott, J.G., 189, 199
Louis, D.R., 185, 198
Ludlow, L., 190, 198

McAnulty, S.J., 189, 199
McCaleb, J.L., 103, 106, 108, 110, 116
McCann, T., 161, 176
McClelland, B.W., 175, 176
McClure, E., 56, 65, 66, 67, 68, 69, 78, 87, 94
McCulley, G.A., 57, 68, 78
McCutchen, D., 57, 59, 62, 63, 64, 67, 68, 69, 78
McGee, L.M., 88, 94, 185, 199
McGinley, W., 251, 252, 259
McKee, J.S., 120n
McKeown, M.G., 75
McKoon, G., 61, 78
McLaren, P., 257, 259
McLeod, A., 158
McNamee, G., 128, 143
McNeil, J., 100, 112, 117
McPeck, J., 168, 176
Macrorie, K., 239, 244
Mailloux, S., 189, 190, 199
Mandel, T.S., 106, 117
Mandl, H., 80, 196
Mandler, J.M., 84, 85, 86, 93
Manicas, P.T., 28
Manning, J., 75
Margolis, J., 28
Markels, R.B., 57, 62, 63, 69, 76, 78
Marshall, J.D., 89, 93, 148, 149, 159, 186, 189, 199
Marshall, N., 56, 63, 65, 66, 78
Martin, B.K., 189, 199
Martin, N., 147, 158, 159, 196
Martinez, M., 128, 139, 143, 144
Marzollo, J., 140, 143
Mason, J., 27, 28, 66, 68, 69, 78, 87, 94, 121, 134, 143, 144
Mathews, S.R., 92
Matsuhashi, A., 69, 78, 144
Mattingly, I.G., 27
Mead, G.H., 15, 28
Medway, P., 146, 151, 159
Meisels, S.J., 123, 143
Meloth, M.S., 76

Meyer, B.J.F., 60, 61, 65, 79, 99, 117
Miall, D.S., 189, 199
Miller, G.E., 92
Miller, J.R., 108, 117
Miller, P.H., 10, 28
Milligan, B., 111, 116
Mitchell, S.P., 189, 199
Moberly, P.C., 65, 66, 79
Moe, A.J., 56, 57, 59, 61, 64, 79, 94
Monson, D., 64, 66, 68, 69, 79
Moore, D.W., 103, 116
Moran, C., 199
Morgan, J.L., 57, 58, 59, 62, 79
Morrow, L.M., 87, 94, 121, 139, 143, 144
Mosenthal, J.H., 59, 60, 62, 63, 76, 79, 80
Murray, D.M., 163, 168, 176
Musgrave, P.W., 189, 199
Muth, K.D., 92
Myers, J.W., 153, 154, 159

Nakamura, G.V., 86, 93
Nelson, J., 252, 259
Nelson, K.E., 117
Newcomer, P., 87, 94
Newell, G.E., 89, 94, 147, 149, 150, 159
Newman, J., 11, 12, 22, 24, 28
Newton, B., 159
Nicholls, J., 198
Niles, J.A., 92, 93, 94, 116, 117, 259
Nodine, B., 87, 94
Norris, J.A., 63, 79
Nystrand, M., 27, 29, 79

Oakley, D.D., 94
Oberg, A., 142, 144
Odell, L., 69, 79
Oka, E.R., 183, 184, 187, 192, 199
Olson, D.R., 92
Omanson, R.C., 75
Onore, C., 178, 199
Osborn, J., 26, 92
Ostertag, J., 8, 26
Otto, B., 128, 143

Paley, V., 128, 143
Palincsar, A., 18, 23, 28, 112, 113, 114, 117, 183, 184, 187, 192, 196, 199
Paris, S.G., 183, 184, 187, 192, 199
Parker, R., 26, 159
Parry, J., 215, 222
Pearson, P.D., 18, 21, 27, 28, 29, 73, 75, 80, 196, 246, 259
Penfield, E.F., 199
Perfetti, C.A., 57, 59, 62, 63, 64, 67, 68, 69, 78
Perkins, K., 57, 77
Petrosky, A.R., 26, 175
Phelps, L.W., 10, 15, 28
Piaget, J., 9, 10, 28, 122, 143
Pierce, C.S., 253, 259
Polya, G., 168, 176
Popham, J.W., 182, 199
Pople, M.T., 75
Powell, W.S., 73f, 76
Pritchard, R.J., 64, 66, 67, 68, 79
Probst, R.E., 189, 199, 200
Propp, V., 82, 94
Pulver, C.J., 60, 65, 66, 77, 79
Putnam, J., 76

Quinn, K., 69, 78

Rabinowitz, M., 103, 105, 106, 107, 108, 116
Rackliffe, G., 76
Raeder, U., 191, 197
Raphael, T.E., 5, 8, 18, 27, 28, 29
Ratcliff, R., 61, 78
Ratliff, J.L., 94
Raynor, J.O., 196
Readence, J.E., 77, 117, 142, 143, 144, 259
Redd-Boyd, T.M., 118
Reder, L.M., 108, 117
Rembold, K.L., 92
Rennert, K., 182, 200
Rensenbrink, C., 177, 200
Rentel, V.M., 60, 67, 68, 78, 79
Resnick, D.P., 16, 29
Resnick, L.B., 16, 29

Rhodes, L., 229, 239, 244
Rice, J.M., 183, 200
Richek, M.A., 65, 66, 79
Riel, M., 194, 197
Rinehart, S.D., 112, 118
Ringle, M.R., 93
Robinson, F., 134
Rodin, J., 182, 200
Roehler, L.R., 28, 76
Roen, D.H., 65, 79
Rogers, T., 189, 200
Rogoff, B., 15, 29
Rohrkemper, M., 183, 200
Roller, C.M., 99, 118
Rosen, H., 83, 94, 158
Rosenblatt, L.M., 189, 200
Rosenshine, B., 182, 200
Ross, G., 18, 30
Rothkopf, E.Z., 143, 198
Rowe, D.W., 251, 259
Rubin, D.L., 198, 199
Rumelhart, D.E., 5, 29, 85, 94
Ryan, E.B., 56, 66, 77
Ryan, R.M., 65, 179, 180, 181, 190, 197

Salomon, G., 191, 200
Samet, M.G., 107, 116
Sampson, M.R., 143
Samuels, S.J., 3, 4, 6, 28, 76, 94
Sanders, M., 178, 200
Scardamalia, M., 4, 8, 29, 57, 79, 86, 87, 89, 91, 93, 187, 192, 196
Schickedanz, J., 128, 143
Schieble, K.M., 103, 105, 106, 107, 108, 116
Schunk, D.H., 181, 183, 191, 200
Schuster, C.I., 186, 200
Scott, L., 94
Scott, S.B., 118
Scribner, S., 14, 16, 18, 29, 60, 63, 66, 75
Sebesta, S.L., 185, 201
Secco, T., 56, 60, 62, 80
Secord, P.F., 28
See, C., 102, 118
Sellner, M.B., 57, 58, 59, 62, 79
Sengul, C.J., 65, 76
Shanahan, T., 7, 29, 191, 200

Subject Index

NOTE: An "f" following a page number indicates that the reference is found in a figure.

ACCOMMODATION, COGNITIVE: 10-11; naturalist theory and, 14-15
ADAPTATION: Piagetian theory of human, 10
ADMINISTRATORS: support of teachers by, 142
ADMIT SLIPS: 154
ADVERBS, CONJUNCTIVE: 66
ADVERSATIVE CLAUSES: 39, 39f, 40, 46, 47, 50, 53
ALITERACY: 177
ALPHABET: 8
ALTERNATIVES: in expository text, 43, 46, 51
ANAPHORA: 58, 59, 60, 64, 65, 66, 68
ANECDOTES: writing stimulated by, 151
ANTECEDENCE: maxim of, 60
ANTECEDENTS: 35f, 58, 61; references and, 65
APOSTROPHE: use of, 229
APPLEBEE, A.N.: 148, 191-192
ARGUMENTATION: 161, 165; connection and, 83
ARISTOTLE: 166, 240
ART CENTERS: kindergarten, 132
ARTWORK: writing and children's, 125. *See also* Drawing(s); Illustrations
ASSIGNMENTS: grading of, 156; in the presentational mode of instruction, 21
ASSIMILATION, COGNITIVE: 10-11; naturalist theory and, 14-15
ATTENTION: reading and, 4-5
ATTRIBUTES: as distinct from definitions, 169-170
AUDIENCE: importance of for writer, 156; writing for, 194, 236, 242, 243
AUDITORY DISCRIMINATION: 124
AUTHORS(S): favorite, 210, 211, 212, 213, 217-218, 220; reader interaction with, 248; student (*see* Books: student-written); techniques of professional, 242
AUTHOR'S CHAIR: 24-25
AUTOMATICITY: 6, 21, 22; subskills and, 9

BALLADS: writing stimulated by, 151
BANDURA, A.: 184
BASAL READERS: 7, 9; literature in lieu of, 185; reading workshops and, 205; stories in, 87; summarizing instruction in, 111; writing style influenced by, 89
BETTS, EMMET: 121
BIG BOOKS: 138-139

BIOGRAPHICAL SKETCHES: writing stimulated by, 151
BIOPOEMS: 154-155
BLUME, JUDY: 2
BOOKS: indexing classroom library, 210; predictable, 22; student-written, 209-210, 211, 212, 215, 216, 220, 223, 253 (*see also* Stories: student-written); in whole language classrooms, 24. *See also* Basal readers; Big Books; Libraries; Literature; Reading; Reference books; Stories; Textbooks; Trade books; Workbooks
BOOK SHARE: 209, 217
BRAINSTORMING: 168, 170; in environmental mode of instruction, 23; as group-discussion alternative, 151; in reading/writing workshops, 239; writing and, 131. *See also* Freewriting
BULLETIN BOARDS: 216

CAPITALIZATION: difficulties with, 229; writing-to-learn activities and, 155
CARLE, ERIC: 218, 219
CAUSALS: 35f, 40, 43, 46, 47, 50, 53
CAUSE-EFFECT TEXTS: summarizing of, 107, 114
CHARACTERS, STORY: 81, 85, 86, 87
CHILDREN: Piagetian view of, 10-12. *See also* Students
CHOICE TIME: kindergarten, 136
CLASSIFICATION, EXPOSITORY: 82
CLASSIFICATION SCHEME: for children's emergent reading, 137f-138f
CLASSROOM ENVIRONMENT: 24-25; low-risk, 157; writing-to-learn activities and, 155-157
CLASSROOMS: context of, 13, 16; environment of (*see* Classroom environment); kindergarten, 124-126, 129, 134-136, 139, 140-142; learning orientation of, 13; literacy-rich, 124-125; reading workshop, 204-205, 216 (*see also* Reading workshops); social-constructivist, 23, 24, 25-26; U.S., 16; whole language, 23-25
CLEMENS, SAMUEL L.: *See* Twain, Mark
CLUES: *See* Context clues; Phonetic clues
CODE: letter/pattern recognition and, 4. *See also* Words: decoding of
COGNITIVE DEVELOPMENT: Piagetian concept of, 10, 12

COHERENCE: cohesion and, 56-57, 59; defined, 57, 59. *See also* Cohesion; Meaning

COHESION: coherence and, 56-57, 59; defined, 56-57, 59; source of, 59. *See also* Coherence; Cohesive ties; Linguistic cohesion

COHESIVE TIES: ix, 58-74; categories of, 64; frequency counts of, 63, 70; manipulation of, 72. *See also* Conjunctions; Lexical repetition; Referents

COLLABORATION: as principle in language arts instruction, 192; among students, 256. *See also* Reading: in pairs

COLLOCATION: 64, 68

COMMENTARY: exposition including, 36, 43-46, 50, 53; written, 151. *See also* Reports; Reviews

COMMUNICATION. *See* Conversation; Exposition; Language; Narration; Speech; Words; Writing

COMPARISON, EXPOSITORY: 82

COMPARISON-CONTRAST TEXTS: 107, 114, 165

COMPETENCE, PERCEIVED STUDENT: 191-192, 193-195; instructional competence and, 192; intrinsic motivation and, 180, 181-182, 190-191; and literature appreciation, 190; reading and, 185; success and, 188; writing and, 185, 186, 187. *See also* Self-determination; Skills

COMPONENT MODELS: 5

COMPOSITION: handwriting as factor during, 6; purposeful, 170

COMPREHENSION: 7, 52; cohesive devices as aid to, 55, 61, 64-66, 70; of literature, 190; reading and, 16, 183; summarizing and, 98-101, 105-106, 109, 111, 115. *See also* Meaning; Words: decoding of

COMPUTERS: as kindergarten Writing Center resource, 132; readers and, 5; spell-checkers of, 232. *See also* Word processors

CONCRETE OPERATIONAL PERIOD: 11

CONDENSATION: and summarizing, 99-100, 103, 104-105, 106, 107, 109, 110-111, 113, 115

CONFERENCES, TEACHER/STUDENT: reading-related, 207, 208, 209-210, 211, 215, 216, 218-219; writing-related, 229, 231, 236

CONJUNCTIONS: 66, 67; as cohesive devices, 58, 60; misuse of, 65; negative, 67; overuse of, 69; positive, 67. *See also* Adverbs, conjunctive; Connectives, implicit

CONJUNCTIVE PHRASES: 74

CONNECTEDNESS, LOCAL. *See* Cohesion

CONNECTICUT YANKEE IN KING ARTHUR'S COURT, A (Twain), 227

CONNECTION: argumentation and, 83

CONNECTIVES, IMPLICIT: 66. *See also* Conjunctions

CONSCIOUSNESS: "landscape" of, 83

CONSTRUCTION: and summarizing, 98-99, 100, 113, 115

CONTENT: form and, 165, 174; story, 82, 86, 88; writing to learn and, 156. *See also* Context

CONTEXT: importance of word, 12; learning and, 9, 252-253

CONTEXT CLUES: to word decoding, 182

CONTRAST. *See* Comparison-contrast texts

CONTROL. *See* Self-determination

CONVERSATION: writing stimulated by, 151

COOPERATIVE LEARNING: 158

COPYING: in summaries, 109

CRITERIA: and attributes, 170; and examples, 167, 169

CULTURE: individual and, 16; phenomenological view of, 10. *See also* Enculturation

CURRICULA: advances in, 249; child-centered, 25; stagnation of, 258; writing across, 249

DE BEAUGRANDE, R.: 61

DECODING. *See* Words: decoding of

DEFINITIONS: 165; student writing of, 166-167

DELETION, PRIOR TO SUMMARIZING: 98, 100, 112, 113

DESCRIPTION: 161, 165; defined, 82; exposition as, 36-46, 47, 48, 50, 53; as rhetorical predicate, 35f

DESCRIPTIVE CLAUSES: 39

DEVELOPMENTAL THEORY OF LEARNING. *See* Learning: Piagetian theory of

DEWEY, JOHN: 121

DIALOGIC STORYTELLING: 137f

DIALOGUE(S): 17, 19; cohesive devices in, 68; internalized, 23; learning logs and, 153; social-constructivist teaching and, 23, 24; writing stimulated by, 151. *See also* Conversation; Discourse

DICTATION: by kindergartners, 128, 129-130

DIDACTICISM: 258

DISCOURSE. *See* Argumentation; Description; Exposition; Narration

DISCUSSIONS: student-led, 23; teacher-led, 21

DITTO SHEETS: 22

DOLCH WORD LISTS: 22

DRACULA: student writing about, 226, 240, 242

DRAFT ANALYSIS: ix

DRAMA: educational potential of, 253. *See also* Plays

DRAWING(S): kindergartners', 126, 128, 133; student, 251; writing and, 13. *See also* Illustrations
DROP-EVERYTHING-AND-READ TIME: 136, 139

EDITING: in process writing, 130; by student writers, 231-235, 236; of writing-to-learn exercises, 156. *See also* Proofreading
EDITORIALS: writing stimulated by, 151
EDUCATION: cognitive psychology and, 178; politics and, x
ELABORATION: exposition including, 36, 38, 40, 43, 44, 46-50, 51, 52, 53; of simple description, 40; in summaries, 99, 108
ELLIPSIS: as cohesive tie, 58
EMERGENT LITERACY: 26, 87, 120-142; defined, 121
EMIG, J.: 164
ENCODING: and summarizing, 101
ENCULTURATION: transformation and, 20
ENGLISH AS A SECOND LANGUAGE (ESL) STUDENTS: 225
ENGLISH TEACHERS: as resources for writing-to-learn activities, 156
ENVIRONMENT: classroom (*See* Classroom environment); naturalist emphasis on, 12-15; Piagetian theory and, 10; as factor in reading/writing ability, 9-12; social constructivism and, 16
EPISODIC MEMORY: 4
ERROR, COHESIVE: 64, 66, 68, 69
ERROR ANALYSIS: ix
ESCHHOLZ, P.: 162-163, 173-174
ESL STUDENTS. *See* English as a Second Language students
ESSAYS: cohesive errors in, 69; extended-definition, 166-167; as inspiration for writing, 160, 161-175; student, 147, 148, 149
EVALUATION: description and, 40; in expository text, 43, 44, 46, 50, 53
EXIT SLIPS: 154
EXOPHORA: 58, 66
EXPLANATION: description and, 40; in expository text, 43, 46, 50, 53
EXPOSITON: 32-34, 53, 161; cohesion in, 63, 69; defined, 34, 82; references and, 64; summarizing of, 97-98, 106-107; text-structure knowledge and, 8. *See also* Reports

FABLES: 97
FAIRY TALES: 84, 211

FANTASY PLAY: of kindergartners, 128
FEEDBACK: as related to presentational mode of instruction, 21; scaffolding, 18
FILMS: as reading/writing resource, 251
FLASHCARDS: 222
FLUENCY: reading and, 5
FOLK TALES: 84
FORESHADOWING: 81, 242
FORM: content and, 165
FORMAL OPERATIONAL PERIOD: 11
FRANKLIN, BENJAMIN: 160-161, 162, 174, 240
FREEWRITING: described, 168; effectiveness of, 174; focused, 152; learning logs and, 152

GAMES: learning-related, 241
GENERALIZATIONS(S): evidence for, 170; prior to summarizing, 98, 100; as summary strategy, 107, 108, 112, 113
GENRE: 256; reading/writing and development of, 32-53; summarizing and, 106-107
GESELL SCREENING: 123
GIST PROCEDURE: 112
GIVEN-NEW CONTRACTS: 60-61, 67
GRADES: inadequacy of letter, 255
GRAMMAR: emphasis on, 166; freewriting and, 152; writing-to-learn activities and, 155. *See also* Syntax
GRAPHEMES: 12
GROUPING: 19

HAHN, MARY: 227, 242
HALLIDAY, M.A.K.: 62, 63-64
HANDWRITING, ILLEGIBLE: 229. *See also* Scribbling
HASAN, R.: 62, 63-64
HINTON, S.E.: 228
HOME: literacy and the, 122, 125; reading at, 134, 136, 210-211, 218, 219; writing samples taken at, 126-128. *See also* Parents
HUEY, E.B.: 121
HULL HOUSE CENTER (Chicago): 128
HUMOR: in student reports, 50
HYPONYMS: 68
HYPOTHESES: oral language – related, 22

ICONIC IMAGES: 5
IDEAS: writing as connection of, 36
ILLUSTRATIONS: allure for children of, 207, 211, 215, 218-219; value of, 253. *See also* Drawing(s)
IMAGES: words and, 253
INDUCTION, EXPOSITORY: 82
INFERENCES: reader-drawn, 16; in summaries, 99, 107

concept of, 11; preschool, 248-249 (*see also* Emergent literacy); social aspects of, 9, 14, 256, 257; sociopolitical aspects of, 257, 258. *See also* Emergent literacy; New Literacy; Reading; Writing
LITERACY CENTER: 2
LITERATURE: basal readers and, 185; cohesive ties in, 74; motivation theory and instruction in, 188-190; personal interpretation of, 189-190, 191; reading/writing programs and, 249, 251; story writing and, 90, 151. *See also* Books; Stories; Writing
LITERATURE LOGS: 228, 238
LONDON, JACK: 226, 242

MACDONALD, BETTY: 228
MACROPOSITIONS: in text, 98, 108, 109, 111
MAGAZINES: as literacy resource, 255
MAPS. *See* Story maps
MARTIN, BILL, JR: 218
MAYER, MERCER: 218
MEANING: constructivist view of, 248; memory and, 5; reading and, 191; text and, 189; writing and, 13, 146
MEMORIZATION: as reading alternative, 215
MEMORY: cohesive devices and, 60, 61; information processing and, 4; reading and, 4-5; rote, 150; summarizing from, 108-109
METACOGNITION: emergent readers and, 183
METACOMPONENTS: and performance components contrasted, 4
MEYER'S PROSE-ANALYSIS SYSTEM: 34-35
MINORITIES: literacy instruction for, 258
MISCUES, READER: 13, 14. *See also* Error, cohesive
MISS PIGGLE WIGGLE (MacDonald): 228
MODELING: participant, 184; for reading programs, 183; scaffolding and, 18; teacher, 23, 141, 158
MODELS: essays as, 161-175; motivational, 178; negotiated curriculum, 178; use of in presentational mode of instruction, 21; value of studying, 162
MONOLOGIC STORYTELLING: 137f
MOTIVATION: extrinsic, 179-180; intrinsic, 178, 179, 180-182, 185, 186, 187, 190-195
MOTIVATIONAL PSYCHOLOGY: 183
MOTIVATION THEORY: 178-190, 191, 195; and metacognitive reading strategies, 184
MULTIPLE-CHOICE QUESTIONS: 100
MURRAY, D.M.: 163-164

NARRATION: 161, 165; cohesion in, 63, 69;

references and, 64. *See also* Stories
NARRATIVE: defined, 82; summarizing, 106-107. *See also* Exposition
NATURALISM: 3; learning as perceived, 9-15, 20, 21, 24-25. *See also* Piaget, Jean; Whole language
NEWELL, G.E.: 149
NEW LITERACY: ix-x
NEWSPAPERS: class, 230-231; as literacy resource, 255
NOTES: story-related, 90; student, 148, 149, 252

OPERATIONAL PERIOD: 11
ORAL LANGUAGE: 9, 12-13, 14, 26; "rules" of, 32. *See also* Speech
ORGANIZATION: as writing element, 5
OUTCOME, STORY: 85, 86
OWNERSHIP: of writing, 185-186, 187, 192, 193, 195

PARAGRAPHS: cohesive devices within, 71-72; freewriting and, 152; main ideas of, 103; *Specific Skills Series*, 112; summarizing, 112, 113 (*see also* GIST procedure; Topic sentences)
PARENTS: and beginning readers, 134; and emergent literacy, 140-141; reading encouraged by, 211, 219. *See also* Home
PARKS, BARBARA: 227
PART-WHOLE RELATIONSHIPS: 123
PEERS: environmental mode of instruction and, 23; knowledge and, 14, 15, 16, 17; instructional support from, 13, 192, 195; as reading/writing resource, 251; in social-constructivist classrooms, 24; writing for, 22
PERFORMANCE COMPONENTS: and metacomponents contrasted, 4
PHENOMENALISM: language learning and, 10
PHONETIC CLUES: to word decoding, 182
PHONETICS: 205
PHONICS: decoding and, 7; dictation and, 130; kindergarten-level, 126. *See also* Invented spelling
PHONOLOGICAL MEMORY: 4
PHONOLOGICAL PROCESSING: 5
PIAGET, JEAN: 10, 11, 121
PICTURES: unscrambling of, 88
PIGMAN, THE (Zindel): 227
PLAGIARISM: 258
PLANNING: as writing phase, 4
PLAY-ACTIVITY CENTERS: kindergarten, 132

PLAYS: student-written/acted, 227, 240. *See also* Drama

PLOT: 97; defined, 82; summary of, 100-101

POINT OF VIEW: narrator's, 82; report writer's, 36, 50-51, 53

PORTFOLIOS, STUDENT: 247, 255, 256-257

POSTTESTS: essay-related, 169

PRAGMATICS: 64, 248

PREDICATES. *See* Lexical predicates; Rhetorical predicates

PREDICTION: comprehension and, 23; as reading/writing skill, 21, 22, 23, 208

PRESCHOOLERS: and literacy, 251; writing of, 87, 128

PRESENTATIONAL INSTRUCTION: 21-22, 188

PRETESTS: essay-related, 169

PREWRITING: 156, 161, 220

PRINT: analysis of, 5, 11; children and, 12-13, 17, 138f; conventions of, 8; and negotiability, 11; writing and, 13. *See also* Letters (symbols); Words

PRIOR KNOWLEDGE: 149; cohesion and, 62, 70; and expressive language, 146; reading and, 182-183, 191; as summary factor, 105, 110, 114

PROCEDURAL FACILITATION: 187, 188; and competence, 192

PROCESSES: reading and writing as, ix. *See also* Subprocesses

PROCESSORS, LIMITED CAPACITY: 5

PROCESS WRITING: x, 141, 249; emergent literacy and, 130-132

PROFILES, STUDENT: 255, 256

PRONOUNS: cohesion and, 72; referents and, 66; use of, 69

PROOFREADING: by kindergartners, 131; as process-writing element, 130. *See also* Editing

PROTOCOL ANALYSIS: ix

PSYCHOLOGISTS, SCHOOL: 225, 226

PUNCTUATION: difficulties with, 229; freewriting and, 152; writing-to-learn activities and, 155

QUESTIONS: comprehension, 16, 149; multiple-choice, 100; open-ended, 22; process, 151; in scaffolding context, 18; study-based, 148, 150; writing-to-learn — related, 158

QUIET READING: 205-206, 207, 215, 217, 218, 228

QUOTATIONS: as writing workshop topic, 229

READER RESPONSE THEORY: x, 188-190

READERS: expert vs. novice, 7-8. *See also* Reading

READING: aspects of, 138f; beginning, 9; components of, 25; comprehension and, 7; cultural aspects of, 19; informational, 223, 239-240; by kindergartners, 134-141; language and, 32; learning and, 248, 254; letter-by-letter, 5; looking at pictures as, 137f; and meaning, 191; motivating student, 177-195; motivation theory and, 182-185, 188 (*see also* Literature: motivation theory and); nature of, 183, 248f, 249f; new approaches to teaching, 247, 248, 248f, 249, 249f, 250-258; oral, 124; in pairs, 209, 215; and prior knowledge, 182-183, 191; as a process, ix; shared, 249 (*see also* Book Share; Reading: in pairs); silent (*see* Silent reading); social aspects of, 16, 17, 24, 26, 248f; strategic (*see* Strategic reading); with strategies imbalanced, 138f; to students, 19, 134, 141 (*see also* Reading workshops); and telling contrasted, 139; and thought, 32, 248f, 249, 252; writing and, 7, 8, 12-14, 19, 33, 51, 73, 96, 121, 147, 163, 166, 191, 204, 211, 220, 248, 248f, 249, 249f, 250-258. *See also* Authors; Basal readers; Books; Exposition; Literacy; Literature; Print; Quiet reading; Reading workshops; Stories; Textbooks; Trade books; Workbooks

READING COMPREHENSION TESTS: 100

READING DISABLED STUDENTS: writing of, 87, 90. *See also* Special needs students

READING INCENTIVE PROGRAMS: 210-211

READING PROGRAMS: inadequacies of commercial, 221-222

READING READINGNESS: 123-124, 249f

READING WORKSHOPS: 204-223, 225, 226-229, 239. *See also* Writing workshops

RECALL: ix, 86; comprehension and, 52; summary and, 97, 99, 102, 115

RECIPROCAL TEACHING: 23, 184, 188; and competence, 192; summarizing instruction in, 113, 115

REFERENCE BOOKS: 251

REFERENTS: 58, 60; ambiguous, 64, 66-67; as cohesive ties, 58, 69; and comprehension, 65; and pronouns, 66, 68

REHEARSAL: cohesive devices and, 60; prewriting, 13

REINFORCEMENT THEORY: 179

REPETITION: cohesion and, 64; variation and, 61. *See also* Lexical repetition

REPORTS: 34, 36-53, 249f; high school, 50; kindergartners' oral, 34. *See also* Commentary; I-Search papers; Reviews; Summaries

REPORT TOPICS: with description and commentary, 36, 40-46; with elaboration, 36, 46-50; sophisticated, 52

RESPONSE, READER. *See* Reader response theory

RESPONSE JOURNALS: 238-239, 240, 241, 242

RETENTION: 257

REVIEW(S): as writing phase, 4; writing stimulated by, 151. *See also* Commentary; Reports; Summaries

REVISION: 13, 161; of criteria for writing, 169; by kindergartners, 131; in process writing, 130; story, 89, 90; of student-written stories/books, 223, 233, 236; of summaries, 113; in whole language method of instruction, 22; writing and, 5; of writing-to-learn activities, 156. *See also* Editing

RHETORIC: "formulary," 161; of ancient Greece, 160

RHETORICAL PREDICTATES: 35f, 44, 46, 48

RHYME: as emergent reading resource, 138-139, 218

RISK-TAKING: by developing readers, 11, 13

SACHAR, LOUIS: 238

SCAFFOLDING: 17-18, 191-193, 195; summarizing and, 113, 114

SCENARIOS: writing stimulated by, 151

SCHEMATA: accommodative, 11; assimilative, 10; learner challenge of, 11; story (*see* Structure: story)

SCHEMA THEORY: 249

SCRIBBLING: 17, 121, 122, 126, 133, 141

SELF: phenomenalogical concept of, 10

SELF-DETERMINATION, STUDENT: 191, 193, 195; intrinsic motivation and, 180, 181-182, 185, 190-191; and literature appreciation, 190; reading and, 191; and self-regulation contrasted, 184; writing and, 185, 186, 187, 188, 191. *See also* Competence; Self-regulation

SELF-DISCOVERY: reading/writing and, 248f

SELF-ESTEEM: learning and, 225

SELF-MONITORING: by emergent readers, 12, 183

SELF-REGULATION, STUDENT: 191, 192; intrinsic motivation and, 190; and self-determination contrasted, 184; writing and, 188

SEMANTIC MEMORY: 4

SEMANTIC PROCESSING: 5

SEMANTIC REPETITION: 70

SENTENCES: 9; cohesion of, 63, 70; freewriting and, 152; summarizing, 107. *See also* Paragraphs; Topic sentences

SEQUENCE TEXTS: summarizing of, 107

SETTING, STORY: 85

SIGNALS, COHESIVE DEVICES AS: 60

SIGNS: 16, 17, 22

SILENT READING: 22. *See also* Sustained silent reading

SKILL CLUSTERS: 257

SKILL FOLDERS: 246

SKILLS: reading, 246, 248f, 249f; writing, 249f

SKILL SHEETS: 246

SKINNYBONES (Parks): 227

SMALL-GROUP DISCUSSIONS: writing-related, 150-151, 152, 158, 188

SOCIAL CONSTRUCTIVISM: viii, 3; and information processing theory contrasted, 16; learning as perceived by, 15-20, 21. *See also* Vygotsky, L.

SONGS: writing stimulated by, 151

SOUNDS: blending of, 124; symbols and, 7; words and, 253

SPECIAL NEEDS STUDENTS: 223, 224, 225-243

SPECIFIC SKILLS SERIES: 112

SPEECH: phenomenological concept of, 10. *See also* Dialogue; Language; Narration; Words

SPELLING: 223; editing of, 156; faulty, 229; freewriting and, 152; invented (*see* Invented spelling); kindergartners and, 126, 130 (*see also* Invented spelling); phonetic (*see* Invented spelling); writing and, 7, 231-233, 236-238, 239, 248f; and writing-to-learn activities, 155

STATEMENTS, INCIDENTAL: 169-170

STEVENSON, JAMES: 228

STORIES: 81-91; conflict in, 86; defined, 81; form of, 33; kindergartners', 122, 126-128, 130; kindergarten-level, 134-141; mechanics of writing, 88; "points" of, 97-98, 101, 103; predictable, 138-139; reading of, 88-89, 90-91; sentences and, 9; within stories, 85; structure of, 7, 81, 82, 84-87, 88, 97; student-written, 231-236 (*see also* Books: student-written); summarizing, 97-115; suspense in, 86, 87, 89; writing of, 87-91; writing stimulated by, 151. *See also* Books; Literature; Reading

STORY GRAMMARS: 84-85, 88, 90

STORY MAPS: 2, 90

STORY REENACTMENT AND WRITING CENTERS: 125, 139

STRATEGIC READING: metacognitive processes in, 183-185, 187
STRUCTURE: story, 7, 81, 82, 84-87, 88, 97; writing, 34, 36-53
STUDENTS: in information processing classroom, 23; mainstream, 19; in social-constructivist classroom, 24; as teachers, 23; in whole language classroom, 23-25
SUBPROCESSES, READING/WRITING: 4-5, 6, 9, 21
SUBSKILLS, READING: 248f; basal reader emphasis on, 9; language learning and, 9
SUBSTITUTION: as cohesive tie, 58
SUBTOPICS: topics and, 43
SUMMARIES: ix, 2-3, 96-115, 153-155; copy-delete, 102, 104, 113; defined, 97-98, 101; forms of, 154; open-text, 108-109, 114; paragraph, 7; reader-based, 109-110, 114; recall and, 97, 99, 102, 115; recursive nature of, 101; rules of, 112, 113-114; writer-based, 109, 114. See also Reports; Reviews
SUSTAINED SILENT READING: 136, 139
SYMBOLS: sounds and, 7. See also Signs
SYNONYMS: 68
SYNTACTIC STRUCTURES: reader comprehension of, 5
SYNTAX: sixth grade – level, 39; sophisticated, 52; of story writers, 88-89; textbook, 13
SYNTHESIS: 7

TALES OF A FOURTH GRADE NOTHING (Blume): 2-3
TALK. *See* Language; Speech
TALKING: writing reinforced through, 146, 147
TAMING THE STAR RUNNER (Hinton): 228
TASK APPROPRIATENESS: 192
TEACHERS: as class-newspaper editors, 231; and cohesive ties, 74; English (*see* English teachers); and environmental mode of instruction, 23, 188; and influence of on students' writing, 150-158, 188; instructional styles of, 193; instructional support from 192, 195; kindergarten, 120, 124, 125-126, 128, 130, 131-132, 134-136, 138-142; and natural instruction, 15, 22; and presentational mode of instruction, 21; and reading/writing connection, 19; role of, 156, 158; and scaffolding, 18; in social-constructivist classrooms, 24, 25; and stories, 87; and story writing, 89-90; student and, 17; students as, 23; and summarizing, 113-114. *See also* Classrooms; Instruction
TEACHING LOGS: 208

TELEVISION: educational potential of, 253-254; reading replaced by, 177; as reading/writing resource, 3
TESTS: cohesion-related, 71-72; end-of-the book, 213; reading, 228; spelling, 237; standardized, 228, 256; weaknesses of, 256, 257. *See also* Iowa Tests of Basic Skills; Pretests; Posttests; Questions
TEXT: making sense of, 11, 13; relationship among (*see* Intertextuality); syntax of, 13. *See also* Exposition; Language: written; Writing
TEXTBOOKS: children's reaction to, 11; literature preferred to, 185; multimedia, 253-254; relating real life to, 19. *See also* Basal readers; Trade books; Workbooks
THEME: five-paragraph, 164; story, 82
THERE'S A BOY IN THE GIRLS' BATHROOM (Sachar): 238
THOUGHT: language and, 150, 151; narrative mode of, 82; paradigmatic, 83, 90-91; Piagetian view of, 10-11; reading and, 32, 248f, 249, 252; social-constructivist view of, 17; text and, 13; writing and, 32, 248f, 249, 252
TIMED WRITING: 223, 239
TOPICS: report (*see* Report topics); response journal, 238
TOPIC SENTENCES: 113
TRADE BOOKS: 22, 247; commercial reading programs and, 222; stories in, 87; student selection of, 204-222
TRANSACTIONAL LANGUAGE: 146
TRANSLATION: as writing phase, 4
TREE DIAGRAMS: 34-35, 35f
TWAIN, MARK: 227

UNSCRAMBLING. *See* Pictures: unscrambling of

VAN DIJK, T.A.: 98, 100, 101
VISUAL DISCRIMINATION: 124
VISUAL IMAGES: 5
VISUAL MEMORY: 4
VISUAL MOTOR INTEGRATION: 225
VISUAL PROCESSING: 5
VOCABULARY: 7; cohesive ties and, 68; control, 222; low-frequency, 107; sixth grade, 39; writing and, 67
VYGOTSKY, L.: 17, 121

WAIT TILL HELEN COMES (Hahn): 227, 242
WEBBING: writing and, 131

WELLS, ROSEMARY: 213
WHOLE LANGUAGE: x, 9, 12, 22, 249; cohesive
ties in, 74; and reading instruction, 185;
writing and, 13. *See also* Naturalism
WHITE FANG (London): 226, 227
WILLINSKY, J.: 194
WORD PROCESSORS: student use of, 223, 229-236,
238, 240, 241, 243
WORDS: 22; decoding of, 5, 6, 8, 182, 205;
images and, 253; letters and, 9; meaning
and, 8, 12; sounds and, 253. *See also*
Language; Letters; Print; Sentences; Speech;
Spelling; Symbols; Vocabulary
WORKBOOKS: 22, 220; basal reading, 9;
readiness, 124
WORKSHEETS: 220, 246; kindergarten-level, 125
WORKSHOPS: Big Books, 138. *See also* Reading
workshops; Writing workshops
WRITING: 194; beginning, 9; cohesion and,
66-74 (*see also* Linguistic cohesion); and
competence, 185, 186, 187; components of,
25; cultural aspects of, 19; defined, 129;
expressive, 194; of extended-definition
essays, 166-167; imaginative uses of, 148;
informational, 38, 148, 223, 239-240 (*see
also* Exposition); by kindergartners,
125-128, 129-134, 140, 141; language and,
32, 150, 249f; learning and, 145-158, 249,
254; and meaning, 13, 146; mechanical use
of, 148; motivating student, 177-195;
motivation theory and, 185-188; nature of,
248f, 249f; new approaches to teaching,
247, 248, 248f, 249, 249f, 250-258;
personal uses of, 148; planning and, 5;
prerequisites of, 15; as process, ix, 161;
publicizing of student, 156; purpose of,
150; reading and, 7, 8, 12-14, 19, 33, 51,
73, 96, 121, 147, 163, 166, 191, 204, 211,
220, 248, 248f, 249, 249f, 250-258;
self-regulation and, 188; sharing of, 247;
social aspects of, 16, 17, 24, 26, 248f, 251;
spelling and, 7, 231-233, 236-238, 239,
248f; story, 88; and thought, 32, 248f, 249,
252; unfinished, 153; uses of, 148. *See also*
Authors; Composition; Essays; Exposition;
Freewriting; Literacy; Literature; Prewriting;
Process writing; Reports; Reviews; Revision;
Scribbling; Stories; Summaries; Timed
writing
WRITING CENTERS: kindergarten, 132
WRITING WORKSHOPS: 204, 205, 209, 217, 219,
223, 225, 229-239; prewriting exercises in,
220. *See also* Reading workshops

YATES, J.M.: 147

ZINDEL, PAUL: 227
ZONE OF PROXIMAL DEVELOPMENT: 16, 17